# Limerick Lions

# Limerick Lions

## Limerick and the British and Irish Lions 1888-1988

By

Des A Ryan
with
Stephen Ruschitzko

Copyright © 2025

All rights reserved. No parts of this book can be reproduced in any manner whatsoever without written permission, except in the case of brief quotations embodied in critical articles and reviews.

First printing 2025

Published by TTT Press

ISBN 9781068672873

For the proud people of Limerick

Luimneach Abú

# Acknowledgements

Carol, Dearbhla, Cormac, Audrey and Grace

Declan O'Reilly (The Lion King), Haroon Mohammed and AJ Whetton for some great nights in New Zealand, John Power for picking a late-night fight with the English rugby captain in Auckland. Phil Gartland, Dave Cunningham, Geoff Boreland, Kev Hickey, Noel Clancy, Mike Richardson, Adrian Halpenny, Cathal O'Reilly, Robi George, Brian Glynn, Jamie O'Sullivan, Niall Byrne, Tom Coleman, Gary Hayes, Sam Shanahan

Mark (Stitch eile), Jack, Heather, Tina, Bayleigh, Shaughan, Dermot, Frank, David, Alan, Sarah, Gareth, Joanna, Finola, Ben, Dick, Esther, Colm, Lorraine, Nicola Elaine and Andy – who each have your own allegiances, tastes and views on rugby.

To the lads of the 150 Club - Eddie Stanley and Philip Smith for all the epic rugby days out, be that on tour, in the stands, on the sidelines or sitting on a high stool - long may they continue kid.

The crew at 'All Things Rugby' – Eoin Grant, Ciaran Doran, Ian Fitzgerald, James O'Dwyer, Ronan Furlong, Andrew Valder, Arthur Riordan, Brendan O'Brien, Declan Burke, Declan Keane, Des Fortune, Kev O'Shea, Sean Devaney, Tim Clifford, Conor Norris and Brendan Grant
John Purcell of Young Munster RFC,
Ron Chiasson and Ian Campos of Town of Mount Royal RFC Montreal,
Dennis Bennett and Kevin Jarvis of Newport RFC,
John Fitzgerald and Olann Kelleher of U.C.C RFC
Frank Kenny of Lansdowne RFC
Sean McMahon at Munster Rugby
Audrey O'Byrne at Rockwell College
Damien Burke of the Jesuit Archives
George Lee of Christian Brothers and Markets Field
Peter Agnew of Hockey Ireland
Sinead O'Riordan of Crescent College Past Pupils Association
Sean Gannon – Limerick Local Studies
John-Mark Griffin
Aiden 'Dano' Hayes of Garryowen RFC
Darryn O'Brien, Niall Moran, Ray Mulligan, Daire Lyons and Bart Vjrihof
Pat McLoughlin
Judie and Tim Barry and the family of Dr WJ Roche
Colm Tucker Jnr (Cullie) and the family of Colm Tucker
Keith Wood and the family of Gordon Wood
Conor English and the English family
Cara Mulcahy and the Mulcahy family
Tony Ward
Gerry McLoughlin

# Sources

In putting together the stories of the players and their tour experiences, we have used a range of sources. Where possible we have spoken directly to the player or a member of their immediate family to get first-hand accounts. We have also found insights in previously published player interviews. We have spoken to historians at their rugby clubs. We have read extensive newspaper accounts and match reports for every game played on each tour along with match reports for significant games in their club, provincial and international careers. These reports were from Local, Irish, UK, Australian, South African and New Zealand newspapers.

We have also consulted a range of books which added insight. These included:
- Rugby Reminiscences and Opinions by Rowe Harding
- Lions Downunder 1950 by Alan Evans
- Lions Rampant by Vivian Jenkins
- Kings of Rugby by Terry McLean
- 125 years of the British and Irish Lions by Clem Thomas
- Behind the Lions by Steve Jones
- Lions Among the Springboks by JBG Thomas
- Lions of Ireland by David Walmsley
- British Lions 1980 by John Hopkins
- The Barbarians: The official history of the Barbarian football club by Nigel Starmer-Smith
- Where Miracles Happen by Charles Mulqueen
- Rockwell College 1864-2014 by Dr Sean O'Donnell
- My Life in Rugby by Donal Lenihan
- Twelve Feet Tall by Tony Ward
- The Green Faded Jersey (Richmond RFC)
- The Home of the Spirit – A celebration of Limerick Rugby
- St Mary's are we… 1943-1993
- The Story of Young Munster
- Shannon Rugby Football Club 1884-1984
- The Carling Story of Munster Rugby by Charles Mulqueen
- Rugby in Munster – A Social and Cultural History by Liam O'Callaghan
- Garryowen FC 1884-1984 by Charles Mulqueen
- The Breaking Rapid by Joe Coleman
- Limerick Rugby History by Charles Mulqueen
- From Ludicrous to Logical: The Transformation of Sport in North Munster, 1850–1890 by Tom Hayes

RUGBY IN LIMERICK ............................................................................. 7
THE BRITISH AND IRISH LIONS ..................................................... 25
1924 ................................................................................................... 33
    WILLIAM ROCHE ............................................................................. 35
    SOUTH AFRICA AND ZIMBABWE (1924) ......................................... 51
1950 ................................................................................................... 81
    TOM CLIFFORD ............................................................................... 83
    NEW ZEALAND, AUSTRALIA & SRI LANKA (1950) ......................... 97
1955 ................................................................................................. 129
    TOM REID ..................................................................................... 131
    SOUTH AFRICA & KENYA (1955) .................................................. 147
1959 ................................................................................................. 179
    GORDON WOOD ............................................................................ 181
    BILL MULCAHY ............................................................................. 197
    MICK ENGLISH .............................................................................. 213
    AUSTRALIA, NEW ZEALAND & CANADA (1959) .......................... 225
1962 ................................................................................................. 261
    BILL MULCAHY ............................................................................. 263
    SOUTH AFRICA, RHODESIA & KENYA (1962) ............................... 265
1980 ................................................................................................. 297
    COLM TUCKER .............................................................................. 299
    TONY WARD ................................................................................. 311
    SOUTH AFRICA (1980) .................................................................. 325
1983 ................................................................................................. 353
    GERRY MCLOUGHLIN .................................................................. 355
    NEW ZEALAND (1983) .................................................................. 381
A TEAM OF LIMERICK LIONS ........................................................ 395

# Preface

A British and Irish Lions tour comes around every four years and players from each of the four home nations do battle to get picked for what many believe to be the pinnacle of rugby.

In the build-up to the squad announcement, everyone has their opinion as to who should be selected. Usually there is a little bias involved, whether that be national bias, provincial bias or club bias, and there is always great debate, over a beer, as to who should wear, first the jersey and then the much-coveted test jersey.

Ireland have provided some of the greatest British and Irish Lions over the years, Willie John McBride, Tony O'Reilly, Jack Kyle, Tom Kiernan, Brian O'Driscoll and Ronan O'Gara for example, these names would feature on many 'greatest ever Lions' lists. Throw into the mix Limerick men like Keith Wood, Paul O'Connell, David Wallace or Conor Murray and they would also be in contention for the best ever list.

One of the problems with best ever lists is recency bias. With professionalism came more games, better playing conditions and mass television coverage. We see players more now. They are celebrities. The game is faster, more high scoring, some would say more exciting. How can you compare a current professional rugby player with someone who only played four international games a year while holding down a job, working as an insurance assessor?

The idea for this book came about when the authors, Des and Stephen, over a beer were debating who the greatest Limerick Lions were. We quickly realised that prior to the professional era, we didn't know enough about the Limerickmen who had played for the Lions to do the debate justice; in fact, neither could comprehensively list the contenders. So, we set out to research and document Limerick's Pride of Lions.

What makes a Limerick Lion? What criteria do you use to decide? Many would say that the great Young Munster legend Tom Clifford was the first Limerickman to play for the British and Irish Lions. The problem is he was born in Limerick Junction in County

Tipperary. Do you include him? If you do, do you include Laurence Bulger who went on the 1896 British and Irish Lions tour? He was born in Kilrush which is as close to Limerick as Limerick Junction. Do you include Tony Ward? Born in Dublin, raised in Leeds but played for Limerick Utd in the League of Ireland, as well as rugby for Garryowen and, of course, was one of the Munster men who beat the All-Blacks in 1978. In the end, we selected nine players who were either born in Limerick or who played a very significant part of their career at Limerick clubs.

The first Limerickman to play for the Lions was William Roche in 1924. He didn't play club rugby in Limerick so is often unfairly overlooked. Since then, our list of Limerick Lions has twenty-three names on it up until the time of writing. We are proud of every one of them and their achievements. We decided to draw the line at 1988 for two reasons. Firstly, these are the ones who are starting to fade from public consciousness and we felt they needed to be restored to the spotlight. Secondly, to go into the level of detail we wanted to, it had to be a manageable number and the dawn of the professional game in the 1990's was a logical cut off point.

We have tried to give a good account of each player's career. We have painstakingly researched and reviewed their club, provincial and national careers. We've also comprehensively reviewed their invitational careers with the Barbarians and then their Lions tour experiences. The farther you go back, before the digital age, it becomes more and more difficult to get access to data but we think we have it right. We know how passionate Limerick people are about their rugby clubs and the honours each has achieved - we hope we have it all accurately accounted for.

So, let us re-introduce you to the first Limerick men who played for the British and Irish Lions. There are some interesting characters here and some interesting anecdotes. We hope you enjoy the book and hopefully you will be able to add some of these older Limerick Lions to your next debate about who is the greatest Limerick Lion.

Des and Stephen
May 2025

# Limerick Lions

Depending on the criteria you use to define a 'Limerickman', up to twenty-three men from the Treaty County have worn the red jersey and played for the Lions. Four of them, Bill Mulcahy, Keith Wood, Paul O'Connell and Conor Murray, led the team out onto the field as captain.

Some came close, Peter Clohessy was picked for the 1997 tour but had to drop out because of injury. He was replaced by Paul Wallace. Likewise, Jerry Flannery was part of the 2009 squad but injury meant he couldn't play. Alan Quinlan was also picked for the Lions tour in 2009 but during Munster's European Cup semi-final against Leinster, he was cited for foul play. He was subsequently suspended and as a result missed the tour.

What follows is our list of Limerick Lions. We know there will be contention about some of those listed. The criteria we used was Limerick born or deeply associated with rugby in Limerick either by playing significant parts of their careers in Limerick or by living for long periods in Limerick. You don't have to agree.

## 1888 -1988

| | |
|---|---|
|  | **William Roche**<br>UCC, Newport RFC, Cardiff RFC<br><br>1924 Tour of South Africa |
|  | **Tom Clifford**<br>Young Munster<br><br>1950 Tour of Australia and New Zealand<br><br>*\* Tipperary born* |

**Tom Reid**
Garryowen, London Irish, TMR RFC

1955 Tour of South Africa

**Gordon Wood**
Old Crescent, Garryowen, Lansdowne

1959 Tour of Australia and New Zealand

**Bill Mulcahy**
Bohs, UCD, Bective, Skerries

1959 Tour of Australia and New Zealand
1962 Tour of South Africa

**Mick English**
Shannon, Bohs, Lansdowne

1959 Tour of Australia and New Zealand

**Colm Tucker**
Richmond, St Mary's, Shannon

1980 Tour of South Africa

### Tony Ward
St Mary's College, Garryowen, Greystones

1980 Tour of South Africa

*\* Dublin born*

### Gerry McLoughlin
St Mary's, UCG, Shannon

1983 Tour of New Zealand

# 1988 – 2025

### Richard Wallace
Garryowen

1993 Tour of New Zealand

*\* Cork born*

### Mick Galwey
Shannon

1993 Tour of New Zealand

*\* Kerry born*

### Keith Wood
Garryowen

1997 Tour of South Africa
2001 Tour of Australia

*Clare born*

### Peter Clohessy
Young Munster

Picked for the 1997 Tour of South Africa but had to drop out due to injury.

### Paul Wallace
Garryowen

1997 Tour of South Africa

*Cork born*

### Rob Henderson
Garryowen

2001 Tour of Australia

*England born*

### David Wallace
Garryowen

2001 Tour of Australia
2009 Tour of South Africa

### John Hayes
Shannon, Bruff

2005 Tour of New Zealand
2009 Tour of South Africa

### Paul O'Connell
Young Munster

2005 Tour of New Zealand
2009 Tour of South Africa
2013 Tour of Australia

### Keith Earls
Thomond, Young Munster

2009 Tour of South Africa

### Alan Quinlan
Shannon

Picked for the 2009 Tour of South Africa but missed out due to suspension.

*Tipperary born*

### Jerry Flannery
Shannon

Picked for the 2009 Tour of South Africa but had to drop out due to injury.

**Conor Murray**
Garryowen

2013 Tour of Australia
2017 Tour of New Zealand
2021 Tour of South Africa

**CJ Stander**
Munster

2017 Tour of New Zealand

*South Africa born*

# Rugby in Limerick

Rugby School in Warwickshire, England is infamous for being the school where in 1823, a sixteen-year-old pupil by the name of William Webb Ellis during a game of football, decided to 'pick up a ball and run with it in his hands, touching in down under the posts' and the first ever 'carrying' game of football started. The game continued to evolve at Rugby School and in 1845, a set of rules were developed, some other schools and universities started to play and a unique game broke away from what became association football.

## Sir Charles Burton Barrington

Limerick has a legitimate claim as being the 'Home of Irish Rugby'. It was a Limerick man, Sir Charles Burton Barrington, who is credited as being the father of the game in Ireland.

The Barrington family, originally from Yorkshire, are synonymous with Limerick. The family estate was at Glenstal Castle in Murroe, County Limerick. Sir Charles' grandfather, Sir Joseph Barrington (1st Baronet) built Barrington's Hospital in 1829 and it was one of the first hospitals in Ireland focused on providing free care to those who could not afford it. Many other well-known Limerick landmarks are named after the family, such as Barrington's Pier, Barrington Street and Barrington's Bridge.

*Sir Charles Burton Barrington of Glenstal*

Sir Charles Burton Barrington (5th Baronet) was born in 1848. He was educated at St Columba's College in Dublin and was then sent to Rugby School where he studied between 1864 and 1866. While there, he learned to play the game of rugby which had been invented at the school forty years earlier. After Rugby School, Barrington returned to Ireland and attended Trinity College Dublin.

Dublin University Football Club (Trinity's team) is the first ever rugby club in Ireland and was founded in 1854 by Trinity College students. Trinity's first ever team comprised of nine men from Rugby school, a dozen from Cheltenham school, and about a dozen more from Irish schools. Early members were disadvantaged by having no one to play against, except other members of their own club. It was also the first 'senior' rugby club founded anywhere in the world. Later, no other Dublin team was allowed to play the Trinity first team without first defeating Trinity's second team.

Having joined the club, Barrington was made team captain in 1867 and he held that position until 1870. When Barrington entered Trinity, he described what he found as 'a rugby of sorts', but with few formal rules and no designated kit.

*Sir Charles Burton Barrington (with the ball) with Trinity rugby team in 1869*

In the 1920s and 30s, Barrington now late in life, corresponded with Edward Watson who was a historian, documenting the history of sport at Trinity. The correspondence was published as part of the book 'The Bold Collegian: The development of sport in Trinity College'. The following are extracted from that.

> *'A little desultory football, with no particular rules to speak, or kit. A good little chap called Wall was running the show. I started away and pulled things together, made a good club out of it with rules of Rugby School, and we were very successful for it caught on at once. I have a photo of our First XV by me, and we are a queer-looking lot judged by modern ideas. We had caps made in Rugby too, but there was no-one in those far-off times to play against. The match of the year was against the Medical School. Sometimes too the Dublin Garrison boiled up a team to play us ... We played matches among ourselves, 'pick up' twice or three times a week ...*
>
> *The Club was really a great success and did introduce the Rugger game into Ireland.'*

Barrington goes on to describe how he and the honorary club secretary, R.M. Wall (whose father, Rev. F.H. Wall, was headmaster on another early rugby nursery, Arlington School, Portarlington), tackled the problems of rules:

> *'The club had no rules, written or unwritten. They just played and ran with the ball, no touch line, no goal lines, our only paraphernalia being the Rugby goal posts. These were all sufficient for the simple tastes of those days in Dublin Football. A Rugbean brought in the new idea of Rules. Rugby [School] itself though had no written rules! They were traditional, like the British Constitution or the Secrets of Free Masonry.'*

In fact, Rugby School had produced written rules in 1845, and a further set had been drawn up by Blackheath FC, one of the earliest of English clubs, founded in 1862. But when Barrington and Wall met to draw up rules in the secretary's rooms in 1868, The Rugby School tradition was paramount:

> *'Wall sat gravely at his little table. A small dark wiry hardy chap with a short back beard and kindly dark eyes. He wrote and I dictated. Gradually and gradually as one could remember them the unwritten laws that govern the immortal Rugby game were put on paper.'*

Below are the rules Barrington and Wall published for Dublin University Football Club in 1868.

> 1) The Kick-off from the middle of must be a place-kick.
> 2) Kick-out must be from 25 yards out of goal, not a place-kick.

3) Charging is fair in case of a place-kick, as soon as the ball has touched the ground; in case of a kick from a catch as soon as the player offers to kick, but he may always draw back, unless he has touched the ball with his foot.
4) If a player makes a Fair Catch, he shall be entitled to a free kick, provided he claims it, by making a mark with his heel at once; and in order to take such kick he may go back as far as he pleases, and no player on the opposite side shall advance beyond his mark until he has kicked.
5) A Fair Catch cannot be made from Touch.
6) A Player is off side when the ball has been kicked, thrown or knocked on, or is being run with by one of his own side behind him.
7) A Player off side may impede the game by standing close to the ball; but he may not, in any case, kick or touch it, charge or put over.
8) A Player is on side when the ball is kicked or thrown or knocked on, or when it has rebounded from the body of another player of the opposite side.
9) It is not lawful to take up the ball when not in touch, except in an evident hop. Lifting the ball is strictly prohibited.
10) Running in is allowed to any player onside, provided he does not run through touch.
11) If in case of a run in, the ball is held in a maul, it shall not be lawful for any other player on his own side to take it from the runner and run with it.
12) It shall be lawful for any player to call upon any other player, holding the ball in a maul, to put it down, when evidently unable to get away.
13) A Player, if he wishes to enter a maul, must do so onside.
14) No Player, out of a maul, may be held or pulled over, unless he himself is holding the ball.
15) No hacking, as distinct from Tripping, is fair.
16) Try at Goal. A ball touched between the goal posts may be brought up to either of them, but not between.
17) When the ball has been touched down behind the goal, the player who touched it down is entitled to walk out straight 25 yards, and any one of his side may take a place-kick, but as soon as the ball had been placed, the opposite side may charge.
18) It shall be a goal if the ball is dropped, but not if punted, hit or thrown, between the posts or posts produced at any height over horizontal bar, whether it touch it or not.
19) No goal may be kicked from touch.
20) A Ball in Touch is dead; consequently, the first player on his side must, in any case, touch it down, bring it to the side of the touch and throw it straight out.
21) Holding and throttling is disallowed.
22) Sneaking in opponents' goal is discountenanced.

Rugby in Limerick

*23) The captains of sides, or any two deputed by them, shall be the sole arbiters of all disputes*

At the club's AGM in 1868, the report of the honorary secretary-treasurer R.M. Wall contained the following reference to the new laws:

*'We have forwarded to the principal leading clubs the rules by which we play, in the hope that for the future we may be able to secure players thoroughly acquainted with the science of the game, a want which has hitherto proved an obstacle to our efficiency in the field. After a careful revision of the rules of all the leading clubs, we have thought fit to compile a code which we hope will meet the approbation of all.'*

It was Sir Charles Barton Barrington's act of writing down a set of rules in 1868, that allowed other teams in Ireland to become established and for teams in Ireland to play against each other. Wanderers Rugby Club was established in 1869 as was Queen's University. Over the following decade, dozens of new clubs sprung up across the country. All of these clubs adhered to the rules as set out by Barrington in 1868. The first club in Limerick was Rathkeale Football Club which was founded in 1874.

Barrington was also instrumental in founding the Irish Football Union in 1874. The Irish Football Union was the governing body for the sport in Leinster, Munster and parts of Ulster. The Northern Football Union of Ireland was founded in January 1875 and controlled the game around Belfast. These two later merged to become the Irish Rugby Football Union (IRFU) in 1879.

Barrington was an all-round sportsman and also rowed for Dublin University and later for Limerick Boat Club. Along with his brother Croker Barrington, the four-oared team from Dublin University won the Visitors' Challenge Cup at Henley Royal Regatta in 1870 and 1873, becoming the first non-British team to do so. They also travelled to Philadelphia in America to complete at an International four-oared race in 1876.

Barrington's only daughter, Winifred Barrington, was shot dead in an IRA ambush at Newport, Co. Tipperary on $14^{th}$ May 1921. She was just twenty-three. She had been travelling in a car with District Inspector Major Harry Biggs of the Royal Irish Constabulary who was the intended target. Shortly after Winifred death, Sir Charles and his family left Ireland to live on their Hampshire estate. He lived there until his death, aged 95 in 1943.

When he left Limerick, Barrington sold his family estate at Glenstal. In 1927 the Benedictine monks of Maredsous Abbey in Belgium acquired it and established a monastic community there. They renamed the castle to Glenstal Abbey and opened a prestigious boarding secondary school for boys in 1932. It remains a working monastery and boarding school up until the present day. Glenstal, perhaps due to the original owner of the estate, is a rugby school and they won their first and only Munster Schools Senior Cup title in 2018. They defeated Christian Brothers Cork 18-17 in the final and were captained on the day by Ben Healy who later played for Munster and Scotland.

## Limerick and the first Irish International rugby team

Seven years after Sir Charles Burton Barrington wrote down the rules for rugby in Ireland, and a year after the formation of the IRFU, Ireland played its first international match. That game, played on 15$^{th}$ February 1875 at Kensington Oval, London was against England.

The Irish team was made up of twenty players with Trinity supplying nine of the team and the remainder coming from Ulster clubs. It wasn't until 1877 that the number of players was reduced from twenty to fifteen. Ireland lost that first game by one try and one goal to no score (7-0).

One of the Irish players supplied by Trinity was Jack Myles. Jack and his younger brother Tom, were the sons of Limerick businessman John Myles and his wife Prudence Bradshaw. The Myles family had a corn merchants' business at 15 Catherine Street in Limerick. Both Jack and Tom entered Trinity in January 1873 to study medicine and both joined the rugby team. Neither was selected for the game in 1875 but when H.L Robinson failed to turn up, Jack Myles took his place in the historic game becoming the first Limerick man to play for Ireland.

Also on the team that day was Abraham Prim Cronyn from Kilkenny. Cronyn's younger brother John George Cronyn was also on the Trinity rugby team at the time though he wasn't selected for Ireland that day. In 1929, he wrote that *"Jack Myles played against me in March 1877 in the first Munster team, against Leinster at College Park on March 26$^{th}$ 1877"*.

Jack Myles' younger brother Tom went on to become Sir Tom Myles. After finishing medical school, he had a successful medical career and became President of the Royal College of Surgeons and was knighted in 1902. He was conferred by the Lord Lieutenant of Ireland, Earl Cadogan in August 1902. Despite being knighted by the crown, Tom Myles was part of the gun running plot, along with Erskine Childers and Conor O'Brien, that smuggled arms and ammunition at Kilcoole, County Wicklow in 1914.

*Jack Myles, seated 4th from left, with the Irish International Rugby team in 1875*

## First Rugby International in Limerick

Between 1875 and 1898, the Irish rugby team played international games in either Dublin or Belfast. Initially, Ballnafeigh and Ormeau were used in Belfast. Rathmines hosted a Dublin game before Lansdowne Road was established. Games were effectively split fifty-fifty between north and south. However, the first international game played outside of Dublin and Belfast, was played in Limerick on 19th March 1898. It took place at the 'Cricket Club' which is now Limerick Lawn Tennis Club on the Ennis Road.

The game took place thanks to the persistence of John M. O'Sullivan, secretary of Garryowen and treasurer of the IRFU, who continuously pressured the IRFU to play a game outside Dublin. When the event came to pass and it is a measure of the strength of Limerick rugby, that Limerick was selected to host the historic game.

Thousands of people turned out at the train station to welcome to teams and the Boherbuoy Band led them as they were paraded down to Cruise's Hotel where they stayed before the game. On the day of the game, thousands of people arrived from around the country and the attendance was estimated at over fifteen thousand for the game itself. The band of the Royal Irish Regiment entertained the crowd before kick-off.

*The Ireland v Wales International played in Limerick in 1898*

Unfortunately, Ireland lost the game (3-11). Ireland's three points came from a penalty goal scored by Lawrence Bulger. Bulger from Kilrush, County Clare, had just returned from the British and Irish Lions 1896 tour to South Africa. He had played twenty-one times on that tour including in four test matches. Bulger died while attending the England v Scotland five nations game at Twickenham on St Patrick's Day 1928.

## Limerick Rugby – William Lamb Stokes

Limerick historian Tom Hayes considered William Lamb Stokes to be the 'Father of Limerick Rugby'. It was he who co-founded, structured and established rugby in Limerick and his legacy lives on today.

Stokes hailed originally from Galway and came from a middle-class protestant background. He was educated at Rathmines School in Dublin where he was first exposed to the game of rugby. Having moved to Limerick, Stokes became a butter merchant and operated out of the Limerick Milk Market, where he bought butter from local producers for export.

During his many years in Limerick, Stokes was involved in many different aspects of life. He was active commercially with his own business and in the Chamber of Commerce. His civil activities saw him elected to the corporation in 1898 and he was High Sheriff of Limerick in 1908. He was also an active member of the Limerick Market Trustees and of the Free Masons.

*William Lamb Stokes*

His contribution to social and sporting life is Stokes' most significant legacy. Stokes co-founded with Barrington and played on the Limerick County Football team. He also contributed to the establishment of Garryowen Football club and became the club's first president. He was also involved in boating, athletics and cycling in the city.

His contribution to Limerick rugby saw Stokes elected as the eighth President of IRFU in 1887 and he held that role when Ireland recorded their first ever victory on 5th February 1887. It took Ireland eight games to score their first try. That was scored against England at Lansdowne Road in January 1880. They were beaten that day. Two years later in February 1882, Ireland drew with England again at Lansdowne Road. Finally, after twelve years and twenty-five attempts Ireland won a game when they beat England by two goals to nil at Lansdowne Road.

*Lamb Stokes (in black) President of IRFU and the Irish team in February 1887*

William Lamb Stokes lived on the North Circular Road in Limerick. He died suddenly there, of a brain aneurysm, in April 1910. He was 59 years old.

## First Limerick Rugby Club

The first rugby club in Limerick was, perhaps surprisingly, **Rathkeale Football Club**, which was founded in 1874. At the time, it was in line with the game elsewhere, in that it was played by the elite and well-to-do. The first rugby game ever played in Limerick was in November 1874, when Rathkeale Football Club played a team organized by a local landlord Mr. Massey. The next two recorded games of Rathkeale Football Club, both played in January 1875, were against Mr. Harkness' team, followed by a game against a combined military and constabulary side.

Rathkeale Football Club didn't last long but it was around long enough to trigger William Lamb Stokes and Sir Charles Burton Barrington to co-found Limerick County Football Club in late 1879. Stokes played for the club and held several positions in it, including captain, club secretary and club president. The designation Football Club as opposed to Rugby Football Club comes from the fact that they were established before the IRFU. Clubs formed after 1879 can only be called RFC.

Having established the cup the year prior, William Lamb Stokes was captain of Limerick County Football Club when they played in the

Munster Senior Cup final in 1887 and again in 1889. They lost on both occasions.

William Lamb Stokes (with the ball) and the Limerick County Football team in 1887

## Club Rugby in Limerick – It was tribal

Twice Oscar nominated actor, Richard Harris was a rugby player. He was on the Crescent College team in 1949 that won the Munster Schools' Senior cup and he played one game of underage rugby for Munster, against Connacht, after which he swore that he never would wash the blood from his jersey.

In an interview with the Sunday Times in May 2002 Richard Harris spoke about Limerick rugby.

> "Intrinsic is exactly what it is to the city. And the game did start on the streets, in little junior, juvenile clubs, in parishes that were all competing against other parishes. And they still go to Thomond Park. For example, St Mary's Parish juveniles versus another parish, and they kill each other! They hate each other. It is tribal fucking warfare. You cross the border into our town, and you will pay for it boy, believe me".
>
> Rugby was life in Limerick. The heroes of Limerick rugby are my heroes. Gladiators, square-jawed warriors who represent us on the battlefield".
>
> Richard Harris

By the early 1880s, **Limerick Football Club** had sixty registered players and it was felt that there was a need for a second prestige club to be formed, this one in the city. Following a series of meetings involving William Lamb Stokes, Alderman Mike Joyce MP, Alderman Tom Prendergast and his brother William Prendergast, Park Rangers Football Club and Catholic Institute Football Club agreed to merge and **Garryowen Football Club** was formally established on 18th September 1884. Stokes became the first president of the club and it was his influence that got Garryowen recognised as the first senior club in Limerick city. Importantly, Stokes was a protestant member of the elite while his new club colleagues were catholic and members of the Labour Party. This became a theme of Limerick rugby. There was no exclusivity involved.

Playing out of the Markets Field, the original idea was that Garryowen would be the senior club to represent Limerick city. Each of the five points of the star on their crest represented one of the five Limerick Boroughs of St Mary's, St Michael's, St Munchin's, St Patrick's and St John's.

In their first year of existence, Garryowen reached the final of the Munster Senior Cup, where they were beaten by Bandon from Cork. Of the first twenty-nine winners (up until the outbreak of WW1), Garryowen won seventeen and were runners-up on another six occasions. This incredible achievement was possible only because they were the only senior club in Limerick city and drew on players from the junior clubs that sprung up across the city in the late 1800s. Garryowen became a graduation point for players who started out in junior clubs.

Other junior clubs began to be established around Limerick at this time:

**Shannon RFC** was formed on 18th February 1884 at the Shamrock Bar on the Corbally Road. They claim to be an older club than Garryowen but because William Lamb Stokes lobbied on their behalf, Garryowen became senior first. Shannon, representing "the parish" (St Mary's parish), remained a junior club for almost seventy years and supplied players to Garryowen. They won the Munster Junior Cup for the first time in 1914. They finally progressed to senior status in 1953/54 and won their first Munster Senior Cup in 1960.

**Young Munster RFC** was founded in 1895. The club originally had ties to the military. Their black and amber colours come from the Bengal tiger. The Royal Munster Fusiliers were known previously as the Royal Bengal Fusiliers. Young Munster drew on players from Boherbuoy (the Yellow Road). In 1928, they became the first and only Limerick club to win the Bateman Cup. The Bateman Cup was an All-Ireland knock out competition that ran from 1922 until 1939. Young Munster became a senior club in the early 1920s and won their first Munster Senior Cup in 1928.

Other clubs that came into existence at the time but didn't survive included Limerick Post Office RFC, Phoenix RFC, Pirates RFC, Summerville and Old Queens. Each of these competed very strongly and even won silverware. Pirates RFC and Old Queens both won the City Cup twice.

Other well-known Limerick Clubs were formed later. Typically, they represented an area or a parish.

**Limerick RFC** – 'The Gaubies' – Formed in 1909. Originally part of Garryowen and known as 'Young Garryowen', they spun out as a standalone club following a dispute about committee representation. Limerick RFC won the Munster Junior Cup in 1912 but eventually re-integrated with their parent club.

**Presentation RFC (1917)**– Presentation was formed on Sexton Street in the city in 1917. They take their name from the girls' school adjacent to where the club was formed. They were originally a city club and drew players from across the city. Now playing at their ground in Ballysheedy, Pres won the Munster Junior Cup in 1929.

**Bohemian Football Club (1922)** – Bohs were originally formed in 1922. They achieved senior status in 1927 and won their first Munster Senior Cup that year. Bohs won the Munster Junior Cup in 1932. In 1999, Bohemians merged with the University of Limerick team to form UL-Bohs.

**Abbey RFC** – Formed in 1926, Abbey RFC also came from St Mary's and comprised of local fishermen and members of the Abbey boat club. They competed in the junior leagues until they disbanded in the 1930s. In their short existence they won the City Cup three times.

**Richmond RFC (1928)** – The Richmond rugby club was formed in 1928. Representing the Richmond Park and Canal Bank area. They won their first Munster Junior Cup in 1934/35.

**St Marys RFC (1943)** – St Marys was formed in 1943, filling the gap left by the disbanding of Abbey RFC, and drew on players from 'the parish' and Corbally. Still a junior club, St Marys won their first City Cup in 1946 and their First Munster Junior Cup in 1968. They have also own multiple Transfield Cups and Munster Junior Plates.

**Thomond RFC (1944)** – Formed in 1944, Thomond RFC originally drew on players from the Thomondgate area of the city. Still a junior club Thomond have won multiple Transfield Cups, North Munster Leagues and Munster Junior Cups.

**Old Crescent (1947)** – Old Crescent were formed out of the successful Crescent College school rugby teams of 1947 and 1949. Established in September 1947, they originally drew from alumni of Crescent. They were promoted to a senior club in 1952. Despite, multiple appearances in the final, Old Crescent have yet to win their first Munster Senior Cup.

With the establishment of all these clubs and the growing interest in the game, William Lamb Stokes became the game administrator in Limerick. Despite the fact that he was playing for Limerick County Football Club (he played until he was thirty-nine years old) and was President of Garryowen Football Club, Stokes was keen to see rugby grow in the region and so was very active in supporting other clubs that were set up. Garryowen too were keen to see more players added to the pool from which they could select players for their senior team.

In 1887, Stokes was involved in the creation of a **Limerick Junior Cup** competition. The competition was set up by members of the Limerick Football Club and Garryowen Football Club as the two senior clubs in the locality. In its first year, it was played on a succession of Sunday afternoons in a field behind Tait's factory. It is an indication of the interest in rugby and the impact of Stokes, that ten clubs entered in that first year; Parteen, Thomond, Kincora, Shannon, Ramblers, Rovers, Star, Sarsfields, Faugh-a-Ballagh and the second Garryowen team. There was huge interest in it and as many as a thousand spectators showed up to watch games.

The tournament was held again the following year and was reported on by the newspapers.

> "I am delighted to perceive the Limerick Junior Clubs Tournament, which was so successfully inaugurated last year, will be held again this season. It is bound to prove most interesting and should be supported by every Knight of the jersey, past and present... They have no lack of clubs – The Rovers, Star, Shannon, North Liberty, Rangers, Pirates, Kincora 2$^{nd}$, Ramblers, Parteen etc. Last year they took £9 in one day and of this generously gave £5 to Barrington's Hospital, medals and other expenses swallowing up the remainder. But they want a cup, and I think this is a thing they well deserve. I am sure that Mr W.L Stokes would give the project his invaluable support. All the leading citizens could subscribe to the cup, and besides entrance fees of 5s and gate money would be a source of income. If it were necessary, Limerick County, Garryowen and Kincora 1$^{st}$ XV would, I am sure, play matches in the Markets Field for the benefit of their junior brethren."

Junior rugby was flourishing in Limerick. Sunday rugby games continued to draw crowds and the introduction of other competitions fuelled that further.

The **Transfield Cup** was established in 1895. The Transfield Cup was named after T.G Transfield who was a Limerick businessman who owned a permanent circus on O'Connell Avenue. It was a competition for junior clubs in the North Munster region. The first winners of the Transfield Cup were Pirates RFC who no longer exist.

The **Munster Junior Challenge Cup** was set up in 1909. This was broader than the Transfield Cup as it took in all of Munster. The first winners were Limerick's Crescent College RFC.

The **North Munster Charity Cup** was established in 1925. This was an open competition for senior and junior clubs. Garryowen won it in its first two years.

**Limerick City Cup** was set up in 1920. The first winners were Young Munster.

## Munster Senior Challenge Cup

In the 1870s, clubs were springing up all over the country. William Lamb Stokes saw the need to establish a competition that was broader than Limerick so, along with John Forbes Maguire from Cork Football Club, they commissioned a trophy and established the Munster Senior Challenge Cup.

The Munster Senior Challenge Cup competition started in 1885 and just eight clubs competed in the first year; Garryowen FC, Nenagh RFC, Clanwilliam FC, Tralee RFC, Cork Football Club, Bandon RFC, Queen's College RFC and Limerick County Football Club. The first game was played at the Markets Field between Garryowen and Nenagh Ormond. Garryowen won by two goals and three tries to nil. Garryowen went on to the final in the inaugural year but were beaten by Bandon.

Since then, the Munster Senior Cup has been the most prestigious competition for rugby clubs in the region. In the one-hundred and thirty-nine years since its inception, Limerick clubs have won the competition seventy-four times. Cork clubs have won it sixty times and Nenagh-Ormond became the sole Tipperary winner in 2025. Garryowen are by far the most successful club in the competition with forty wins.

## Rugby is just different in Limerick

It is often said that rugby is different in Limerick to other parts of the country and world. Limerick is compared to Wales and New Zealand, as places where the game isn't elitist and is instead played by the average man or woman. There are a number of theories as to why this is the case. The reality is probably a mix of all of them.

**Limerick's Demographic** - When the game of rugby arrived in Ireland, it was embraced by the upper class and in cities like Dublin, Belfast and Cork, there was enough of that demographic to supply players to feed the clubs. Limerick didn't have a large enough middle/upper class so William Lamb Stokes had to embrace a broader demographic to get enough players to make the game viable in the city. This is the biggest single factor that differentiates Limerick rugby from elsewhere.

**Sunday Rugby Games** - As early as 1887, William Lamb Stokes was arranging for junior clubs to play each other on Sundays. The fact that the majority of the players were working class, meant that they worked six days a week. They didn't have the leisure time on a Saturday which was when rugby games were typically scheduled in other parts of the country. Sunday games and the lack of traction that the GAA had in the city, gave rugby in Limerick a huge pool of potential players. Supporters too could turn out on a Sunday to watch their friends and family play.

**Limerick's Working Class Legacy** - While not exclusively, the game in Limerick has always been played by the working classes. Men who, during the week, were labourers, working on the docks, in the mills and doing manual labour in the bacon factories. They had a physicality and strength that a doctor or banker simply couldn't have. That strength fed into the style of rugby played in Limerick. For years, the stereotype Limerick player was forward dominated, 'ball up the jersey' and run at your opponent. Physical, strong, uncompromising and perhaps with little flair. This is evidenced in the fact that, of the nine players we cover in this book, seven were forwards and two played out-half. Limerick rugby wasn't known for its pacy wingers until more recent years. Back then it was nine-and-a-half-man rugby.

**Local Rivalry** - Limerick rugby clubs belong to a defined local area and it has always been that way. Clubs like Shannon, St Marys and Abbey were formed from St Mary's Parish; Garryowen was originally from Garryowen before they moved to Dooradoyle; Young Munster came out of the Yellow Road; Richmond from Rhebogue, Thomond from the north side of the city and Presentation from the south side. What part of Limerick you come from matters, it's what binds people together and gives them an identity. Having pride in where you come from, what rugby club you play for or support, creates the rivalries that fuelled Limerick rugby. During the week a Limerick working class man was just like the next but on Sunday, when they put on their club's jersey and took to the field marching behind their local marching band, class disappeared. Now they were local heroes to their family, neighbours, supporters. Families watched on with pride as their sons, brothers, husbands and fathers battled it out against their local arch enemy.

**Social Unity** - The phrase that epitomises rugby in Limerick, that it is played by *'the Docker and the Doctor'*, alludes to the fact that all classes played the game in the city. Rugby in Limerick had/has broad appeal and more so than in other places, allows everyone to be included. In Limerick rugby was about pride in your locality, family tradition, representing the jersey with bravery. These things cross social classes and allow people with very different social and economic backgrounds to play together for the shared vision of representing your locality and beat your neighbouring club.

**Rugby Vs GAA** - Rugby was already being played in Limerick city for ten years by the time the Gaelic Athletic Association was formed in 1884. While some GAA clubs did form in the late 1880s such as St Patricks, Commercials (which no longer exists) and Old Christians, rugby clubs easily outnumbered them and already had their members locked in.

Things were different outside the city boundaries. Limerick County Football Club which had been formed in 1879, was made up of the military and landlord classes. They were pulling from a different clientele than the GAA clubs that formed across the county. The GAA also had to contend with the Parnell split which was about who would control and run the GAA. For ten years, this divided the GAA community between the nationalist Fenians (pro-Parnell) and the Clergy (anti-Parnell). It was only in the early 1900s that the GAA started to recover.

Even the introduction of Rule 27 which banned GAA members from supporting foreign sports, made no impact in Limerick city. Players just played under assumed names and administrators looked the other way.

While the GAA did not directly control any schools' curriculum, they did discourage schools from playing in foreign sports. For example, C.B.S Sexton Street was a rugby school and won the Munster Schools' Senior Cup in 1926, 1931, 1933 and 1934 but then effectively stopped playing rugby completely.

# The British and Irish Lions

The British and Irish Lions is a huge commercial entity these days. Every four years the elite players from each of the Home Unions travel to the southern hemisphere to play games against the big three rugby counties down there. It is the pinnacle of the rugby career for most. The twelve-year time gap between visits means that for some southern hemisphere players, their entire career is played between visits and they miss out.

The first tour of what is now The British and Irish Lions took place in 1888. A squad of twenty-one players from England, Scotland and Wales travelled to Australia and New Zealand. That group played thirty-five games, including some that were not even rugby. They played nineteen games of 'Aussie Rules' in Victoria and South Australia and somehow managed to win six of those. That tour was a successful venture and established the concept of a northern team touring the southern hemisphere.

Three years after that first tour, a South African rugby union invited the rugby unions of Great Britain to tour there. Sanctioned by the English Rugby Union, a squad of twenty-one players from England, Scotland and Wales toured what is now South Africa, playing twenty games. The team, named British Isles Rugby Union Team (BIRUT) presented a cup to the team that they felt performed best against them. The first winners of what is now the Currie Cup, was Griqualand West from that tour. This tour formalised the concept and included official test matches which could not be played on the previous unsanctioned trip.

In 1896, another tour to South Africa was undertaken. This group of twenty-one players was the first to have Irish players included. That tour had twenty-one games and four test matches, three of which were won by BIRUT.

Tours continued with an 1899 tour to Australia, 1903 tour to South Africa and then a 1904 tour to Australia and New Zealand. In 1910, 1927 and 1936 tours were undertaken to Argentina but as these were less commercially successful, Argentina fell off the schedule.

No tour was undertaken between 1910 and 1924 or between 1938 and 1950 because of the World Wars in which some BIRUT players died in the fighting.

After WW2, the tours started again. The BIRUT team was christened The Lions for the 1950 tour of Australia and New Zealand. The press had coined the phrase and it stuck. The 1950 team was also the first to wear the now famous red jersey. Prior to that tour BIRUT played in blue jerseys.

The current format where the Lions travel every four years, alternating between South Africa, New Zealand and Australia has been in place since 1989. Prior to that tours were loosely every four years but not strictly so.

The first Irish captain of a British and Irish Lions tour team was Sam Walker who led the 1938 tour to South Africa. He was the first of four in a row with Karl Mullen leading the 1950 tour down under, Robin Thompson leading the 1955 South African tour, and Ronnie Dawson leading the 1959 tour of Australia and New Zealand. Other Irish captains include Tom Kiernan in 1968, Willie John McBride in 1974, Ciaran Fitzgerald in 1983. More recently Brian O'Driscoll, **Paul O'Connell**, Peter O'Mahony and **Conor Murray** have been named Lions Captain. Limerick's **Bill Mulcahy** and **Keith Wood** have both led the Lions for specific non-test matches.

Irishmen have also been selected to be Lions head-coach on a number of occasions. Jack Siggins was the first in 1955. O.B Glasgow in 1959, Harry McKibbon 1962, Ronnie Dawson 1968, Syd Millar 1974, and Noel Murphy in 1980.

The most capped Lion of all time is Ireland's Willie John McBride who played in an astonishing seventeen Lions test matches. He toured with the team on five occasions. The top Lions test try scorer is also an Irishman; Tony O'Reilly scored six tries in ten tests across the 1955 and 1959 tours.

Since 1955, The Lions have also played occasional one-off games outside of the southern hemisphere countries. The first was a 1955 game at Cardiff Arms Park to make the 75th anniversary of the Welsh Rugby Union. In 1977 a "home" game against the Barbarians was played to mark the Queen's Silver Jubilee. To mark the centenary of the International Rugby Board, a Lions team took on a 'Rest of the World' team at Cardiff Arms Park. As part of France's celebration of the bi-centennial of the French Revolution, a Lions team took on a French team at Parc des Princes. Finally, in 1990 a Lions team took on a 'Rest of Europe' team in a charity fundraiser in support of Romania following the overthrow of Nicolae Ceausescu. A number of other games have been arranged as warm up fixtures ahead of tours or occasionally to mark their return from a tour.

The concept of the Lions tour has always been popular with rugby fans in the destination countries. Home fans started to travel in large numbers on the tours in support of the team. The tour documentary film, 'Living with the Lions', which gave fans behind the scenes views of the 1997 tour to South Africa, raised that to another level completely and tours since then have seen huge numbers travelling long distances to watch the team.

The camaraderie that surrounds the Lions both between the players and the fans who follow them is a joyous thing. Strangers who would normally be committed adversaries, commonly sing their adversaries' rugby songs in far flung places to the delight of the host countries.

There is little doubt that the sum is greater than the parts. When a Lions team gels, the standard of rugby can be sublime. Injuries often prevent the best fifteen players from turning out but when they do it fuels the old adage that 'rugby is the game they play in heaven'.

## Early Tours

**1888 – New Zealand and Australia.** There were no Irish men on this, the first tour. Thirty-five matches were played on the tour but no tests.

**1891 – South Africa.** No Irish amongst the touring party who won the test series three nil.

**1896 – South Africa.** Ireland won the 1896 Home Nation Championship and that was reflected in the selection of nine Irish men in the squad including Laurence Bugler from Kilrush just outside Limerick in County Clare. The squad played twenty-one matches in South Africa winning all but one. They won the test series 3-1.

**1899 – Australia.** Three Irish men were among the party that won the series to Australia three tests to one.

**1903 – South Africa.** There were five Irish men on the first British and Irish Lions teams to lose a test series. On this tour the team played twenty-two games. Three were test matches against the Springboks. The first two were drawn and South Africa won the third, giving them the series.

**1904 – Australia and New Zealand.** Two Irish men were selected for the sixth tour, a nineteen-game tour with fourteen games in Australia and a further five in New Zealand. There were four test matches on this tour. The Lions won the three against Australia but lost the test in New Zealand.

**1908 – New Zealand and Australia.** There were no Irishmen on the 1908 tour when the Lions played twenty-six matches (nine in Australia and seventeen in New Zealand). The Lions lost the test series in New Zealand having lost two and drew one.

**1910 – Argentina.** There were again no Irishmen on this tour to Argentina. There were six games played including one test. The Lions won all the games. The test game, played in Buenos Aires was the first test that Argentina had ever played in the sport.

**1910 – South Africa.** Coming just after the 1910 tour to Argentina, there were six Irish selected for the tour to South Africa. Irishman Tommy Smyth who was playing his rugby at Newport in Wales became the first Irish man to captain the Lions on this tour. The team played twenty-four games including three test matches. The Lions lost two and won one test losing the series.

## Limerick and the British and Irish Lions

You can't write a history of the British and Irish Lions without mentioning Limerick rugby. Names like Conor Murray, Paul O'Connell, Keith Wood, Bill Mulcahy, Tom Clifford and Tom Reid are deeply engraved into the story of the Lions.

The first Limerick connection to the British and Irish Lions was in 1904 but it was a Limerickman playing against the Lions. Edmund (Ned)

Dore was born at Mount David in Shanagolden on 9th November 1879. He was the third child born to Robert Dore and Sarah Jane Cregan. Within months of his birth, the family moved to Australia and arrived in Rockhampton in Queensland aboard the Sir William Wallace on 12th March 1880.

Robert Dore joined the police force in Brisbane and the family grew to ten children. As well as Ned, the family included another Australian international rugby player, Michael (Mickey) Dore and a Queensland Rugby League player, Vince Dore.

Ned attended St. Joseph's Christian Brothers' College at Gregory Terrace in Brisbane and played rugby for the North Brisbane Rugby Club.

Dore was selected for the Queensland team in 1904 and newspapers reported him as being "a hard-working prop and good in the loose". Following a Queensland game against New South Wales in Sydney, he was selected to play for the Australian team to play against the British and Irish Lions in Sydney on 2nd July 1904.

The Lions won the game 17-0. Dore injured his back during the game and wasn't selected for the other tests. His back injury ended his career and prevented him from going back to his work as a barrel-maker. In search of non-manual labour, Dore joined the Queensland Police Service and worked for them for the rest of his life. Dore died on 3rd September 1964.

*Edmund (Ned) Dore wearing his Wallaby cap and holding his Queensland cap.*

## 'Limerick based players' who played against the British and Irish Lions

Many players who have called Limerick home while playing for Munster have played against the British and Irish Lions over the years.

During the 2021 tour of South Africa, current Munster full back **Thaakir Abrahams** played on the wing for the Sharks in their 7-54 defeat by the Lions. He also played in their second game, another loss (31-71) but did score a try. **Damien de Allende** played for the South Africa A team that defeated the Lions 17-13 at Cape Town Stadium. He also played in the 1$^{st}$ Test (17-22 Loss), 2$^{nd}$ Test (27-9 Win) and the 3$^{rd}$ Test (a 19-16 win). **RG Snyman** was also part of the Springbok squad for this tour however, due to a burn injury, he didn't play in any of the games.

On the 2017 tour of New Zealand, current Munster prop **Oli Jager**, played for the New Zealand Provincial Barbarians in their 7-13 loss to the Lions. Former Munster player, **Malakai Fekitoa** played for the Highlanders team that beat the Lions 23-22. He also came on as a substitute in the final test at Eden Park which ended in a 15-15 draw.

Ahead of the 2013 tour, the British and Irish Lions played the Barbarians in Hong Kong. Ex-Munster player, **Casey Laulala** played for the defeated Barbarians team.

During the 2009 tour of South Africa, **Jean de Villiers** played in the first two test matches, a 26-21 win in Durban and a 28-25 win at Loftus Versfeld in Pretoria.

For the 2005 tour of New Zealand, the All Blacks had **Doug Howlett** on their team. He played in the first test at Lancaster Park, Christchurch which New Zealand won 21-3 and he was a replacement for the third test at Eden Park which the New Zealand also won, 38-19. Also during the tour, **Rua Tipoki** played for the New Zealand Māori team that defeated the Lions for the first time in their history. **Lifeimi Mafi** also played against the Lions on the tour. He was on the Taranaki team that were beaten 14-46 in New Plymouth.

On the 2001 tour of Australia, **Big Jim (Seamus) Williams** captained the Australia A team that won 28-25 at Gosford Stadium. He also played for the ACT Brumbies who narrowly lost 28-30 at Bruce Stadium in Canberra. On the same tour, future Munster coach **Stephen**

**Larkham** played in the first two test matches, losing the first at the Gabba in Brisbane and then winning the second in Melbourne. He was injured and replaced by Elton Flatley for the deciding test which Australia won.

Lastly, future Munster coach **Rassie Erasmus**, played in the 3$^{rd}$ Test for South Africa in 1997. The game was played at Ellis Park and the Springboks won 35-16. The Lions had already won the series having won the first two tests.

# 1924
# South Africa

William Roche

# William Roche
# Lion #220

**William Joseph Roche**
Born - 27 March 1895, Limerick

School – Mungret College
Club – UCC, Cardiff & Newport (Wales)
Ireland Caps - 3
Lions Tour(s) - 1924
Lions Appearances – 12
Lions Tests – n/a
Position – Prop/Back Row

The first Limerickman to play for the British and Irish Lions was **William Joseph Roche**. His Irish rugby career was relatively short but his achievements were considerable. He played for Munster and Ireland, played for and against the Barbarians and he toured South Africa with the British and Irish Lions. He was also a champion boxer, a consultant physician, a successful businessman, and to top it off, he had an interesting run-in with Hitler's second in command - Herr Rudolf Hess during World War II.

## Early Life

William Joseph Roche was born at 46 Upper William Street, Limerick on 27$^{th}$ March 1895. Mysteriously, William's birth certificate records his date of birth as 28$^{th}$ March, however he and his family, always celebrated his birthday on 27$^{th}$.

*William Roche's birth cert - 1895*

William's father James Hogan Roche was a flour merchant and set up a business that is still in operation today, Roche's Feeds on the Dock Road in Limerick. William's mother was Mary Jane Roche (nee Roche), the daughter of a farmer named Thomas Roche.

James and Mary Jane had ten children during their marriage. Six of those survived with William being the youngest. He had three older sisters and two older brothers.

## School

William attended Mungret College on the outskirts of Limerick City. In later life he would maintain that the school only started a rugby team because of his insistence that Association Football was *"not manly enough for growing boys"*. While at school he played football, cricket and was involved in the theatrical society.

*William Roche seated second from the right with the Mungret College team*

During his school years the Munster Schools Senior Cup competition was dominated by Rockwell and Christian Brothers Cork. Mungret wouldn't win their first Munster Schools Cup until 1941.

## Club Rugby

After finishing school William went to University College Cork to study medicine. Rugby at the turn of the century was deeply entrenched in the medical community, particularly so in Cork and Roche played with the U.C.C. rugby team and was captain of the team in 1919. While playing on this team he was selected on three occasions to play for the Irish national side. U.C.C. didn't win any honours during his time with them. While at U.C.C William was also the university heavy weight champion for four consecutive years from 1915-1919. He was also on the university hockey and cricket teams.

After World War I, William moved to Wales where he took up an appointment at Royal Gwent Hospital. Keen to continue his rugby exploits, he signed up to play for Newport RFC in 1920 and in his first season with them made over thirty appearances.

Newport had a tremendous start to the season and went unbeaten until the end of January 1921 but injuries affected the back end of the season but they still won the Welsh Club Championship. In their final game of the season in April 1921, Newport fielded a team of fifteen international players. In that game, against Bristol, they fielded ten Welsh, three English, one Scottish and one Irish international; WJ Roche.

At the end of that first season, William took up an appointment in Cardiff and so switched his rugby playing allegiance to Cardiff RFC where he played the 1921/22 season.

*The all-international team that played for Newport against Bristol in 1921*
**Back row** *– Reg Edwards (England), L Attewell (Wales), H Uzzell (Wales), R Dibble (England), J Whitfield (Wales), P Jones (Wales)*
**Middle row** *– J Wetter (Wales), E Hammett (England), F Birt (Wales), Reg Plummer (Wales), N McPherson (Scotland), J Shea (Wales),* **William J Roche (Ireland)**
**Front row** *– A Brown (Wales), T Vile (Wales), W J Martin (Wales)*

*William Roche (seated far right) with the Cardiff team in 1921/22*

Cardiff lost thirteen games that season but did better than either of their two bitter rivals Newport and Swansea. Their best win of the season came in the Barbarian's Easter 'tour' when Cardiff beat them 28-3. Roche, however, missed that game. They also did a double over William's previous team, Newport. As William played over fifteen games during the season, he was awarded a cap by the club.

In 1922 William Roche was appointed as Medical Officer for the Shipping Federation at Newport and so moved back to Newport RFC in the 1922/23 season and played there for the next five seasons becoming team captain in his final season in 1926/27.

In his first season back with Newport the team went undefeated in their thirty-nine-game season. They won thirty-five and drew four of their games on their way to winning the Wales Club Championship. In the third game of the season William played his old team mates at Cardiff in a 0-0 draw but beat them later in the season 16-3. The team also won away at Olympique Paris that season winning 6-21. They also won the

South Wales and Monmouthshire Knock-out Cup beating Treherbert in the final at Rodney Parade (4-3).

The team, nicknamed the 'Invincibles', went down in the history books of Newport RFU and each member of the team was issued with a gold watch by a local businessman. There was uproar because of this as rugby was strictly an amateur sport and gifts like this were deemed payment. Roche's future Lions teammate, Neil McPherson was suspended by the Scottish Rugby Union because of this. In the end the watches had to be returned and McPherson was re-instated.

The 1923/24 season was perhaps a highlight as William, despite not being on the Irish international team, along with two of his Newport teammates were selected to tour South Africa with the British and Irish Lions. The other two being Vince Griffiths and Neil McPherson. Another colleague, Harold Davies would also join the tour later as injury cover.

Newport had a very difficult season in 1924/25 with a record number of losses. They did manage to score an away win against Racing Club de France (3-24). William and his Newport team mates also played the touring New Zealand All-Blacks. The All-Black team of 1924 were, like Newport a few seasons earlier, given the nickname The Invincibles because of their success on this tour. In thirty-two games on the tour, they won every one of them including their game against Newport. Despite it being only Newport's fourth game of the season, they narrowly lost by 10-13.

Another difficult season followed in 1925/26 with William as Vice-Captain of the team. The following year William was made Club Captain but the 1926/27 season was again difficult. He was unable to stem the tide and Newport for the first time lost sixteen games in a season. They also conceded three times as many tries as they had in his first season with the club. The highlight of the season was William Roche leading Newport in a game against the New Zealand Māori. That game ended in a 0-0 draw.

After his season as captain of Newport, William Roche retired from playing first team rugby and, after a year with Newport's seconds, he decided to concentrate on refereeing. He had played one hundred and fifty-six times for Newport and scored twenty-two tries. Dr William

Roche was inducted into the Newport RFU Rugby Hall of Fame on March 25th 2022.

The Newport team that played the Māori in 1927
(Captain Roche - centre with the ball)

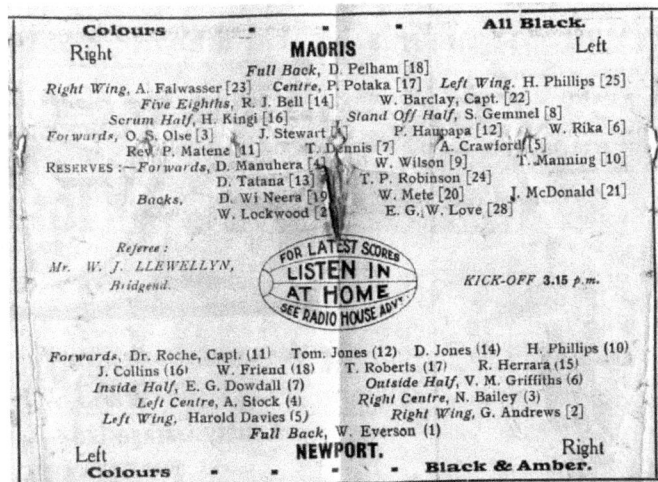

The Newport team that played the Māori in 1927

During his time at Newport, William had also helped out training and supporting the team at Risca RFC which is a nearby feeder club for Newport.

## Munster Rugby

World War I significantly limited William Roche's opportunities with Munster. There was no provincial team selected during the war period when he was at his peak playing for U.C.C. He was selected in the first Munster team after the war in 1920. At the time there was no formal Interprovincial competition so he would have played in some one-off games. Even after he moved to Wales, he continued playing for Munster until 1922. In 1950, Roche was one of the Munster Rugby selectors.

## International Rugby

# William Roche

The Five Nations championship was not held between 1915 and 1919 because of the war. It resumed for 1920. At the time, trial games were played ahead of the team being selected for the Five Nations. In 1920, William was called into the 'possibles' team to play the 'probables'. He had an outstanding trial and was selected for the Irish team. The Evening Herald had this to say about his selection, *"The surprise selection of the team, even to most of the Munster division. Roche is a genuine, hard-working forward, and thoroughly enjoys a good, lively, hustling game."*

He played in two games in that year's championship. The first an 11-14 loss to England at Lansdowne Road. He then played in Ireland's 19-0 loss at Murrayfield. He was named to play in the final game, their 28-4 loss in Wales however he withdrew at the last minute due to ill-health. He didn't play in the final game of the season against France.

*William Roche, standing on left, with the Irish team that played England in 1920*

The following year he was again called into the trial games ahead of the international season. He travelled back from Wales. There was stiff competition with the Irish Independent saying, *"Many good judges consider that any two out of Collis, Clancy, Roche and Thompson were vying for their places before either of the two named."* Roche was unlucky and missed out.

## The Barbarians

During his time with Newport and Cardiff, the Barbarians were not a touring side as they are today. The Barbarians played an annual Easter festival against Welsh and English clubs. Basing themselves at the Penarth Españade Hotel, they would play games on successive days against challenge clubs.

*William Roche, 3rd from left, at the 1925 Barbarians Easter Tour event
The gentleman sitting beside him is William Percy Carpmael who founded the
Barbarian Football Club in 1890*

William Roche played for the Barbarians on two occasions.

During their 1921/22 Easter event, while he was playing for Cardiff, William was selected to play for the Barbarians in their 15-6 loss to Newport. He played for them again on 10th April 1924/25 season against Penarth when they won 11-22. According to William's son-in-law Tim Barry, his Barbarian's blazer was a prized possession.

William Roche also played against the Barbarians four times.

In 1920 he was on the Newport side that beat them 39-0. (7 tries, 2 goals and 2 drop goals). On April 14$^{th}$ 1925, he was again victorious over the Barbarians. Three days after he had played for them against Penarth, he played on the Newport team that beat them 15-10. On April 6$^{th}$ 1926, he again played for Newport against the Barbarians. On this occasion he was on the losing side 5-6. Finally, on April 19$^{th}$ 1927, William Roche captained the Newport team that beat the Barbarians 9-8.

## The British and Irish Lions

William Roche became the first Limerickman to play for the British and Irish Lions when he was called up for the tour to South Africa in 1924. On that tour Roche played in twelve games but was not on the test team during either of the four tests. He also scored one try.

To read more about his Lions tour – Refer chapter South Africa and Zimbabwe (1924).

## Hockey

During his lifetime, Dr Roche recounted a story to his family about playing hockey for Ireland. The story goes that he was holidaying in Scotland (year unknown). The Irish national team were also in the country touring and playing the Scottish national side. William was a spectator for a game but, due to illness, the Irish side were short a player. A very capable all-round sportsman, William agreed to fill the vacancy and played in two matches over the course of a weekend. Unfortunately, Hockey Ireland were unable to corroborate the story.

## Boxing

Outside of rugby William Roche was a promising amateur boxer. Competing as a heavyweight he won the Welsh Amateur Championship in 1923.

Having won that he went on to compete for the British Heavyweight Championship in the Grand Hall at Alexandra Palace in London. Fighting Harry Mitchell, Roche broke his thumb in the first round but fought on bravely until the referee stopped the fight in the second round.

*The cup won by Dr William Roche when he competed in the Welsh Amateur Boxing Association Championships.*

*Below is the inscription.*

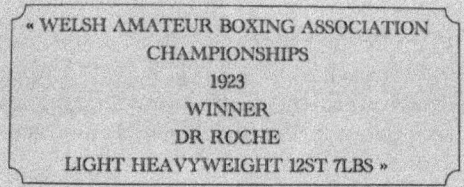

« WELSH AMATEUR BOXING ASSOCIATION
CHAMPIONSHIPS
1923
WINNER
DR ROCHE
LIGHT HEAVYWEIGHT 12ST 7LBS »

160.

**Dr. Roche's Titles.**

Dr. W. J. Roche, the Newport and Irish Rugby international forward, was on Saturday, at Cardiff, declared the winner of the light-heavyweight Welsh amateur boxing championship, and so becomes possessed of the Welsh Cup. Dr. Roche also entered for the heavy-weight championship, but his doctors would not allow him to compete owing to an injury to his shoulder. He was regarded as a "cert" in this contest. Mr. Tom White, president of the Association, was one of the judges.

**Army Cross-Country.**

Lance-corpl. W. M. Cotterell (Signals) retained the Army cross-country championship (about six miles) at Aldershot on Tuesday, winning by over 100 yards from Lieut. J.

# Post Rugby Career

After finishing his playing career William Roche became a referee and travelled all over Britain refereeing rugby games. The following appeared in the London Evening News in 1930, *"Really good rugby referees have always been scarcer than really good players and it was therefore very pleasant to hear compliments passed on the control of Dr WJ Roche in the Blackheath and Birkenhead Park match...... Good players do not necessarily make good referees but when they do, as Dr. Roche has shown, they command respect. I know few who could be said to be more competent to take charge of an international match than Dr. Roche and I am sure London will welcome him whenever he can spare the time".*

In March 1928, William Roche was invited to be the commentator on the RTE broadcast of the Wales v Ireland rugby game. The press gave great praise for his clear and interesting running commentary as Ireland won the game 10-13.

In his professional career he became a visiting Ophthalmic (eye) Surgeon to Oakdale and Caerphilly hospitals before returning to Ireland to be an eye specialist in Cork.

William Roche was a long-time friend and financial supporter of Sir Julian Hodge, a successful Cardiff banker and was for years a director of many of Julian Hodge's Companies. When these were taken over by Standard Chartered Bank, he became a Director of the Irish side of Standard Chartered Bank, a position he held for the rest of his life.

## World War II

While living in Wales in 1923, Roche was commissioned into the Royal Army Medical Corp. He was attached to the 1st Monmouthshire Battalion based in Newport. In 1927 he was promoted to Captain and he continued to serve right through to the end of the second world war by which time he had risen to the rank of Lieutenant Colonel. During WWII, he had an interesting encounter.

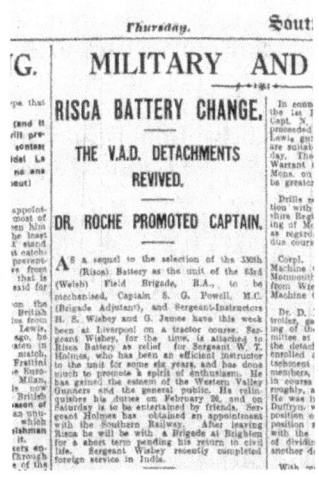

On 10th May 1941, a plane crashed in Scotland. When approached by the local farmers, the pilot identified himself as Hauptmann Alfred Horn and said he had an important message and he wanted to meet the Duke of Hamilton immediately. Speculation rose as to the actual identity of Herr Horn, with some recognising him and suspecting that he was in fact, Hitler's second in command, Rudolph Hess. Dr Roche was summonsed and was asked to verify that it was Hess from available medical records. He confirmed that it was and Hess would spend the rest of the war in prison.

On 26th June 1942, after an attempted suicide, Hess was relocated to Maindiff Court Military Hospital just north of Newport. Dr Roche was commander of six RAMC medical orderlies who looked after Hess' health while there. Hess remained in South Wales until October 1945 when he was transferred to Nuremberg for trial alongside other high-profile Nazis. He was found guilty and sentenced to life-imprisonment. Hess died by suicide in 1987.

## Personal Life

Roche's son in law Tim Barry relayed the story of how, while still at U.C.C, William witnessed the bodies of the victims of the Lusitania being brought ashore in Cobh harbour. A harrowing experience that no doubt left a mark on his character and perhaps prompted his military career.

William Roche married Marie Callaghan in July 1938. They had a daughter Judie born in 1942. When the second world war ended, the family moved back to Ireland and settled in Cork where Roche became Ophthalmic surgeon at the Mercy Hospital, The Bons Secours Hospital and St. Finbarr's Hospital. He had built up great insight into eye medicine from treating workers from the coal mines during his time in Wales. who were afflicted by coal dust.

The Roche family moved to the village of Innishannon in County Cork on 17th March 1958. He lived out his days there fishing on the Bandon and Blackwater Rivers. Dr William Joseph Roche passed away on 26th June 1983. He was eighty-eight years old. He is buried in Innishannon, Co. Cork.

Sadly, almost all of William Roche's rugby memorabilia was destroyed in a house fire in the 1950s. The only memory the family now have of his Lions adventure is a rugby ball signed by both teams on the tour and the more recently issued Lions cap.

William Roche's great grandson Sam Barry is currently training with Munster's underage team.

*William Roche's Lions Cap*

*William Roche – Sports All-Rounder*

*William Roche (1895-1983)*

# South Africa and Zimbabwe (1924)

This would be the tenth British and Irish Lions tour and the fifth to South Africa. It was also the first tour since the end of the first world war.

There were no Five Nations championships held between 1915 and 1919 because of the war effort. England had dominated the competition from its resumption until the 1924 tour, winning three Grand Slams (1921, 1923 and 1924).

On the other hand, Ireland struggled in the Five Nations after the war. They came last in each Five Nations between 1920 and 1923. 1924 was marginally better with a third-place finish after they beat France in Dublin and Wales away in Cardiff.

In Munster, Garryowen was the dominant club on the Munster Senior Cup front. In 1924 they won the first of three in a row, having been beaten by Cork Constitution in the previous two finals. Despite this dominance in Munster, none of their team were selected in the 1924 Lions squad.

## Touring party

This touring party would be the first to be given the nickname The Lions. The term would be officially adopted on the 1950 tour.

The tour was to be managed by former Welsh international Harry Packer (an English born prop who played his rugby for Newport and the Welsh international team. William Roche hadn't played on the international stage since 1920. He was playing well with Newport and perhaps because the tour manager was an ex-Newport player, he caught the eye and was selected for the tour.

Ultimately, the tour was not viewed as successful. In part that was put down to the fact that those selected were not reflective of the very best that the four nations had to offer. Coming so soon after the war, not everyone wanted to travel. The economy was recovering and money was tight. There was also the prospect of an inbound tour by the New

Zealand All-Blacks that was scheduled to overlap with the end of the tour.

*William Roche (far left) with the 1924 British Lions squad*

England's dominance in the Five Nations was reflected in the selection of eleven English players for the tour squad, including tour captain Ronald Cove-Smith. There were ten Scots and four Welsh. Given Ireland's poor performance in the previous few Five Nations championships, the selection of six Irish on the squad was somewhat flattering.

For William Roche, there was familiarity in the squad. Two of his teammates from Newport had been selected; Neil McPherson a Scottish international was part of the Newport forward pack with him, and Harold Davies out in the backs was also a colleague from the Newport team. Irish man Bill Cunningham who would later be drafted into the squad made his debut in the Irish team with Roche in 1920, as had Michael Bradley who was also a Munster teammate.

Among those selected there were some interesting characters:

Stanley Harris had been born in South Africa. With two caps for England under his belt, he was the only member of the touring party who had been in South Africa before. Harris had been commissioned

1924 South Africa

into the Royal Field Artillery in 1915 and was severely wounded during the Battle of the Somme in 1916. After recovering, he returned to active duty to serve in both Flanders and North Russia. Like William Roche, he was first capped at international level in 1920. Later in his life he would represent England in polo and become a boxing champion in South Africa. When the second world war broke out, he re-enlisted and was taken prisoner by the Japanese when they took Singapore. He would spend the rest of the war working on the Burmese Railway.

Englishman Arthur Blakiston also had a war service pedigree. He had served in the Royal Field Artillery and had been awarded the Military Cross - *"For conspicuous gallantry and devotion to duty. When a convoy of ammunition wagons, of which he was in charge, was heavily shelled and suffered casualties, he succeeded in removing all the wounded men, under continuous fire, and by his coolness and initiative prevented further casualties among the convoy".*

Another who was impacted by the war was Scotsman Bob Howie who had lost his brother David during the war.

In an administrative mix up, Englishman Reg Maxwell almost missed out on the tour. Invitations to join the tour were sent to the players' clubs. Maxwell's club, Birkenhead Park, hadn't opened the invite. With no response heard back, Maxwell's spot on the tour was offered to Mel Rosser. Luckily for Maxwell, Rosser was unable to get approval from his employer to attend the long tour and he was forced to decline. A second invite was sent to Maxwell, this time to his personal address. This time Maxwell received the invite and accepted.

The following was the tour party selected for the tour:

**Manager**
Harry Packer (Wales)

**Forwards**
R. Cove-Smith (Old Merchant Taylors and England) (captain), Arthur Frederick "Freddie" Blakiston (Blackheath and England), A. Thomas "Tom" Voyce (Gloucester and England), Neil McPherson (Newport and Scotland), R.G. Henderson (Northern and Scotland), K.G.P. Hendrie (Heriots FP and Scotland), D.S. Davies (Hawick and Scotland), R.A. Howie (Kirkcaldy RFC and Scotland), Douglas Marsden-Jones (London

1924 South Africa

Welsh and Wales), Andrew Ross (Kilmarnock and Scotland), Jammie Clinch (Dublin University and Ireland), **William Roche (Newport and Ireland)**, Jim McVicker (Collegians and Ireland), Michael Bradley (Dolphin and Ireland), Norman Brand (North of Ireland FC and Ireland)

**Backs**
D Drysdale (Heriots FP and Scotland), W.F. Gainsford (St. Bart's Hospital and England), T.E. Holliday (Aspatria and England), Rowe Harding (Swansea and Wales), Ian Smith (Oxford University and Scotland), Stanley "Stan" Wakefield Harris (Blackheath and England), William "Bill" Wallace (Percy Park and England), Roy Kinnear (Heriots FP and Scotland), James Bordass (Cambridge University and England), Reginald "Reg" Bellamy Maxwell (Birkenhead Park and England), Harold Davies (Newport and Wales), Vince Griffiths (Newport and Wales), Herbert Waddell (Glasgow Academicals and Scotland), Bill Cunningham (Lansdowne and Ireland), Arthur Young (Blackheath and England), Herbert Whitley (Northern and England)

# The Tour

Ahead of the tour the Western Mail newspaper reported a 'Presentation to Dr Roche'. *"Dr W.J Roche, the well-known Newport and ex-Cardiff ex-Irish Rugby forward was given a cordial send-off by a number of his personal friends of Dock Street, Newport prior to his departure with the British Rugby team to South Africa. Mr Guy Treverton Jones, chairman of the local Shipping Federation committee, entertained a large company to tea and presented Dr. Roche with a dressing case inscribed 'From his shipping pals at Newport'."* The case, no doubt packed with food supplies, would go on the tour with him.

This being in the days before commercial air travel, the team took a train from Waterloo station in London to Southampton where they boarded the ship Edinburgh Castle and set sail on 21$^{st}$ June for South Africa.

In his 1929 book Rugby Reminiscences and Opinions, Rowe Harding said that *"We were a happy party, and the voyage was one unending round of fun, frolics and food"*.

1924 South Africa

The voyage from Southampton to Cape Town would take seventeen days. The only break from the ship the team got was a few hours stop off on the Portuguese island of Madeira, off the coast of Morocco, where the captain took on supplies and the passengers were able to stretch their legs. Before they left Madeira, the team were entertained by locals who dove off the ship's deck, into the crystal-clear water to retrieve coins that the team were tossing for them. Irishman Norman Brand went so far as to dive in with them.

*William Roche (for right) with the Lions at Waterloo Station*

Newspaper reported that the journey was *"seventeen glorious days. Up to the Friday of last weekend the weather was hot – too sultry perhaps for perfect enjoyment of deck games"*.

There were all kinds of entertainment during the trip. A tug of war was held between first class passengers (including the team) and second class, there was a fancy-dress dinner and one newspaper reported that William Roche *"took a prominent part in the concert on board and got a rousing chorus going with McNamara's Band"*. He was also noted for taking part in *'The Beauty Chorus'* when a selection of the footballers dressed as women entertained all with a rowdy sing-song. It wasn't

55

1924 South Africa

all fun though; the team trained on board every morning and would discuss tactics in afternoon sessions.

*The Lions departing Southampton on the Edinburgh Castle
Roche is noticeable in the centre of the photo*

*The ship Edinburgh Castle which took the Lions to and from South Africa in 1924*

1924 South Africa

The Edinburgh Castle pulled into Cape Town harbour on 6th July. Harding said, "We got a very cordial welcome on our arrival at Cape Town and indeed, wherever we went in the Union and Rhodesia we were overwhelmed with hospitality and kindness".

There were just six days until the Lions played their first game against Western Province. In the meantime, there were a lot of formal engagements to be attended. The team were formally welcomed by the South African Rugby Union who were accompanied by the South African Football Association, the Local Lawn Tennis Club and the Bowling Association. There was also a civic reception at Town Hall where members of parliament and city councillors were among almost two hundred guests who welcomed them.

The team stayed at the Arthurs Seat Hotel about five miles out of town. They hoped that the location would allow them some privacy but the hotel became a beacon for the locals wanting to spot the players.

None of the party had ever been to South Africa before with the exception of Harris who was born there. In the short time they had available to them, they tried to get used to the local conditions; the heat, the hard dry pitches and the food.

In a tour that would be heavily impacted by injuries, the first struck before the team had even departed England. During the very first training session Wilf Gaisford dislocated his knee and didn't play in any games on the tour. Things got worse for the team when, during a training session ahead of this first game, Rob Henderson also dislocated his knee and missed the first six weeks of the tour.

## The Games

### Game One
v Western Province (Town & Country)
Cape Town, South Africa 12/7/1924
6–7 - Loss

**Lions Team** – Drysdale (Scotland), Harris (England), Wallace (England), Kinnear (Scotland), Holliday (England), Young (England), Waddell (Scotland), Cove Smith (England), McPherson (Scotland),

1924 South Africa

Howie (Scotland), McVicker (Ireland), Ross (Scotland), Hendrie (Scotland), Blakiston (England), Marsden Jones (Wales)

The Lions opened their 1924 tour with a game against Western Province (Town and Country) at Newlands in Cape Town. William Roche wasn't selected for the game.

A record crowd of 15,000 watched as the Lions got off to a good start, taking the lead with a Wallace try after fifteen minutes. Drysdale missed the conversion which would prove to be costly. Krige kicked a drop goal and then a few minutes later du Toit scored a try giving the home team a 7-3 advantage a half time.

England's Tom Holliday was injured at the start of the second half, breaking his collarbone, and didn't play again on the tour. Wallace scored a second try but the Lions again missed the conversion and the tour got off to a losing start.

That evening, while the rest of the tour party went to a local music hall, Roche's medical skills were required and he stayed behind at the hotel with Holliday.

*The 1924 Lions pictured ahead of a training game in Cape Town Roche is seated at the front in white – third from the right*

1924 South Africa

## Game Two
v Western Province (Universities)
Cape Town, South Africa 14/7/1924
9–8 - Win

**Lions Team** – Drysdale (Scotland), Harding (Wales), Smith (Scotland), Bordass (England), Waddell (Scotland), Griffiths (Wales), Young (England), Cove Smith (England), **Roche (Ireland)**, McPherson (Scotland), Howie (Scotland), Davies (Scotland), Voyce (England), Clinch (Ireland), Ross (Scotland)

William Roche got his first run out of the tour in the second game against the Western Province Universities side. 14,000 spectators turned out in what the newspapers described as a game *"begun in delightful weather, and the ground was in splendid condition."*

After fifteen minutes, the Lions went behind when de Villiers scored from an intercept. His try was converted by another man named de Villiers on the team. The Universities side went further ahead when Truter scored with a run from midfield after thirty minutes. With a minute to go in the first half, the Lions pulled one back when Welshman Griffiths scored after a brilliant break-through from Indian born Arthur Young. Newspaper reported that the game was very open and fast but the South Africans went into the break ahead by five points.

In the second half the Lions forward pack dominated the game and after seventeen minutes Tom Voyce scored. Voyce then put Smith through in the corner a few minutes later securing the victory for the Lions.

Irishman James Clinch was selected in this game and became the first son of a Lions player to play for the British and Irish Lions. His father Andrew Clinch had been on the South Africa tour in 1896.

Other than playing conditions and injuries, the other hindrance on the tour was the long distances that had to be travelled between games. After the first two games in Cape Town the team had just four days to get to Kimberley and prepare for the next game. This involved an incredible twenty-eight-hour train journey. To make matters worse, a fire broke out in one of the carriages on the way further delaying them.

1924 South Africa

**Game Three**
**v Griqualand West**
**Kimberley, South Africa 19/7/1924**
**26–0 - Win**

**Lions Team** – Drysdale (Scotland), Wallace (England), Maxwell (England), Bordass (England), Harris (England), Griffiths (Wales), Whitley (England), Blakiston (England), Bradley (Ireland), Brand (Ireland), Clinch (Ireland), Davies (Scotland), Hendrie (Scotland), Marsden Jones (Wales), McVicker (Ireland)

Roche missed out on the third game of the tour against Griqualand West in Kimberley.

In a very one-sided game, Griqualand West lost a man in the first five minutes and from there, there was only ever going to be one outcome. Billy Wallace set a record for the most tries scored by an individual in a Lions match. The record of five tries would stand until 1971.

After this game the team travelled to Salisbury (now Harare in Zimbabwe). This involved an even longer train journey than a few days earlier. Two days on a train to reach Salisbury and then another two days to get to the next game.

The newspapers gave a feel for how the team were greeted. The Evening Express reported, *"Tremendous enthusiasm has been aroused by the visit of the British Rugby team, who are playing against a fifteen representing Rhodesia here this afternoon. It will be the first occasion on which an overseas team has played at Salisbury "*.

**Game Four**
**v Southern Rhodesia**
**Salisbury, Zimbabwe 24/7/1924**
**16–3 – Win**

**Lions Team** – Clinch (Ireland), Smith (Scotland), Kinnear (Scotland), Maxwell (England), Rowe (Wales), Harding (Wales), Waddell (Scotland), Young (England), McPherson (Scotland), Voyce (England), **Roche (Ireland)**, Davies (Scotland), Bradley (Ireland), Brand (Ireland), Ross (Scotland), McVicker (Ireland)

1924 South Africa

William Roche was selected for the first international team to play a game in Zimbabwe when he turned out against Southern Rhodesia in Salisbury.

To mark their arrival, a government luncheon was held in their honour hosted by Charles Coghlan the Premier and parliament was postponed for the day so that people could attend the game.

Southern Rhodesia had the better of the first half and were rewarded for their efforts when they were awarded a penalty close to the Lions' line. Coaton kicked them into the lead. There was no further score in the first half and the Lions went into the break down by three.

There was a much-improved Lions performance in the second half. Voyce, Smith and Harding each scored tries. Australian born Scotland winger Ian Smith also scored a second try. In the closing stages the Lions were in complete control and could have scored more.

Rowe Harding said this of the conditions, *"When a scrum was formed, clouds of dust rose in such a volume that the scrum was hardly visible, and the ball emerged like a smoke bomb from its cloud of smoke".*

Scottish hooker Andrew Ross injured his knee so badly in this game that he never played again on the tour.

*Roche (on the left) with a Lions hunting party during the tour*

1924 South Africa

## Game Five
## v Western Transvaal
## Potchefstroom, South Africa 30/7/1924
## 8-7 - Win

Lions Team – Voyce (England), Wallace (England), Bordass (England), Griffiths (Wales), Harding (Wales), Waddell (Scotland), Young (England), Cove Smith (England), Howie (Scotland), Marsden Jones (Wales), McVicker (Ireland), Bradley (Ireland), Harris (England), **Roche (Ireland)**, Blakiston (England)

After only four games the Lions were already in a crisis with six players down before this game with flu and injuries. This would become a recurring theme on the tour. Brand and Clinch were originally named in the team but were unavailable. Harris and McVicker were brought in as late replacements.

This was expected to be the stiffest test to date and it proved to be a tight affair. Western Transvaal had the better of the opening stages and went ahead after twenty minutes with a penalty kick from du Plessis. At the end of the half, the Transvaal side lost Bodenstein to injury and played the rest of the game down a man as there were no substitutes allowed under rugby rules at the time. From that point on, the Lions took control up front.

In the second half Transvaal went further ahead from a drop goal. Griffiths scored for the Lions. With ten minutes to go Voyce put the Lions ahead with a penalty. That was enough to give the Lions victory.

## Game Six
## v Transvaal
## Johannesburg, South Africa 2/8/1924
## 12-12 - Draw

Lions Tour – Drysdale (Scotland), Wallace (England), Kinnear (Scotland), Maxwell (England), Harding (Wales), Young (England), Waddell (Scotland), Cove Smith (England), Blakiston (England), McPherson (Scotland), Voyce (England), Davies (England), Howie (Scotland), McVicker (Ireland), Marsden Jones (Wales)

1924 South Africa

The newspapers reported this as a "credible draw" for the Lions against the strongest provincial side in the country. 15,000 spectators attended the game and witnessed a sensational opening as Waddell scored a drop goal after just two minutes. Transvaal immediately went down the other end of the field and scored a try but it was disallowed because of offside. Waddell then scored again after four minutes picking up a loose ball and running over the line. Voyce converted. After seven minutes Transvaal got on the score sheet when Bosman kicked a penalty. The Lions went into half time 9-3 up.

Transvaal scored five minutes into the second half when Van Druten got over the line. His try was converted by Bosman. Transvaal then went ahead when Hudson kicked a drop goal. The Lions pulled back level when Harding scored an unconverted try. For the rest of the game, the Lions launched wave after wave of attacks but Transvaal held them out and the game finished 12-12.

This draw started an unwanted record. It was the longest winless run in Lions matches and it would take eight games and a full month before they won again.

**Game Seven**
**v Orange Free State (Country)**
**Kroonstad, South Africa 6/8/1924**
**0–6 - Loss**

**Lions Team** – Drysdale (Scotland), Wallace (England), Maxwell (England), Harding (Wales), Harris (England), Griffiths (Wales), Bordass (England), McPherson (Scotland), Clinch (Ireland), Davies (Scotland), Howie (Scotland), Bradley (Ireland), **Roche (Ireland)**, Marsden Jones (Wales), Brand (Ireland)

Barely half of the squad were fit and available for this game. A team was picked but it had players playing out of position. There was even talk that the next four games (up until the first test) should be cancelled to allow the Lions to get back to strength. To make matters worse, the hotel the team were staying in was overbooked and the Lions had to sleep three in a bed the night before the game.

Wind was blowing more than usual and the dry dusty field was whipped up into a spiral dust cloud. The Lions lost the toss and played into the win and dust in the first half. The managed to keep the game tight and went into the break only 3-0 down. The team were confident that they could overcome the opposition with the breeze in the second half.

Just as the whistle went to signal the start of the second half, the breeze mysteriously changed direction completely and the Lions again played into the wind and dust in the second half. It felt like everything had gone wrong for them and they surrendered to a 6-0 loss.

**Game Eight**
**v Orange Free State**
**Bloemfontein, South Africa 9/8/1924**
**3–6 - Loss**

**Lions Team** – Drysdale (Scotland), Wallace (England), Kinnear (Scotland), Griffiths (Wales), Maxwell (England), Whitley (England), Waddell (Scotland), Blakiston (England), Brand (Ireland), Bradley (Ireland), Clinch (Ireland), Davies (Scotland), McVicker (Ireland), Marsden Jones (Wales), **Roche (Ireland)**

The newspaper report summed up this game with the line *"Orange Free State had three chances and scored two of them. We had five times as many opportunities and scored just once"*.

**Game Nine**
**v Natal**
**Pietermaritzburg, South Africa 13/8/1924**
**3–3 - Draw**

**Lions Team** – Harris (England), Smith (Scotland), Bordass (England), Maxwell (England), Harding (Wales), Young (England), Griffiths (Wales), Cove Smith (England), Blakiston (England), Bradley (Ireland), Clinch (Ireland), Howie (Scotland), McPherson (Scotland), McVicker (Ireland), **Roche (Ireland)**

With only seven fit forwards, Vincent Griffiths had to be drafted in from the backs to make up the pack. Harold Davies had been drafted in as injury cover. He was named in the team despite only being

1924 South Africa

expected to arrive in Pietermaritzburg that morning. In the end he was delayed and Maxwell played instead.

It had been raining for the previous two days but on the day the sun appeared and the weather was glorious.

Natal scored after fifteen minutes when their winger Tod scored a try which went unconverted. Although the Lions had the better of the first half they didn't score and went into half time 3-0 down.

The Lions continued to pressure Natal during the second half and Ian Smith scored after eighteen minutes with a break away from the halfway line. The easy conversion was missed by Waddell which proved costly. In an *"uninspiring"* game, there were no further scores.

The newspapers at this point in the tour started to talk about off field activities being a reason for the Lions' poor form. *"It is only the ghost of the side that landed a month ago. The team deserves to be beaten. If Britain wants to maintain the excellent standard set hitherto, certain of her players must cut out the jollification part of the business. It is only fair to their opponents, who put the game first and the gaiety afterwards,"* said the Daily Express. In response, the team pulled out of an after-game function at Pietermaritzburg much to the disgust of their hosts.

**Game Ten**
**v South Africa (First Test)**
**Durban, South Africa 16/8/1924**
**3-7 - Loss**

**Lions Team** – Drysdale (Scotland), Smith (Scotland), Wallace (England), Maxwell (England), Kinnear (Scotland), Whitley (England), Waddell (Scotland), Cove Smith (England), Blakiston (England), Brand (Ireland), Davies (Scotland), Howie (Scotland), Marsden Jones (Wales), McPherson (Scotland), McVicker (Ireland)

**South Africa** – Ellis, van Druton, Kruger, du Plessis, Clarkson, Walker, Payn, Mellish, Bester, Myburgh, Osler, Truter, Tindal, Albertjn, Mostert, Aucamp, van der Plank, Starke

Ahead of the first test the Lions named a panel of seventeen players from whom the match day fifteen would be picked. The reason being

1924 South Africa

that such was the length of the injury list, they didn't know who would be fit to play.

With the breeze and the sun at their backs, the Springboks took a 7-0 half time lead through a Hans Aucamp try which many in the crowd felt was knocked on. Nonetheless, the try was awarded and an Osler drop goal extended their lead. Bennie Osler, who would go on to be one of South Africa's greatest ever players, was a renowned goal kicker and could convert kicks from vast distances.

The Lions pulled back a try in the second half from scrum-half Herbert Whitley, who scored under the posts. Despite the apparent easy conversion kick, it was missed. In a valiant effort the Lions battered the Springboks in the second half but couldn't score again and lost the test.

The Lions lost centre Reg Maxwell with a dislocated shoulder during this game and played for a long period down a man. Maxwell joined the list of injured and wouldn't play again for six weeks.

**Game Eleven
v Witwatersrand
Johannesburg, South Africa 20/8/1924
6–10 - Loss**

**Lions Team** – Harris (England), Smith (Scotland), Bordass (England), Harris (England), Davies (Wales), Harding (Wales), Whitley (England), Griffiths (Wales), McPherson (Scotland), Hendrie (Scotland), Clinch (Ireland), **Roche (Ireland)**, Bradley (Ireland), Voyce (England), Marsden Jones (Wales), Davies (Scotland).

Another man down; McVicker had an operation the morning of the game for a splintered bone in his nose.

The Lions showed their superior skills in the first half and went ahead through a Voyce penalty after an offside infringement. Within a few minutes they went further ahead when Whitley scored a try.

1924 South Africa

In the second half Witwatersrand came back into the game. After five minutes they scored a penalty, kicked by de Villiers. De Villiers went on to score a drop goal and another penalty as the Lions went down to another defeat. The headlines at home simply read "Beaten Again". They were now six games without a win with the second test up next.

**Game Twelve**
**v South Africa (Second Test)**
**Johannesburg, South Africa 23/8/1924**
**0–17 - Loss**

**Lions Team** – Drysdale (Scotland), Smith (Scotland), Harding (Wales), Kinnear (Scotland), Davies (Wales), Young (England), Waddell (Scotland), Cove Smith (England), Blakiston (England), Brand (Ireland), Davies (Scotland), Hendrie (Scotland), Howe (Scotland), Marsden Jones (Wales), McPherson (Scotland)

**South Africa** – Bosman, Aucamp, Bester, Starke, Albertjn, Osler, Truter, Mostert, Kruger, Ellis, van Druten, du Plessis, Walker, Payn, Mellish

*The Lions take the field for the 2nd Test in Johannesburg*

The capacity of the stadium was just 15,000 but with great excitement after a close first test, spectators broke down the fence and the number

1924 South Africa

swelled dramatically. The estimate is that 25,000 or more watched the game.

The first half was a titanic battle between the two sets of forwards. The only score coming on the brink of half time when Osler scored a penalty.

Early in second half Blakiston scored a try but it was disallowed for a forward pass. This borderline decision knocked the confidence of the Lions and the South Africans took control of the game. They ran in four unanswered tries from Kenny Starke, Phil Mostert, Jack van Druten and Pierre Albertyn, to easily win the game. The best the Lions could do now was to draw the four game test series.

Before leaving Johannesburg, the team were taken to a Zulu dance to experience Zulu culture. They were each presented with a shield and the Zulu stabbing sword called an assegai as mementos of the tour.

> *"The British team arriving at a town after a night in the dusty train, with a day's growth of beard, a day's deposit of train dust, shirts open at the neck, disreputable pairs of old flannels covering our legs, and assegais and Zulu shields clutched in either had, gave the impression of a band of lawless ruffians descending upon the town."*
>
> Rowe Harding

**Game Thirteen**
**v Pretoria**
**Pretoria, South Africa 27/8/1924**
**0–6 - Loss**

**Lions Team** – Davies (Wales), Harris (England), Bordass (England), Kinnear (Scotland), Waddell (Scotland), Harding (Wales), Whitley (England), Griffiths (Wales), Cove Smith (England), Henderson (Scotland), Hendrie (Scotland), Howie (Scotland), McVicker (Ireland), **Roche (Ireland)**

The Lions still struggling with injuries played eight backs and seven forwards in this game. Scot Henderson was recovered finally from his dislocated knee and got to play his first game on tour.

1924 South Africa

The first half was a scrappy affair with no scores. After five minutes of the second half Malherbe scored for Pretoria. Twelve minutes later Borman kicked a penalty to make it 6-0 at the final whistle.

The Lions had now gone eight games without a win. Interest from back home was starting to fade. They needed a win badly.

**Game Fourteen**
**v Cape Colony**
**Kimberley, South Africa 30/8/1924**
**13 – 3 – Win**

**Lions Team** – Voyce (England), Wallace (England), Kinnear (Scotland), Davies (Wales), Harris (England), Whitley (England), Cunningham (Ireland), Cove Smith (England), Clinch (Ireland), Davies (Scotland), Henderson (Scotland), Hendrie (Scotland), Marsden Jones (Wales), McPherson (Scotland), McVicker (Ireland)

A win at last. Injuries meant the Lions called up Bill Cunningham. Cunningham was an ex-Ireland fly half who was now living in Johannesburg where he was working as a dentist. Cunningham had eight Irish caps between 1921 and 1923 but hadn't played high level rugby since then.

In his second game back from injury, Henderson scored the only try of the first half which Voyce converted. In the second half the Lions pushed out their lead with tries from Harris and Wallace to make it 17-0. Right at the death the Cape Colony team scored through Slater.

**Game Fifteen**
**v North Eastern Districts**
**Aliwal North, South Africa 3/9/1924**
**20–12 - Win**

**Lions Team** – Davies (Wales), Harris (England), Griffiths (Wales), Waddell (Scotland), Harding (Wales), Whitley (England), Cunningham (Ireland), Blakiston (England), Bradley (Ireland), Clinch (Ireland), Henderson (Scotland), Hendrie (Scotland), Howie Scotland), Marsden Jones (Wales), **Roche (Ireland)**

1924 South Africa

The North Eastern team played well in front of a crowd of 2,500 but the Lions were just too strong. Davies opened the scoring with a penalty. Shortly afterwards his cross-field kick opened up the chance and Bradley scored in the corner. Griffiths scored another try for the Lions before the African team rallied with a try and a penalty to make it 13-6 at half time.

The second half was a very open contest. Cunningham dropped a goal and Griffiths got his second try. Duplessis scored two penalties to keep the North Eastern team in the game but the game was won.

Game Sixteen
v Border
East London, South Africa 6/9/1924
12–3 - Win

Lions Team – Bordass (England), Harding (Wales), Davies (Wales), Waddell (Scotland), Harris (England), Young (England), Clinch (Ireland), Cove Smith (England), Blakiston (England), Davies (Scotland), Henderson (Scotland), Howie (Scotland), McPherson (Scotland), McVicker (Ireland), Voyce (England)

Harris opened the scoring as the Lions had the better start to the game but the rest of the half went by without another score. Howie, Voyce and Blakiston scored tries in the second period. None of the Lions conversions were successful.

Game Seventeen
v Eastern Province
Port Elizabeth, South Africa 10/9/1924
6–14 - Loss

Lions Team – Drysdale (Scotland), Voyce (England), Davies (Wales), Bordass (England), Harris (England), Young (England), Griffiths (Wales), Bradley (Ireland), Clinch (Ireland), Hendrie (Scotland), Marsden Jones (Wales), McVicker (Ireland), **Roche (Ireland),** Voyce (England)

Eastern Province opened the scoring with a penalty for an offside infringement. Five minutes later Loftus scored a try to put them further ahead. They went into the break with an 8-0 lead.

Seven minutes into the second half the Lions scored from a forward play that put McVicker over the line. Not long after, Eastern Province scored again when Jeffreys intercepted a poor pass from Young and ran over the line. The Lions came back though and **William Roche** scored his one and only try for the Lions but unfortunately, the Africans scored again and the game was gone. Unfortunately, there is no description of Roche's try in the newspaper reports other than a mention that it was a 'lucky try'.

**Game Eighteen**
**v South Africa (Third Test)**
**Port Elizabeth, South Africa 13/9/1924**
**3–3 - Draw**

**Lion Team** – Drysdale (Scotland), Harris (England), Griffiths (Wales), Kinnear (Scotland), Harding (Wales), Whitley (England), Cove Smith (England), McPherson (Scotland), McVicker (Ireland), Blakiston (England), Howie (Scotland), Henderson (Scotland), Davies (Scotland), Voyce (England), Cunningham (Ireland)

**South Africa** – du Plessis, Grange, van Druten, Bosman, Mellish, Ellis, Devine, Osler, Albertjn, Kruger, Walker, van der Plank, Slater, de Kock, Starke

The Lions went ahead when Bill Cunningham darted over from the back of a five-yard scrum. Drysdale missed what was viewed as an easy conversion that ultimately would have won the game.

Drysdale missed a penalty in the second half that he really should have scored. The South Africans levelled with a try from Jack van Druten and the game finished in a draw.

The Lions could easily have won this game but didn't and as a result the test series was gone. All they had left to play for is pride in the final test in Cape Town.

1924 South Africa

## Game Nineteen
v South Western Districts
Oudtshoorn, South Africa 16/9/1924
12–6 - Win

**Lions Team** – Drysdale (Scotland), Harris (England), Davies (Wales), Voyce (England), Bordass (England), Young (England), Griffiths (Wales), Blakiston (England), Bradley (Ireland), Clinch (Ireland), Davies (Scotland), Henderson (Scotland), Hendrie (Scotland), Marsden Jones (Wales), **Roche (Ireland)**

Just three days after the test match, many of the same players played again against South Western Districts.

In a fast and open first half Voyce, Clinch and Davies scored for the Lions. Ravenscroft scored a penalty for the local team and the teams went into the break with the score at 9-3 to the Lions.

Hendrie didn't return for the second half due to injury. With a man's advantage, de Kock scored for South Western Districts. With the score at 9-6 and tension rising as the clock wound down, Voyce scored a late try giving the Lions victory.


## Game Twenty
v South Africa (Fourth Test)
Cape Town, South Africa 20/9/1924
9–16 - Loss

**Lions Team** – Drysdale (Scotland), Harris (England), Griffiths (Wales), Kinnear (Scotland), Harding (Wales), Whitley (England), Waddell (Scotland), Cove Smith (England), McPherson (Scotland), McVicker (Ireland), Blakiston (England), Howie (Scotland), Henderson (Scotland), Davies (England), Voyce (England)

**South Africa** – Bosman, Slater, Bester, Albertjn, Starke, Osler, Truter, Mostert, Kruger, Ellis, van Druten, Grange, Walker, van der Plank, Mellish

The Lions had already lost the series. All they had to play for was pride. In a tough game during which an unspecified Lions player was reprimanded for fighting like a boxer, the Springboks took a 7-3 first half lead. A try from Bester and a fifty-yard drop goal a minute later from Starke was more than the Lions' penalty goal from Tom Voyce.

Springboks led throughout and in the second half Starke scored again to extend the lead. Harris got one back for the Lions to make it 10-6 but then Starke scored his third. In a back-and-forth half, Voyce again scored for the Lions to make it 13-9 going into the closing stages but Jack Slater scored in the final minute to confirm the victory for South Africa.

**Game Twenty-One**
**v Western Province**
**Cape Town, South Africa 25/9/1924**
**8–6 – Win**

**Lions Team** – Drysdale (Scotland), Harris (England), Davies (Wales), Griffiths (Wales), Harding (Wales), Whitley (England), Bordass (England), Cove Smith (England), Bradley (Ireland), Clinch (Ireland), Howie (Scotland), Marsden Jones (Wales), Blakiston (England), McPherson (Scotland), **Roche (Ireland)**

In the final game of the tour against Western Province, William Roche made his twelfth and final appearance for the British and Irish Lions.

An estimated eight thousand spectators turned out in fine but windy weather to watch the last game. The home side scored first with a try from Weepner after twenty-six minutes. The Lions responded strongly and seven minutes later they scored with Welshman Rowe Harding scoring and unconverted try. It was 3-3 at the break.

Drysdale took a heavy knock during the first half and was unable to return for the second half. The Lions played on with fourteen men. Despite being a man down, the Lions pressured well and Blakiston caught Tindell in possession near his own goal line. The ball went to Cove-Smith who went over to give the Lions a lead. He also converted the try. After twenty-six minutes, Osler scored a penalty to keep Western Province in the game. The closing stages were 'vigorous' but there was no further scoring and the Lions closed their tour with a win.

The Edinburgh Castle left Cape Town on September 27th and arrived back in Southampton on 28th October 1924. It had been a disappointing tour. The 1924 Lions were the first to lose more games than they won on a tour.

## Tour Reflections

William Roche had played in twelve games for the 1924 Lions. He didn't make the test team that lost the series in what was a disappointing tour. It's impossible to know from this vantage point a century later why he didn't get a test game. He was however, a Lion and Limerick's first one at that.

> *"The popular impression of us, I am afraid, was that we were a hard-drinking set of wastrels who never tried to keep fit. I will not deny that there was occasionally what is termed a "blind", but I have known much more successful teams who drank much more, and nothing was ever said about their bad habits".*
>
> Rowe Harding

1924 South Africa

*"The British team record was, bluntly, one that did British sporting prestige in South Africa a good deal of harm. Not only did we suffer from a lack of good reserves, but we never got properly together as a team. Most of us had never met till we embarked at Southampton and it took us a good may days before we got to know each other.*

*We had practically no team practice before we took to the field for our first match, and half the tour was over before the selection committee could decide on the relative merits of individual players.*

*Furthermore, our programme was compressed into an absurdly short space of time. We played twenty-two matches in ten weeks, an average of two matches a week, and in between we sometimes travelled forty-eight hours in the train, so that anything more than a perfunctory practice the day before the match was impossible.*

*Even before a test match, most of the players were called upon to play a midweek match, while the Springboks were collected together and given a week's rest before playing against us.*

*Little wonder then that we were a tired, dispirited, demoralised collection of units and failed to live up to the high-sounding name we bore."*
Rowe Harding

While researching this book, we discovered a letter that was sent by William Roche to his alma mater, Mungret College, in 1925. The letter was published in the school yearbook for that year and probably hasn't been read since. Who better to recount his tour reflections than William Roche himself.

*"I have many happy rugby memories, but none to surpass my visit with the 1924 British Test side which toured South Africa. We were a very happy family – ten Englishmen, ten Scotchmen, four Welshmen and five Irishmen. With four exceptions all were international, and since then two others have been capped. Needless to mention, on the passage out, we won all the events in the ship's sports with the exception of the Ladies' Race. All the players were very popular on board, in fact, so popular was one member that he was engaged before arriving in South Africa. We were more than a little thrilled when, on the morning of the seventeenth day, we were in sight of Cape Town, and we were very much impressed by Table Mountain, with its tablecloth of white cloud, its peaks which are known as the Twelve Apostles, and the Lion's Head standing out in clear silhouette and*

overhanging the beautiful South African Capital. Our first experience of South African hospitality was our reception on board by the President and many members of the Rugby Union at 5.45am. It was indeed a very pleasant surprise. We had expected at that hour to see Dock Officials on the Quay, but there were hundreds of Britishers and Afrikaners who gave us a cheery welcome on coming ashore, which was very enjoyable after seventeen days at sea. South Africa was in spring attire, blue skies and much warmer than home in August. We thought, surely this is not 'rugger' weather but the South Africans were in the height of their season and they had been anxiously awaiting our arrival. Our first days were one round of pleasure and training. We played our first two games at Newlands, Cape Town, which is a grass pitch. It was as hard as a rock and it is not surprising that two of our players sustained fractured bones in the first game. Unfortunately, one was Holliday, this year's English full back. He never played again during the tour.

After ten happy days in Cape Town, we left for Kimberley by Express Train. We were surprised when it stopped at every station and averaged fourteen miles per hour. Yet it was the National Express train. However, it had its advantages. We saw the scenery, and in a few hours, we were in the Karoo, which is practically desert, and we had our one and only experience of a sand storm. I can assure you it is very unpleasant, and it raises your laundry bill considerably. After two days of this, we arrived in Kimberley, famous for its diamond mines. All Kimberley met us on arrival, and they were very much surprised to see Britishers in Plus Fours and Oxford Bags. They had never seen either before. I have on only one previous occasion played rugby on a gravel pitch and that was at Mungret, outside the gymnasium. On that occasion I received 'twice nine' for promoting a rugby match. Rugby was taboo – Mungret was a soccer school then. On this occasion I received deep cuts on knees, elbows and hips. The only consolation was that we won the match, twenty-six points to nil. Kimberley District, even with two feet of dust on the roads, was interesting. There was a drought on and a plague of locusts, things that farmers fear most, for the plague spells ruin to many. The locusts had eaten every blade of grass for hundreds to miles on their flight to the coast. Every foot of the ground was covered with ravenous, dead and spent locusts. It was estimated by the local papers that some of the swarms were one mile wide and half a mile high. Tom Voyce, the English forward, stated that when motoring in the country, the locusts were so numerous that, although only mid-day, it was quite dark, and it was necessary to change from top to second gear to get through them. We accused him of spinning yarns. I have no doubt he exaggerated somewhat, but in many places the trains were

1924 South Africa

*not able to travel, as the crunching of the dead locusts on the lines made the wheel and lines so greasy that the wheels could not grip them.*

*Another experience worthy of note was indirectly due to the drought. The river and ponds were dry, but there was a reservoir near Kimberley, and thousands of partridges from the neighbouring country came to appease their thirst, and we shot one hundred and sixty-five drive birds in two hours. There were six guns, Scotch Moor owners would be envious of our bag.*

*Our next temporary home was Rhodesia, the English Colony, most of which is virgin soil, but so beautiful and famous for big game shooting. We were received on our arrival in Salisbury by the Prime Minister of Rhodesia, Sir James Coughlan, a son of an Irish pioneer. When we visited the sportsground – another gravel footer pitch – we all hoped we should not be selected, still feeling very sore after our Kimberley experience. I was, however, one of the unlucky ones. Andrew Ross, the famous Scotch forward, was injured there; he never played since. I have never seen so many injuries at footer; every match there were three or four casualties, and although there were thirty players, after the sixth match we had only fifteen fit. Fortunately, towards the end of the tour there were twenty-four available. At this stage we were beginning to tire of railway journeys – every place we visited seemed to mean at least two days' journey.*

*From Salisbury we went to Bulawayo. We visited the Matoppes (The World View). It is a high granite Kopje, from which can be seen nearly a thousand smaller Kopjes, and in between them verdant foliage, on which is buried one of England's most famous sons, Cecil Rhodes.*

*What a change it was, coming from the wilds, to Johannesburg, which is the centre of the gold mining industry and the pleasure City of South Africa! Again, we were overwhelmed with hospitality. The only thing we did not like in Johannesburg was playing football. Salisbury was four hundred feet above sea level, Johannesburg is six thousand feet. You can imagine the effect on the players. To walk upstairs slowly meant you were out of breath. It takes one month to become acclimatised, and we played two days after our arrival, and we had to run about one and a half miles before going on the field to get our second wind. We did not do well in Johannesburg. We drew with the Transvaal and lost a test match. At Kroonstad, Orange Free state, we had two days' big game shooting on a preserve nearly the size of County Limerick. You cannot imagine anything more thrilling. We crossed the veldt in three Ford cars, until the buck and wildebeests (S.A buffalo) were in sight – a herd of about three*

1924 South Africa

*hundred. Then the cars went full speed in their direction. These animals do forty-five miles per hour comfortably, and when within five hundred yards range we jumped from the cars and took aim. If you were fortunate enough to strike your objective you would hear a distinct "plonk" as the bullet entered the beast, and then the victim gradually tailed off from his fellows. I shall never forget one bull I wounded in the foreleg. We followed him in the car and when within fifty yards I left the car to give him the 'coup de grace'. As I fired, he charged me – I missed – again I fired and missed; fortunately, the third bullet reached its objective and the bull fell five yards from me. I was lucky. If I had missed again there was no escape; I should have been killed or gored.*

*Some further weary days in a train and we arrived at Durban, which is semi tropical. It was ninety-nine in the shade – surely not football weather, but we succeeded in beating Natal Province. Here we were initiated into the art of surf-bathing, much to the amusement of the onlookers. There is a trick to manipulating a surfboard. Our best exponent was Waddell, the Scottish outside half. At this period, we were more interested in surf-bathing than in football, and we were comparatively efficient, after further endeavours at East London and Port Elisabeth and Muizenburg, where we stayed on our return to Cape Town. Muizenburg is supposed to be the second surf-bathing beach in the world, Honolulu being the best. Traveling one hundred and fifty yards on a broken wave is quite ordinary.*

*I will not write further about our travels and pleasure, or the Editor will frown on the length of my letter. I must comment on South African football. I have never seen such hefty forwards. The test team pack averaged thirteen- and three-quarter stone and six feet in height. Their backs were very orthodox; they invariably played to their wings; an outside half never made an opening; a centre never broke though. From a match-winning point of view, their football was most effective, but from a spectacular viewpoint the British style of play is preferable.*

*I cannot possibly finish without commenting on the South African hospitality. Irish and Scotch hospitality is proverbial, but the hospitality of the Colonial Britisher and the Afrikander, is difficult to imagine. On occasions it was well-nigh embarrassing. We were sorry when our four months' tour, which for most of us will be an outstanding event of our lives, was over, and it was with heavy hearts we waved farewell to three thousand well-wishers on the pier at Cape Town."*

William Joseph Roche 1925

Two of Roche's tour colleagues had early and sudden deaths. Roy Kinnear collapsed and died while playing rugby union with the RAF during World War II in 1942. He was just thirty-eight years old. Irishman Norman Brand would later drown in Poole harbour aged just thirty-nine. On a more positive note, Arthur Blakiston would later inherit his father's baronetcy and become 7th Baronet Blakiston, of London and Master of Hounds in Hampshire.

1924 South Africa

# 1950
# New Zealand, Australia and Sri Lanka

Tom Clifford

# Tom Clifford
# Lion #327

**Tom Clifford**
Born - 15 November 1923, Limerick Junction

School – Christian Brothers
Club – Young Munster
Ireland Caps - 14
Lions Tour(s) - 1950
Lions Appearances – 20
Lions Tests – 5
Position – Full back, Out-half, Flanker, Prop

The phrase 'legend of the game' is often thrown about too generously. If there was one person in Limerick rugby to which they are an undoubted fit, it is **Tom Clifford**. Tom was a true sportsman. He represented Limerick in the League of Ireland, as well as reaching the very peak of what can be achieved in the game of rugby. His legacy in Limerick Rugby continues to today with Young Munster's home ground, Tom Clifford Park, named after him.

## Early Life

Tom Clifford was born Jeremiah Thomas Clifford just outside Limerick Junction, Co. Tipperary on 15th November 1923.

*Tom Clifford's Birth Cert*

Tom's father, also Jeremiah, was a gardener. When Tom was three years old, his family moved to Limerick and lived at Newtown House in Upper William Street.

## School

Tom Clifford was educated at Christian Brothers on Sexton Street secondary school, where he played on the school's hurling team. Unlike their counterparts in Cork, Limerick CBS at that time were known predominantly as a hurling school.

## Club Rugby

In 1938 Tom made his senior debut for Young Munster in a friendly match against Cork Constitution. He was fifteen years old and played at fullback. As early as January 1939 he was being noticed. The Sunday Independent saying on 15th January after a loss to Cork Con in the Munster League that *"T Clifford was a safe full back for the losers but the only other to merit praise was Cyril Lee"*. He continued to play on the Young Munster team in the Limerick Charity Cup and Munster League. In 1943 he was on the Young Munster team that lost the final of the Charity Cup to an Army team (after a replay).

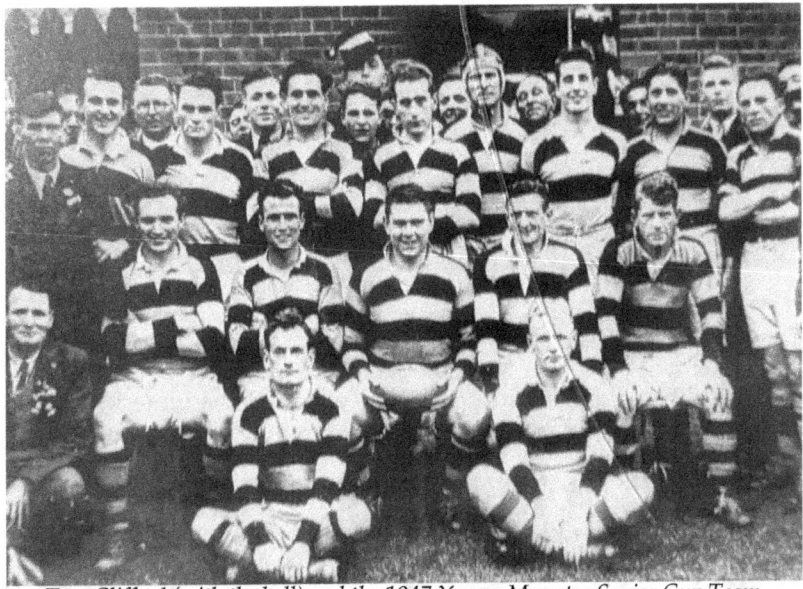

*Tom Clifford (with the ball) and the 1947 Young Munster Senior Cup Team*

He made his first Munster Senior Cup appearance in 1943. This time he was playing as a wing-forward.

Tom Clifford twice led Young Munster to the Munster Senior Cup final. In 1947, they came up against Garryowen and were beaten by a team featuring another Limerick Lion, **Tom Reid.**

The following year, Young Munster again made it to the final of the Munster Senior Cup. This time they came up against Dolphin from

Cork and they again fell short. Many reflect on Tom Clifford's career and feel that it is an injustice that he never got to lift that cup.

*Tom Clifford (with the ball) and the 1949/50 Young Munster Team*

Tom did have success with Young Munster. During his time with the club, they twice won the Munster Senior League title. Bookending his career in 1944 and again in 1952. They also won the Limerick Charity Cup in 1949, 1951, 1955 and in 1956.

*Tom seated 4$^{th}$ from left - Young Munster v Cardiff 1952*

In October 1952, Tom led a Young Munster select XV against the visiting Cardiff side at Thomond Park. The select side which included Tom Reid (Garryowen) and Tom's Lions colleague Jack Kyle were well beaten in an exhibition of running rugby. Cardiff won 31-17 in front of a crowd of five thousand spectators.

## Munster Rugby

Tom Clifford was first called into the Munster squad in November 1943. He played in the inaugural Interprovincial Championship in 1946 when Munster came third. The following year Clifford was also on the team when Munster won the Interpro Championship scoring a penalty in the Munster game against defending champions Ulster.

*The Munster team that lost to Australia at the Mardyke in December 1947*

The following year, 1947, saw Munster take on the touring Australia team. In the game which was played in December at the Mardyke in Cork, Munster were narrowly defeated 6-5. There is an anecdote from that game regarding Tom. Australian Nick Shehadie was one of their best players. After the game Shehadie recounted how Tom Clifford said to him at one ruck *"Come in here, son. You may as well die here as in fuckin Sydney"*.

Tom Clifford played in 1948, 1949, 1950 and 1951 in what were poor championships for the Munster team. In 1952 Tom was on the team that won the Interpro Championship a second time and again for a third time in 1954.

At the end of the 1951 season, Tom was on the team that played against the Springboks at Thomond Park. Munster lost 11-6. Tom had played with the Irish team against them at Lansdowne Road four days earlier but backed it up and the Munster team gave the Springboks a scare. A late try swung the game to the South Africans. That Springbok team were on a Grand Slam tour of Europe and won thirty of their thirty-one games.

*Tom Clifford (on the right) during the Munster All-Blacks game of 1954*

During the 1954 season Munster also took on the All-Blacks with Clifford an important member of the team. Munster went down 6-3 at the Mardyke in Cork.

After twelve years in the team, Tom Clifford played his last game for Munster in 1955. He was thirty-two years old.

Tom was interviewed on camera in 1974 and was asked about Munster tactics. *'There is a wonderful tradition down here that you kick anything above grass height.'*, the interviewer said smugly. *"Well, we don't do it amongst ourselves. We might do it to the Leinster team or the Ulster people coming down here"*, was Tom's response.

## Wolfhounds and Charity Matches

Having returned from his Lions experience with new fame and a high profile, Tom Clifford used it as a source of charitable funds for local causes.

*Tom Clifford with his 'rugby team' that played hurling at the Markets Field in 1951*

On 1st June 1951, Tom was involved in a novel fundraiser in support of the St John's Cathedral Repair Fund. A Tom Clifford 'Rugby XV' took on a 'Soccer XV' selected by former soccer International Rory Keane. The neutral sport of hurling was selected for the competition and dispersed within each team were 'real hurlers' like Paddy Fitzgerald from Askeaton, International hockey players like Eamon O'Conner alongside the likes of Mick Lane, Jim McCarthy and John O'Meara from the rugby ranks and Pike Rovers' Mike Penny, Aberdeen's Tony McKeown and Limerick's Sean Cusack. The game was played at the Markets Field. Tom's team wore Young Munster jerseys and the game must have been a huge hit with the spectators.

The Limerick Leader reported on the game:

*"There were hurling thrills and some good bouts of clever play at the Crescent Field last night when the foreign games specialists – styling themselves 'rugby' and 'soccer' hurling selections – came into contact in a challenge match. The rugbyites were just too good for their opposing friends on the score 6-3 to 3-4.*

*The match proved a fine attraction due to the talent on view. Fielding out were such as Jim McCarthy, Dave O'Loughlin, Tom Clifford, Mick Lane, Paddy Reid and John O'Mara of Irish rugby international fame; while Eddie O'Connor, the Irish international hockey goalie was a star in the same position for the winners.*

*The losers had the services of such as Eamon O'Connor, the Irish National pole vault champion, and Tony McKeown (Aberdeen) and Sonny Price (Derby County).*

*Stars of the match were Paddy Fitzgerald, the former County Limerick hurling stalwart, from Askeaton; J Madden, who in the past distinguished himself in Young Munster colours."*

As Tom's career began to wind down, he started to play more and more charity games including some against the newly formed Irish Wolfhounds. The Irish Wolfhounds are now the Ireland second team, used to give emerging players development opportunity. The original Irish Wolfhounds were very different.

The Wolfhounds were established by Karl Mullen, Jackie Kyle and Tony O'Reilly in July 1956. They were an Irish invitational side modelled on the Barbarians and they would invite international players together to play games, mostly for charity, around Ireland. Their first game was in September 1956 at Donnybrook against a Jean Pratt XV. Tom Reid turned out for the Jean Pratt XV. The Wolfhounds won.

The second Wolfhounds game was at Winsor Park in Belfast. The Wolfhounds, featuring Limerick Lion **Gordon Wood**, played an all-Ulster team named the Vigilantes. The Wolfhounds won.

The Wolfhounds then brought their unbeaten record to Thomond Park on 29th December 1956 to play against a Tom Clifford XV with the money raised going to Cork and Limerick charities.

Tom Clifford's XV, wearing Young Munster jerseys and including Limerick Lion **Mick English**, and of course Tom Clifford beat the Wolfhounds team which had Tony O'Reilly, and Limerick Lions **Tom Reid** and **Gordon Wood**. Tom Clifford's side won 19-16. Mick English dropped a goal and Tom Clifford scored a try for his side.

*The Wolfhounds v Tom Clifford XV 1956*
*Back row – A O'Riordan, A Mulligan, Mick English, P Davies, T McGrath, W O'Gorman, D Barry, JF Horrocks-Taylor, G Spillane, A O'Sullivan, M Spillane, J Stevenson, T Cleary, G Hastings, P Frawley (referee)*
*Front row – J Roche, T O'Toole, P Downes, R Lee, V Gintenane, H O'Connor, C Greally, Tom Reid, M Mortell, Tony O'Reilly, Tom Clifford, D O'Brien, D McCormack, Gordon Wood, M O'Connor, R Tucker*

The following day, Tom Clifford, Bill Mulcahy and Tom Reid, turned out to play for the Wolfhounds in a game against Galwegians at the Sportsground in Galway. The game was played in a mud-bath and ended in a 9-9 draw.

Tom continued to be associated with the Wolfhounds charity games right up until the late 1960s.

## International Rugby

In 1944, Tom was very much on the radar as a possible international. In January 1944 he played for "Rest of Ireland" against a "Combined Universities" team. A month later he played out-half in an Irish XV against a Defence Forces XV at Lansdowne Road. It would take a few more years before he broke into the Irish national side.

Tom Clifford made his debut for Ireland against France at Lansdowne Road on 29th January 1949 in Ireland's first game of the 1949 Five Nations Championship. He played in all four of Ireland's matches in the 1949 tournament which ended with Ireland being crowned the champions and winning the Triple Crown.

Tom Clifford also played in all of Ireland's games during the 1950 Five Nations Championship. Ireland had an indifferent season. Wales won a Grand Slam while Ireland only registered one win at home against Scotland (21-0) and a 3-3 draw away in Paris.

*Tom Clifford (extreme right) in action against England in the 1949 Five Nations*

The 1951 Five Nations Championship was again won by Ireland, with Clifford playing in the home wins against France (9-8) and England (3-0).

*Tom Clifford (sitting 2$^{nd}$ from right) with the Irish team*

*Tom Clifford (bottom left) with Irish team mates (McKibbin, O'Hanlon, Henderson, Nelson and Kyle) en-route to the Paris game against France in 1950*

Tom Clifford's final international appearances came during the 1952 Five Nations Championship. He won his fourteenth cap in the away win in France (8-11), the home win to Scotland (12-8) and his last game being away against Wales on 8th March when Ireland were soundly beaten 3-14.

Tom's only appearance at home outside of the Five Nations Championship came in December 1951, as South Africa played Ireland as part of their European tour. Ireland lost that game 5-17.

*Tom Clifford runs onto the field at Lansdowne Road*

## The Barbarians

*Tom Clifford (back left) with 1951 Barbarians Team*

Ireland's win in the Five Nations in 1951 prompted Tom to be invited to play in the Barbarian's Easter 'tour'.

He played in two games, a 13-3 loss to Cardiff at the National Stadium in Wales and a 9-17 win against Swansea at St Helens.

## The British and Irish Lions

Tom Clifford was the second Limerickman and the first from a Limerick club to play for the British and Irish Lions in 1950.

The 1950 British and Irish Lions would play twenty-nine games on the tour. Tom Clifford played in twenty of those, including all five test matches; three in New Zealand and two in Australia. When he returned to Limerick after the tour, a huge crowd of an estimated eight thousand turned out to welcome him at the railway station.

To read more about his Lions tour – Refer chapter New Zealand, Australia and Sri Lanka (1950)

## Post Rugby Career

Tom Clifford retired from playing rugby in 1957.

During his life, Tom Clifford had a few jobs. Before he went on the 1950 Lions tour, he worked for the City Council cleaning public toilets. After he returned his title had been upgraded to "Sanitation Engineer" which was more in line with his newfound fame. Later he worked in a tannery before he got a job at Shannon Airport, working for ESSO refuelling aircraft.

Outside of rugby, Tom also played hurling for Claughan GAA club and soccer for Wembley Rovers.

## Personal Life

Tom Clifford married his wife, Virginia Keyes at St John's Cathedral in August 1957. As a measure of his fame at the time, the happy event was covered in the national newspapers. Tom and Virginia had three children; two sons (Michael and Gerry) and a daughter (Mary). The family lived at Newtownmahon House on Upper William St, across from St John's Pavilion.

It was a sad day in Limerick on 1$^{st}$ Oct 1990 when Tom Clifford passed away aged 67. He is buried at Mount St Lawrence Cemetery in Limerick. Young Munster's home ground, Tom Clifford Park, is named after him. His Lions tour blazer and other pieces of memorabilia are on display there in the Tom Clifford bar.

*Tom Clifford (1923-1990)*

# New Zealand, Australia & Sri Lanka (1950)

The British and Irish Lions had lost the last tour test series against South Africa in 1938. They had also lost the last test series in New Zealand and Australia in 1930. With the second world war now over, it was important that they get back to winning ways in New Zealand and Australia.

Englishman Leslie Osbourne was appointed to manage the Lions tour, which was only confirmed as going ahead a little before Christmas 1949. He appointed Irishman Karl Mullen as tour captain.

In the aftermath of World War Two, Ireland and Wales had taken the Five Nations by storm. Ireland won a Grand Slam in 1948 and won the championship and a triple crown again the following year in 1949. In 1950 Wales won a Grand Slam. That was reflected in the squad that was announced on 13th February with fourteen Welshmen, nine Irish, five Scots and just three English selected. Most of the players had been given a heads up of their likely selection when they were polled to check their availability just after Christmas.

Tom Clifford was the first man to go on a Lions tour from a Limerick rugby club but he was well acquainted with many of his colleagues from his Irish and Barbarians games. As well as the Irish team captain Karl Mullen, Tom would know Bill McKay, Jack Kyle, Noel Henderson, Jimmy Nelson and Mick Lane from Ireland. He would be even better acquainted with Jim McCarthy, a colleague from the Munster team.

Amongst his new team mates were Bleddyn Williams who had served as a fighter pilot during the war and Welshman Ken Jones, a sprinter, had won an Olympic silver medal for the 4x100m relay in the 1948 London games.

## Touring Party

The following was the tour party selected for the tour:

**Manager**
Leslie 'Ginger' Osbourne (England)

1950 New Zealand, Australia & Sri Lanka

**Forwards**
Grahame Budge (Edinburgh Wanderers and Scotland), **Tom Clifford (Young Munster and Ireland)**, Cliff Davies (Cardiff and Wales), John Robins (Birkenhead Park and Wales), Dai Davies (Somerset Police and Wales), Karl Mullen (c) (Old Belvedere and Ireland), Roy John (Neath and Wales), Don Hayward (Newbridge and Wales), Jimmy Nelson (Malone and Ireland), Bob Evans (Newport and Wales), Jim McCarthy (Dolphin and Ireland), Bill McKay (Queen's University and Ireland), Vic Roberts (Penryn and Wales), Peter Kininmonth (Richmond and Scotland), Rees Stephens (Neath and Wales)

**Backs**
Angus Black (Edinburgh and Scotland), Gordon Rimmer (Waterloo and England), Rex Willis (Cardiff and Wales), Jack Kyle (Queen's University and Ireland), Noel Henderson (Queen's University and Ireland), Jack Mathews (Cardiff and Wales), Ivor Preece (Coventry and England), Bleddyn Williams (Cardiff and Wales), Ken Jones (Newport and Wales), Mick Lane (UCC and Ireland), Ronald MacDonald (Edinburgh University and Scotland), George Norton (Bective and Ireland), Doug Smith (London Scottish and Scotland), Malcolm Thomas (Newport and Wales), Bill Cleaver (Cardiff and Wales), Lewis Jones (Llanelli and Wales)

*Tom Clifford (back row on extreme right) and the 1950 British Lions team*

1950 New Zealand, Australia & Sri Lanka

## The Tour

John Purcell of Young Munster tells the story that before Tom Clifford went on the tour a collection was made around Limerick to raise money for him to go on the tour. Twenty pounds was raised. Then before he headed off, Tom Clifford's mother baked a huge amount of cake which she steeped in alcohol and packed in a big wooden crate. Right through the boat journey down under, the Lions would eat Tom Clifford's mother's cake. Some of the players even sent letters to Mrs Clifford to thank her and compliment her on her baking. There are other stories that suggests that a flotilla of boats had to follow the Ceramic on its voyage so that Tom's supplies could be kept topped up.

*Tom Clifford (front left) at a send-off party held for him ahead of the tour*
*The event was held at Fitzpatrick's bar on William Street*

On 30th March, just six weeks after the squad was announced, the Lions met for the first time at the Mayfair Hotel in London. That evening they were transferred by coach to the Savoy Hotel where they were guests of honour at the annual New Zealand Society dinner. They would need to get used to the attention as these sorts of events would happen at every stop on the tour.

The following day, the team were brought to Twickenham to be issued with their tour blazer and jersey. All other clothing had to be self-

1950 New Zealand, Australia & Sri Lanka

supplied. For the first time, this Lions team would wear the now familiar red jersey. On previous tours the Lions wore blue. The official team photo was taken while they were at Twickenham.

*Tom Clifford (4th left) with his new colleagues and new blazer at Twickenham*

On Saturday 1$^{st}$ April, they were off on their adventure. They took a train from London's Euston Station to the docks at Liverpool where they boarded the Ship Ceramic at 3.30 in the afternoon and forty-five minutes later, they were off. This was the Ceramic II. The original Ceramic had been torpedoed by a German U-boat two year earlier. Perhaps not a good omen for the forthcoming tour.

An anecdote about Tom Clifford comes from the second night of their voyage. Sitting down for a meal while most of the rest of the squad were seasick, Tom was handed a menu to which he replied *"I'll have the lot"*. He then proceeded to eat an eighteen-course meal which the records show included; Hors d'Ouvres, Crème de Tomato, Fillets of Sole Tarte, Sweetcorn en Corotte, Lamb Cutlets Parisienne, Braised York Ham Oporto, French Beans, Boiled and Roast Potatoes, Roast Norfolk Turkey with Cranberry Jelly, Rolled Ox Tongue with Leg of Pork and Apple Sauce, Salad with Mayonnaise Dressing, Plum Pudding with Brandy Sauce, Peach Melba, Dessert Fruit, Coffee and Fromage. His Irish team mate Bill McKay tried to match him course for course but retired half way through the competition.

1950 New Zealand, Australia & Sri Lanka

*Tom Clifford (left) and tour captain Karl Mullen at Twickenham before the tour*

With a long voyage ahead of them, the team set up a routine where they would have team practice each day on deck at 11.30 in the morning and they would have tactical discussions twice a week in the evenings. By all accounts the tactical discussions lasted hours and came to no conclusions as everyone had a strong opinion.

Along the way Jack Matthews who was a doctor and the ship's surgeon gave everyone vaccinations which left a few people unwell. Nonetheless, the team settled into a routine with light entertainment in the form of sing songs, treasure hunts, race meetings and a cinema to keep people occupied.

Eleven days into the journey, the Ceramic docked at Curacao in the Dutch West Indies (off the coast of Venezuela). The team had the opportunity to get off the ship and walk around for a few hours while the ship was restocked. Two days later the ship went through the Panama Canal and stopped for the night in Panama City where again the team got out and had some time on firm ground.

1950 New Zealand, Australia & Sri Lanka

*The Ceramic*

The Ceramic crossed the equator on 17<sup>th</sup> April and they still had two weeks to go before they finally arrived in Wellington on 2<sup>nd</sup> May. It had taken them thirty-one days to get to their destination.

This was the first Lions tour since the war and the first to New Zealand for twenty years. There was huge goodwill towards the touring party and the tourists were quick to acknowledge the support that New Zealand had given Great Britain during the war.

First game was in Nelson which is at the top of the South Island of New Zealand. The Ceramic had docked in Wellington on southern tip of the North Island. After a few days of acclimatisation in Wellington, the team crossed the Cook Straits on board a small ship called the Matai and landed in Nelson the day before the game. A brass band was there to welcome them. The band led the team to their hotel with Tom Clifford marching behind insisting that the band was there for him and him alone.

1950 New Zealand, Australia & Sri Lanka

# The Games

## Game One
## v Nelson-Marlborough-Golden Bay-Motueka
## Nelson, New Zealand 10/5/1950
## 24 – 3 - Win

**Lions Team** –Clever (Wales), Lane (Ireland), Matthews (Wales), Macdonald (Scotland), Thomas (Wales), Preece (England), Rimmer (England), **Clifford (Ireland),** Mullen (Ireland), Budge (Scotland), Hayward (Wales), Nelson (Ireland), McCarthy (Ireland), Stephens (Wales), Roberts (England)

Tom Clifford played in the first game of the 1950 British and Irish Lions tour at Trafalgar Park in Nelson. On a bright and sunny Wednesday afternoon the tour got underway. The team were led out onto the field by a piper amid great excitement from the 8,000 attendees. Half of the town of Nelson had turned out.

*Tom Clifford (Standing 2nd Left) with the team for the first game in Nelson*

The Lions looked a little rusty in the opening stages which was to be expected. There is only so much training you can do on a ship's deck. Malcolm Thomas scored the first points of the tour when he kicked the first of six penalties for the Lions. He kicked two more in quick succession as the local team were infringing offside. Irishman Mick

1950 New Zealand, Australia & Sri Lanka

Lane had to leave the field in the first half with an ankle injury but was able to return before the interval. Tom Clifford stepped up during the half to try a long-range penalty kick form deep inside the Lions' half. His accuracy was off and he missed. A fourth penalty goal for Malcolm Thomas before half time gave the Lions a 12-0 lead at the break.

The second half was a tight affair and a real tussle developed. By the end of the game there would have been forty scrums and seventy-four lineouts, crazy figures by today's standards. Thomas kicked two more penalties to stretch the lead and as the teams began to tire, the game opened up and Thomas and Preece scored tries for the Lions. A late consolation try for the home team went unconverted. The Lions were off to a winning start.

After the post-game function, the Lions boarded their bus and headed to their next venue which was one hundred and forty-two miles away in Westport.

*Tom Clifford showing his dribbling skills in New Zealand*

1950 New Zealand, Australia & Sri Lanka

**Game Two**
**v Buller**
**Westport, New Zealand 13/5/1950**
**24 – 9 – Win**

**Lions Team** –Norton (Ireland), Jones (Wales), Matthews (Wales), Macdonald (Scotland), Thomas (Wales), Kyle (Ireland), Black (Scotland), Davies (Wales), Mullen (Ireland), Robins (Wales), Hayward (Wales), John (Wales), McKay (Ireland), Kininmonth (Scotland), Evans (Wales)

Tom Clifford was among the eleven changes made for the second game against Buller and sat the game out. Irish colleagues Norton, Kyle, Mullen and McKay played.

The Lions led the game 21-0 at half time. The highlight of the first half was the sight of Olympic sprinter Ken Jones running onto a kick through ball from Jack Kyle and leaving everyone in his wake to score a try.

Bill McKay was injured in the first half and was unable to return to the field in the second. The Lions played on with a man down but were comfortable and won the game at a canter.

**Game Three**
**v West Coast**
**Greymouth, New Zealand 16/5/1950**
**32 – 3 - Win**

**Lions Team** – Cleaver (Wales), Jones (Wales), Matthews (Wales), Henderson (Ireland), Thomas (Wales), Kyle (Ireland), Willis (Wales), **Clifford (Ireland)**, Davies, Budge (Scotland), Hayward (Wales), John (Wales), McCarthy (Ireland), Kininmonth (Scotland), Roberts (England)

Greymouth is only sixty-five miles from Westport so there wasn't a burdensome travel effort to get to the next game. That gave the team a free day in Westport before they headed off. The extra day suited Tom who had strained knee ligaments.

1950 New Zealand, Australia & Sri Lanka

Recovered enough, Tom Clifford was again called into action against West Coast. There had been heavy rain in Greymouth so the pitch was soggy and soft which suited the Lions.

The Lions got off to a very strong start. Jack Kyle scored a try after just two minutes. Welshman Matthews also went over and the Lions were ahead by ten after just ten minutes. The flying Welshman Jones scored another before Tom Clifford stepped up to take one of his long-range penalties. On this occasion he missed and the Lions went into the break 13-3 up.

In the second half it was all one way. Roberts and Kyle scored tries before Tom Clifford again stepped up to take a penalty. This one, from thirty yards, went over having clipped the upright. Jones scored another try and confident Clifford converted it. A third try for Jack Kyle completed the scoring.

**Game Four
v Otago
Dunedin, New Zealand 19/5/1950
9 – 23 - Loss**

Lions Team – Norton (Ireland), Jones (Wales), Matthews (Wales), Williams (Wales), Thomas (Wales), Kyle (Ireland), Willis (Wales), **Clifford (Ireland),** Mullen (Ireland), Robins, Hayward (Wales), John (Wales), Evans (Wales), Kininmonth (Scotland), Roberts (England)

A week out from the first test match which would be held at the same ground, the Lions next faced Otago down in Dunedin at the bottom of the South Island. Travel time meant that they didn't have much time ahead of the game. They trained on arrival on the Thursday evening and again on the Friday before announcing the team that had a distinctly test feel about it.

The 35,000-capacity crowd at Carrisbrook watched as the Lions played into a strong breeze in the first half. They also had to contend with a glaring sun. An early penalty chance to the Lions was held up in the wind and fell short. Shortly afterward Otago took the lead that they wouldn't relinquish. First, they scored a penalty after the Lions handled in the ruck. Then, within minutes, out-half Haig scored an individual try after side-stepping Jack Kyle. Another missed Lions penalty chance passed by before Meates scored a try and in the last minute of the half Haig scored another penalty to give Otago as 12-0 half time lead.

Malcolm Thomas had to leave the field injured soon after the second half started. He put the Lions on the scoreboard before he left when he kicked a penalty. Robins took over penalty duties for the Lions and missed two. In a poor second half, albeit down a man, the Lions let the Otago team in for two more tries, one from Meates and the other from Haig.

The Evening Post summed the game up by saying *"Whatever the reason, the Lions picked their biggest occasion to date to give one of their poorest performances".*

**Game Five
v Southland
Invercargill, New Zealand 23/5/1950
0 – 11 - Loss**

**Lions Team** – Norton (Ireland), Jones (Wales), Cleaver (Wales), Macdonald (Scotland), Lane (Ireland), Preece (England), Black (Scotland), **Clifford (Ireland)**, Davies (Wales), Davies (Wales), Hayward (Wales), Nelson (Ireland), Budge (Scotland), John (Wales), McCarthy (Ireland)

Tom Clifford played his fourth game for the Lions and his third game in the space of a week when he turned out against Southland in Invercargill. Invercargill is as far south as you can go in New Zealand. Next stop after than is the Antarctic. Conditions there can be punishing but, on this occasion, the weather was fine and clear.

Southland's JF. Butt scored the only points of the first half when he kicked a drop goal to give the home side a 3-0 advantage. Norton missed two kicked for the Lions before Tom Clifford took over kicking duties but he also couldn't score. Norton broke his arm in a tackle and had to leave the field. He played no further part in the tour. The home side, growing in confidence as the game went on, sensed a historic victory was there for the taking and tries for Butt and Inder gave them just that. It had been a poor Lions performance.

1950 New Zealand, Australia & Sri Lanka

The team quickly returned to Dunedin to prepare for the first test against the All-Blacks. Back-to-back losses and mounting injuries wasn't the preparation the Lions needed.

**Game Six**
**v New Zealand (First Test)**
**Carrisbrook, Dunedin, New Zealand 27/5/1950**
**9 – 9 – Draw**

**Lions Team** – Cleaver (Wales), Jones (Wales), Matthews (Wales), Preece (England), Macdonald (Scotland), Kyle (Ireland), Black (Scotland), Robins (Wales), Mullen (Ireland), **Clifford (Ireland)**, Hayward (Wales), John (Wales), Kininmonth (Scotland), McKay (Ireland)

**New Zealand** – Scott, Meates, Roper, Cherrington, Elvidge, Beatty, Bevan, Simpson, Hughes, Skinner, Harvey, White, McNab, Johnstone, Crowley

*Tom Clifford (front left) and the team for the first test against NZ in Dunedin*

Seven of the players who had played in the loss against Otago four days earlier were named in the test team. Tom Clifford was playing his fourth game in ten days.

1950 New Zealand, Australia & Sri Lanka

The Lions took the lead after eight minutes with a successful penalty from Robins. In an all-out attack the Lions had the better of the first half but they couldn't get over the line. Robins missed three further penalty attempts. 3-0 at half time.

The first try of the game came early in the second half when Jack Kyle scored after running forty yards. The conversion was missed by Robins though. Midway through the half the All-Blacks scored a try after Kininmonth was caught in possession. The Lions then scored after Ken Jones picked up a through kick from Jack Kyle. Clifford stepped up to convert it but missed. The All-Blacks scored a penalty to make it 9-6 going into the closing stages and then seven minutes from time Elvidge scored a try for New Zealand to level the score. The game ended in a 9-9 draw.

*Tom Clifford (left) during the first test against NZ in Dunedin*

**Game Seven**
**v South Canterbury**
**Timaru, New Zealand 30/5/1950**
**27 – 8 - Win**

**Lions Team** – Cleaver (Wales), Jones (Wales), Henderson (Ireland), Preece (England), Macdonald (Scotland), Kyle (Ireland), Willis (Wales), Robins (Wales), Davies (Wales), Budge (Scotland), Nelson (Ireland), **Clifford (Ireland)**, Roberts (England), Kininmonth (Scotland), McKay (Ireland)

Tom Clifford was again selected for the game in Timaru. 12,000 spectators watched a fairly one-sided game. The first points came from a Preece drop-goal from the back of a scrum. Macdonald scored a try in one corner and then Jones showed his pace and scored in the other to give the Lions a 13-0 lead at half time.

Two quick tries from Bill McKay at the start of the second half made sure of the game. In the closing stages the local team pushed hard and Hobbs scored. They followed that with a penalty from a Lions scrum infringement. The Lions closed out the scoring with a try to flanker Roberts and, two minutes from time, Henderson went over to push the score to 27-8 to the Lions.

**Game Eight
v Canterbury
Christchurch, New Zealand 3/6/1950
16 – 5 - Win**

**Lions Team** – Cleaver (Wales), Jones (Wales), Henderson (Ireland), Williams (Wales), Macdonald (Scotland), Kyle (Ireland), Rimmer (England), **Clifford (Ireland)**, Mullen (Ireland), Robins (Wales), Hayward (Wales), John (Wales), Evans (Wales), Kininmonth (Scotland), McCarthy (Ireland)

There was a half empty stadium to meet Tom Clifford as he ran out for his sixth game on the trot at Lancaster Park. That didn't stop the Lions from adding another win to their belt. Robins scored a penalty after five minutes. Jones again showed his phenomenal pace to score a try from a Williams pass. Williams then scored from a pass off the back of the scrum and the Lions led 11-0 at half time.

The game tightened up in the second half. Reid scored for the home team. They could have scored again but didn't. The Lions' Hayward scored at the death to confirm the win.

1950 New Zealand, Australia & Sri Lanka

Game Nine
v Ashburton County - North Otago
Ashburton, New Zealand 6/6/1950
29 – 6 - Win

Lions Team – Preece (England), Lane (Ireland), Henderson (Ireland), Williams (Wales), Thomas (Wales), Rimmer (England), Willis (Wales), Budge (Scotland), Mullen (Ireland), Davies (Wales), Hayward (Wales), Nelson (Ireland), Roberts (England), **Clifford (Ireland),** McKay (Ireland)

In challenging conditions both in terms of the weather and the style of play from the opposition, the Lions played against the wind and with the sun in their eyes in the first half. The home team missed two penalties before the Lions took the lead in the fifteenth minute.

Bleddyn Williams scored after a pass from Henderson. Williams then scored a second off the blind-side of a scrum. The Lions were looking comfortable but the Ashburton side scored twice in two minutes late in the half, first with a drop goal and then a try in the corner by Tait. 6-6 at the break.

The Lions took control in the second half. A penalty was scored by Thomas before Tom Clifford set up a try for Mick Lane. Thomas scored again. Further tries from Lane and a third by Thomas completed the scoring in an important win ahead of the second test.

Game Ten
v New Zealand (Second Test)
Christchurch, New Zealand 10/6/1950
0 – 8 – Loss

Lions Team – Cleaver (Wales), Jones (Wales), Matthews (Wales), Williams (Wales), Thomas (Wales), Kyle (Ireland), Black (Scotland), **Clifford (Ireland),** Mullen (Ireland), Robins (Wales), Hayward (Wales), John (Wales), Evans (Wales), Kininmonth (Scotland), McKay (Ireland)

**New Zealand** – Scott, Meates, Roper, Henderson, Elvidge, Haig, Bevan, Simpson, Hughes, Skinner, Harvey, White, McNab, Johnson, Crowley

1950 New Zealand, Australia & Sri Lanka

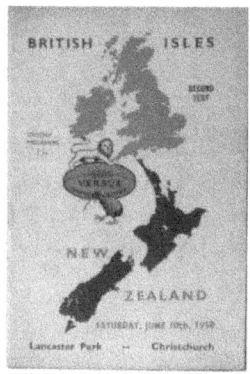

Remarkably Tom Clifford was selected for the eighth successive game when he was picked to play in the second test match in Christchurch.

For a lot of the opening half the Lions were under siege in their own half. Three missed penalties to New Zealand and two to the Lions kept the scoring to zero until the fifteenth minute. Crowley scored a try for the All-Blacks after he broke from a strong New Zealand scrum. To make matters worse, Bill McKay was stretchered off with a broken nose and concussion before the half was out. Another blow was struck when Roper scored another try for the All-Blacks on the cusp of half time.

In the second half the All-Blacks launched waves of attack but the Lions defence stood firm and kept them out. There was no further score.

This was the last game played on the South Island. The remaining thirteen games in New Zealand would be across the Cook Strait to the north.

**Game Eleven**
**v Wairarapa Bush**
**Masterton, New Zealand 10/6/1950**
**27 - 13  - Win**

**Lions Team** – Cleaver (Wales), Lane (Ireland), Matthews (Wales), Henderson (Ireland), Thomas (Wales), Williams (Wales), Willis (Wales), Davies (Wales), Davies (Wales), Budge (Scotland), Hayward (Wales), Nelson (Ireland), Roberts (England), Stephens (Wales), McCarthy (Ireland)

The Lions stayed in the small town of Carterton not far from the venue of the next game in Masterton. There wasn't a hotel that could fit the travelling party so the Lions team was split between two hotels, the Marquis of Normandy and the Club.

Tom Clifford was finally given a break from playing in the game in Masterton. He had played eight games straight and nine of the ten games on tour. The game was a little bit of a non-event with the Lions streaking out to a 24-0 lead in the first half.

**Game Twelve**
**v Hawke's Bay**
**Napier, New Zealand 17/6/1950**
**20 – 0 – Win**

**Lions Team** – Cleaver (Wales), Jones (Wales), Matthews (Wales), Williams (Wales), Thomas (Wales), Kyle (Ireland), Rimmer (England), Davies (Wales), Mullen (Ireland), **Clifford (Ireland),** Hayward (Wales), Nelson (Ireland), Evans (Wales), John (Wales), McCarthy (Ireland)

With a week's rest under his belt, Tom Clifford was again called into action in Napier for the game against Hawke's Bay. Tom's scrummaging skills were on show during this game. There were seventeen scrums and the Lions won ten of them.

It took seventeen minutes for the Lions to score but they were in complete control throughout the game. The Lions were up 9-0 at half time. In the second half Tom also showed his kicking skills by landing a huge forty-five-yard penalty and then followed it up with one from closer range.

*Tom Clifford getting up close to the Kiwis*

1950 New Zealand, Australia & Sri Lanka

Game Thirteen
v East Coast - Poverty Bay - Bay of Plenty
Gisborne, New Zealand 21/6/1950
27 – 3 – Win

Lions Team – Jones (Wales), Lane (Ireland), Matthews (Wales), Henderson (Ireland), Macdonald (Scotland), Preece (England), Black (Scotland), Davies (Wales), Davies (Wales), Robins (Wales), Stephens (Wales), Nelson (Ireland), Budge (Scotland), Kininmonth (Scotland), Evans (Wales)

After his goal kicking exploits in Napier, Tom was again given the opportunity to sit out a game and rest. The Lions easily won against the East Coast side with tries from Matthews, Lane, Macdonald and Henderson. They were then on a thirteen-hour train journey to Wellington where the next two games were being held.

*Tom Clifford kneeling on the left with team mates during downtime on tour*

Game Fourteen
v Wellington
Athletic Park, Wellington, New Zealand 24/6/1950
12 – 6 - Win

1950 New Zealand, Australia & Sri Lanka

**Lions Team** – Cleaver (Wales), Jones (Wales), Matthews (Wales), Williams (Wales), Thomas (Wales), Kyle (Ireland), Rimmer (England), **Clifford (Ireland),** Mullen (Ireland), Robins (Wales), Hayward (Wales), Stephens (Wales), Evans (Wales), John (Wales), McCarthy (Ireland)

On a windy Wellington day, 32,000 people turned out at Athletic Park to see the Lions play their last game ahead of the third test. The Lions put out a slightly weakened team against Wellington but Tom Clifford was called back into action for the game.

Williams scored an early try after five minutes. Jim McCarthy scored another after eighteen minutes. The Wellington team were trying to play open rugby which meant that there was planet of loose ball and the Lions scored two more tries before the break. Williams sidestepped a defender and sent Jones over. Williams then scored again after a dazzling back play move. 12-0 at half time.

In the second half the Lions took their foot off the gas a little and Hourigan scored a try and Phillips landed a penalty. It had been a brilliant spectacle and the newspapers were glowing in their praise for the open rugby that both sides played.

**Game Fifteen**
**v New Zealand (Third Test)**
**Athletic Park, Wellington, New Zealand 1/7/1950**
**3 – 6 - Loss**

**Lions Team** – Cleaver (Wales), Henderson (Ireland), Matthews (Wales), Williams (Wales), Thomas (Wales), Kyle (Ireland), Rimmer (England), **Clifford (Ireland),** Davies (Wales), Robins (Wales), Hayward (Wales), Nelson (Ireland), Evans (Wales), John (Wales), McKay (Ireland)

**New Zealand** – Scott, Meates, Roper, Henderson, Elvidge, Haig, Bevan, Simpson, Hughes, Skinner, Harvey, White, McNab, Johnstone, Crowley

After a draw in the first test and a loss in the second, the pressure was on the Lions to win the third or the series was gone.

115

It had rained a lot in the lead up to the game but it eased on the day with just a few showers. 40,000 spectators turned out anticipating an All-Black series winner.

The All-Blacks kick off went straight into touch and there was scrum on halfway. Within three minutes the Lions were ahead from a penalty after the All-Blacks were penalised for an improper put in to their scrum. The Lions kept the pressure on but couldn't score again. The All-Blacks then came into the game and an almighty tussle evolved. All Black prop, Johnny Simpson, got injured and left the field (his career ended with this injury) and then just before half time their captain Ron Elvidge was hammered in a tackle from Jack Matthews and also left the field. At half time the Lions were up 3-0.

Elvidge returned for the second half with four stitches in his head. He recovered enough to score a great try from twenty-five yards. The battle continued through the second half. Then with fourteen minutes to go the All-Blacks scored again from a penalty after the Lions were called for offside. That was it. The series was lost. Despite a man advantage for the best part of an hour and a two-man advantage for ten minutes in the first half, the Lions had come up short.

**Game Sixteen
v Wanganui
Wanganui, New Zealand 5/7/1950
31 – 3 - Win**

**Lions Team** – Jones (Wales), Thomas (Wales), Henderson (Ireland), Williams (Wales), Macdonald (Scotland), Preece (England), Willis (Wales), Davies (Wales), Davies (Wales), Budge (Scotland), John (Wales), Stephens (Wales), Roberts (England), Kininmonth (Scotland), McCarthy (Ireland)

Wanganui marked the half way point on the tour. The Lions made thirteen changes from the test team and Tom Clifford got a well-earned breather.

Fifteen Māori welcomed the Lions onto the field with a Haka but that was really the only challenge this day. The Lions easily ran out winners scoring five tries to just a penalty to Wanganui.

1950 New Zealand, Australia & Sri Lanka

Game Seventeen
v Taranaki
New Plymouth, New Zealand 8/7/1950
25 – 3 - Win

Lions Team – Jones (Wales), Jones (Wales), Matthews (Wales), Williams (Wales), Macdonald (Scotland), Kyle (Ireland), Black (Scotland), Davies (Wales), Mullen (Ireland), **Clifford (Ireland)**, Hayward (Wales), Nelson (Ireland), Roberts (England), Stephens (Wales), McKay (Ireland)

Tom Clifford was back in action against the strong provincial town of Taranaki. Taranaki is farming country and the locals pride themselves on tough but fair rugby. They had beaten the Wellington team recently and the Lions expected a stern test. In the end it didn't materialise and the Lions were easy winners.

Tom Clifford was on kicking duty during this game. Having missed his first attempt, he scored on thirty-seven minutes. He went on to miss three in the second half but it didn't matter. Tries from Jones (2), Williams (2), McKay and Macdonald gave the Lions the win.

Game Eighteen
v Manawatu-Horowhenua
Palmerston North, New Zealand 12/7/1950
13 – 8 - Win

Lions Team – Cleaver (Wales), Thomas (Wales), Henderson (Ireland), Williams (Wales), Smith (Scotland), Preece (England), Rimmer (England), Budge (Scotland), Davies (Wales), Robins (Wales), John (Wales), Stephens (Wales), Evans (Wales), Kininmonth (Scotland), McCarthy (Ireland)

Tom Clifford was again given a rest for the game at Palmerston and so was on the sideline watching as a bizarre episode occurred during the game. Half way through the second half the scores were locked at 3-3. A Manawatu kick rolled harmlessly over the Lions' dead ball line. The Lions players lined up awaiting the drop out which should have been the next play. The ball was caught by the Manawatu prop (Wehi) who ran in and scored under the posts. The Lions were expecting a penalty but the referee instead awarded the try, saying the ball had not gone over the dead ball line previously so the prop was entitled to catch the drop out. Nonetheless, the Lions won the game and protested the referee's performance.

*Tom Clifford (back right) in the days after the Waikato game*

**Game Nineteen**
**v Waikato-Thames Valley-King County**
**Hamilton, New Zealand 15/7/1950**
**30 – 0 - Win**

**Lions Team** – Jones (Wales), Jones (Wales), Matthews (Wales), Henderson (Ireland), Smith (Scotland), Kyle (Ireland), Willis (Wales), Davies (Wales), Davies (Wales), Budge (Scotland), John (Wales), Nelson (Ireland), Roberts (England), Kininmonth (Scotland), McCarthy (Ireland)

Tom Clifford had the unusual experience of two games off back-to-back which no doubt was very welcome. He had played thirteen games in the eight weeks. He wasn't needed as the Lions turned in a dominant

1950 New Zealand, Australia & Sri Lanka

display scoring seven tries. Jones (2), Willis, Matthews, McCarthy, Henderson and Nelson all scored.

Game Twenty
v North Auckland
Whangarei, New Zealand 19/7/1950
8 – 6 – Win

**Lions Team** – Cleaver (Wales), Jones (Wales), Matthews (Wales), Williams (Wales), Macdonald (Scotland), Kyle (Ireland), Black (Scotland), **Clifford (Ireland)**, Mullen (Ireland), Robins (Wales), Hayward (Wales), Nelson (Ireland), Kininmonth (Scotland), John (Wales), McCarthy (Ireland)

In front of 4,000 spectators the Lions continued their winning streak. Tom Clifford was recalled to the team after a week off and the Lions got off to a great start with two tries in the opening fifteen minutes. The first came from a lineout. The ball went to Jack Kyle who slipped a reverse pass to Bill McKay who scored without being touched. The second try was a sixty-five-yard run from speedy Ken Jones. It wasn't all one way. North Auckland had two tries disallowed. Half time 8-0.

In the second half Auckland came back into it and scored a try followed by a penalty. Auckland had a chance late in the game to win with a penalty but missed and the Lions held on.

Game Twenty-One
v Auckland
Auckland, New Zealand 22/7/1950
32 – 9 – Win

**Lions Team** – Jones (Wales), Jones (Wales), Henderson (Ireland), Williams (Wales), Lane (Ireland), Kyle (Ireland), Willis (Wales), Davies (Wales), Mullen (Ireland), Budge (Scotland), John (Wales), Nelson (Ireland), Evans (Wales), Kininmonth (Scotland), McKay (Ireland)

Clifford sat out the game against Auckland at Eden Park a week out from the fourth test. The Lions ran out easy winners with McKay (2), Jones (2) and Davies each scoring tries.

1950 New Zealand, Australia & Sri Lanka

With a week before the next game, the team went to Rotorua for some downtime. Rotorua is a noted Māori cultural city and so the team got to experience dancing, singing, hakas and the hot springs that surround the town.

Game Twenty-Two
v New Zealand (Fourth Test)
Eden Park, Auckland, New Zealand 29/7/1950
8 – 11 - Loss

Lions Team – Jones (Wales), Jones (Wales), Matthews (Wales), Williams (Wales), Lane (Ireland), Kyle (Ireland), Willis (Wales), Davies (Wales), Davies (Wales), Budge (Scotland), John (Wales), Nelson (Ireland), Evans (Wales), Kininmonth (Scotland), McKay (Ireland)

New Zealand – Scott, Meates, Roper, Henderson, Tanner, Haig, Bevan, Wilson, Hughes, Skinner, Harvey, White, Johnstone, Mexted, Crowley

Tom was left out of the team for the fourth and final test against New Zealand in Auckland. The Lions ultimately lost the game but for a fleeting moment late in the second half, both sets of supporters were on their feet roaring for the Lions. With the All-Blacks 11-3 up and just five minutes remaining, Lewis Jones intercepted his own team's pass which was destined for Bleddyn Williams. Jones was deep in his own half and he took off. He sidestepped a defender before passing to Ken Jones and the Olympic sprinter, still in his own half, pinned back his ears and ran. With four All-Blacks left in his wake, he flew up the field and over the line to score one of the Lions' greatest ever test tries.

In the last few minutes, the Lions threw everything at their hosts and came close but didn't score again.

Game Twenty-Three
v New Zealand Māori
Athletic Park, Wellington, New Zealand 2/8/1950
14 – 9 – Win

Lions Team – Jones (Wales), Jones (Wales), Henderson (Ireland), Williams (Wales), Macdonald (Scotland), Kyle (Ireland), Black (Scotland), **Clifford (Ireland),** Mullen (Ireland), Robins (Wales),

1950 New Zealand, Australia & Sri Lanka

Hayward (Wales), John (Wales), Roberts (England), Stephens (Wales), McCarthy (Ireland)

The final game of the New Zealand leg of the tour was back in Wellington from where the team would depart for Sydney. Tom Clifford was recalled. Determined to end the tour on a high a conscious effort was made to ensure an open running game against the Māori. That effort was immediately visible when Ken Jones scored his sixteenth try of the tour. The Lions scored a drop goal followed by a forty-five-yard penalty to go 11-0 up. Percy Erceg scored a try for the Māori before Henderson got another for the Lions. 14-6 at the break. The Māori scored again early in the second half and the game got a little scrappy. The Lions held on to ensure a winning end to the tour.

The end of the game triggered a field invasion as the locals started a party that would run into the night. The Lions had an early boat to catch and as they boarded the Wanganella, hundreds of the locals came down to see them off.

*Tom Clifford enjoying a healing volcanic mud facial in Rotorua*

It took three days to cross the Tasman Sea. In very stormy conditions most of the players spent the journey in their cabins. Having arrived in Sydney the team spent a night in a hotel before a five-hour drive south

1950 New Zealand, Australia & Sri Lanka

to Canberra for the first game. After a formal reception at the Governor General's mansion and another at the British High Commission, the Lions set about preparing for the game against Combined Country.

Game Twenty-Four
v Combined Country
Manuka Oval, Canberra, Australia 9/8/1950
47-3 – Win

Lions Team – Cleaver (Wales), Thomas (Wales), Matthews (Wales), Henderson (Ireland), Smith (Scotland), Preece (England), Rimmer (England), Davies (Wales), Davies (Wales), Budge (Scotland), Stephens (Wales), Nelson (Ireland), Evans (Wales), Kininmonth (Scotland), McKay (Ireland)

Clifford sat out the first game in Australia which was played at Manuka Oval, a cricket ground. It proved the be a one-sided game with the Lions scoring ten tries to a single penalty to the home side.

Game Twenty-Five
v New South Wales
Sydney Cricket Ground, Australia 12/8/1950
22 – 6 - Win

Lions Team – Jones (Wales), Thomas (Wales), Matthews (Wales), Williams (Wales), Smith (Scotland), Kyle (Ireland), Willis (Wales), **Clifford (Ireland),** Mullen (Ireland), Robins (Wales), Stephens (Wales), Nelson (Ireland), McKay (Ireland), John (Wales), Evans (Wales)

Tom Clifford turned out in the second game of the Australian leg which was played at the famous Sydney Cricket Ground. The centre of the field was hard and grassless because of the wicket that was usually there. As would be the case in all of the Australian games, the local team was no match for the Lions. The Lions ran in six tries in the New South Wales game.

Game Twenty-Six
v Australia (First Test)
The Gabba, Brisbane, Australia 19/8/1950

1950 New Zealand, Australia & Sri Lanka

19 – 6 - Win

**Lions Team** – Jones (Wales), Thomas (Wales), Matthews (Wales), Williams (Wales), Smith (Scotland), Kyle (Ireland), Willis (Wales), **Clifford (Ireland),** Davies (Wales), Robins (Wales), Stephens (Wales), Nelson (Ireland), Evans (Wales), John (Wales), McKay (Ireland)

**Australia** – Gardner, Thompson, Walker, Bromley, Hills, Solomon, Burke, Gordon, Cottrell, McCarthy, Mossop, Shehadie, Macmillan, Cross, Brockhoff

Tom Clifford was restored to the test team for the first test at the Gabba in Queensland. The Gabba would in future tours be the site of *"Waltzing O'Driscoll"* bursting onto the scene in 2001.

Lewis Jones scored all of the Lions' eleven points in the first half. In the fourteenth minute he started with a penalty. Twelve minutes later he scored and converted his own try and then after thirty-three minutes he scored a drop goal. The first half was marred by an injury to Malcolm Thomas who fractured his cheek and didn't play again on the tour.

Bill Gardner added to the penalty he scored in the first half twelve minutes into the second. Jones hit back shortly after with a penalty for the Lions. Not long before the end Bleddyn Williams rounded out the scoring with a try.

The tour was starting to wind down and the team had a few days off in Sydney ahead of the second test.

**Game Twenty-Seven**
**v Australia (Second Test)**
**Sydney Cricket Ground, Australia 26/8/1950**
**24 – 3 - Win**

**Lions Team** – Jones (Wales), Lane (Ireland), Matthews (Wales), Williams (Wales), Macdonald (Scotland), Kyle (Ireland), Willis (Wales), **Clifford (Ireland),** Mullen (Ireland), Robins (Wales), Stephens (Wales), Nelson (Ireland), Evans (Wales), John (Wales), McKay (Ireland)

1950 New Zealand, Australia & Sri Lanka

**Australia** – Costello, Tonkin, Walker, Bromley, Hills, Solomon, Burke, Gordon, Cottrell, Shehadie, Mossop, Cornforth, Macmillan

Tom Clifford was again the test side for the second game in Sydney, back at the Sydney Cricket Ground. The Lions were more convincing winners this time. The Lions were 16-0 up at half time after Kyle, John and Macdonald scored tries. Nelson scored twice in the second half and the test series in Australia was won.

**Game Twenty-Eight**
**v Metropolitan Union**
**Sydney Cricket Ground, Australia 29/8/1950**
**26 - 17  - Win**

**Lions Team** – Cleaver (Wales), Lane (Ireland), Henderson (Ireland), Williams (Wales), Macdonald (Scotland), Preece (England), Black (Scotland), Davies (Wales), Davies (Wales), Budge (Scotland), Hayward (Wales), Nelson (Ireland), Roberts (England), Kininmonth (Scotland), McCarthy (Ireland)

Three days after the second test, Clifford sat out a game against Metropolitan Union. The Lions got out to a 13-3 lead and never looked back. Henderson scored twice and Williams and Macdonald also scored.

**Game Twenty-Nine**
**v New South Wales**
**Newcastle, Australia 2/9/1950**
**12 - 17  - Loss**

**Lions Team** – Jones (Wales), Jones (Wales), Matthews (Wales), Williams (Wales), Lane (Ireland), Preece (England), Black (Scotland), **Clifford (Ireland),** Mullen (Ireland), Robins (Wales), Hayward (Wales), Stephens (Wales), Evans (Wales), John (Wales), McKay (Ireland)

The final game of the tour in Australia was played two hours north of Sydney in the mining town of Newcastle. By this stage the Lions had stopped training, had one eye on a long journey home and were tired. The sides were level at half time and then the Lions took a lead early in

1950 New Zealand, Australia & Sri Lanka

the second half but weariness showed and the New South Wales team finished the stronger winning well.

The long journey home started in Newcastle from where the team took a train back to Sydney for some formal send offs and then another train from there to Albany where they switched trains and got the last one two hundred more miles to Melbourne. There the boarded the Strathnavar which would take them home. Their trip home took a different route to the one they took on the way out.

After thirteen days and stops in Adelaide and Fremantle, they docked in Colombo in what was then called Ceylon (now Sri Lanka). In these very unusual surroundings Tom Clifford was selected for what was an un-official game, played against mostly ex-pats living on the island.

The Strathnavar

**Game Thirty**
**v Ceylon**
**Colombo, Sri Lanka 18/9/1950**
**44 -6 - Win**

**Lions Team** – Jones (Wales), Lane (Ireland), Henderson (Ireland), Williams (Wales), Macdonald (Scotland), Kyle (Ireland), Willis (Wales),

Clifford (Ireland), Mullen (Ireland), Robins (Wales), Stephens (Wales), Nelson (Ireland), Roberts (England), John (Wales), McCarthy (Ireland)

This game was played at the Colombo Racecourse in front of 4,000 spectators. Because of the heat and humidity, it was agreed ahead of the game that there would only be thirty minutes a half. Even still, the Lions put on an exhibition. Roberts (4), Macdonald (2), Jones and Lane scored tries. There was perhaps some embarrassment that the local team scored two tries, both by Roelofsz.

The Lions were only in Colombo for the day, that night they continued their voyage stopping briefly in Bombay, Aden and Marseilles on their way home.

In much the same was as he had kicked off the tour with team building eating performance, he again contributed on the way home. Jack Kyle remembered, *"We were somewhere in the Bay of Biscay having a final party among ourselves. The call came out for a last rendition of O'Reilly's Daughter but Tommy was nowhere to be seen. Suffering the effects of over six months as a Lion he had finally succumbed and taken to his bed. So, six of the boys went down to his cabin, lifted him, still in the horizontal position, and carried him into the party. Responding to our musical request, he sat up, sang his favourite song, and then laid back down again. We did the only decent thing and carried him back to where we had found him ten minutes before."*

The Strathnavar finally arrived at Tilbury Docks in London on Sunday 8$^{th}$ October. Tom Clifford had been away from home since the end March. Six and a half months on tour. A couple of days later he arrived at the train station in Limerick where an estimated crowd of eight thousand turned out to greet him. As had been the case in most towns the tour party had arrived in, a brass band was also there to welcome home a legend of Limerick rugby.

## Post Tour Game

The 1950 Lions came together a year after the tour for a game at Cardiff Arms Park. The game played on 22$^{nd}$ September 1951 was to mark the seventy-fifth anniversary of Cardiff RFC. It was Tom Clifford's final appearance in the red of the British and Irish Lions.

1950 New Zealand, Australia & Sri Lanka

## Tour Reflections

While they had lost the test series in New Zealand, the 1950 Lions tour was a success. They won the series in Australia and had won twenty-three of the thirty games on their gruelling six-month tour. Excluding this post tour game, Tom Clifford had played in twenty Lions games, including five tests. He had scored fourteen points for the team (four penalties and one conversion). Tom Clifford is undoubtedly one of the greatest Limerick Lions.

> *"Clifford had a brilliant tour, and his performance in New Zealand and Australia are well documented. He played in five of the six tests and if one outstanding forward had to be chosen, then Clifford was strongly challenging McKay for that honour."*
> Tour Captain Karl Mullen

*Tom Clifford leaving the field after the 1951 Lions v Cardiff game*

1950 New Zealand, Australia & Sri Lanka

# 1955
# South Africa

## Tom Reid

# Tom Reid
# Lion #383

**Tom Reid**
Born - 3 March 1926, Limerick

School – Christian Brothers
Club – Garryowen, London Irish, Town of Mount Royal
Ireland Caps - 13
Lions Tour(s) – 1955
Lions Appearances - 12
Lions Tests – 2
Position – 2nd Row, back row

Limerick Lion **Tom Reid**'s rugby career includes success with Garryowen, Munster and Ireland. He was the first person to play both **for** and **against** the British and Irish Lions. He played on the first Barbarians team to tour internationally and ended up staying on tour, as he met his future wife on that tour to Canada. Reid went on to become a legend of Montreal rugby.

## Early Life

Tom Reid (Thomas Eymard Reid) was the son of Joe Reid, a carpenter from Athlunkard Street and Elizabeth Ryan (grand-aunt of author Des Ryan) from Singland. He was born on $3^{rd}$ March 1926 and was the eldest of five children.

Tom's father Joe was a rugby player and played for Garryowen as was his first cousin Paddy Reid. Paddy played both rugby union and rugby league for Ireland and was on the Irish team that won the Grand Slam in the Five Nations of 1948.

## School

The Reid family lived on Sexton Street and Tom went to school around the corner with the Christian Brothers. Unfortunately, it's not clear what sports he participated in during his schooling. Christian Brothers was not a rugby school at that time so it's likely that Tom played hurling.

## Club Rugby

### Garryowen

Tom followed his father Joe and cousin Paddy in joining Garryowen. He had huge success with the club, first winning the Munster Senior League in 1946, the Munster Senior Cup and the Munster Charity Shield in 1946/47 on a team captained by his cousin Paddy.

In the 1949/50 season, Reid was a beaten finalist in the Munster Senior Cup coming up short in the final against U.C.C but two years later, he again won the Munster Senior Cup avenging the defeat from two years earlier by beating U.C.C. in the final.

*The victorious Garryowen team of 1947. Tom Reid is seated on the far right*

The following year 1951/52 saw Garryowen again defeated in the Munster Senior Cup final, this time by Sundays Well but perhaps Tom's proudest moment in the Garryowen shirt was when he led them to the Munster Senior Cup in the 1953/54 season beating defending champions Sundays Well in the final. That year he also captained them to a Munster Senior League title. That Garryowen team in 1952 also featured Tom's brother John Reid, his two cousins Paddy and Kevin Quilligan and future Limerick Lion, **Gordon Wood**.

During his time at Garryowen, Tom played in a few other interesting games. On St Stephens Day 1951, Reid played in a Garryowen/Shannon select XV team that played the first Italian team to come to Ireland, Roma-Rugby. Roma where four times Italian champions and had been unbeaten that season. He was also on the Garryowen team that played away at against Lourdes the then French champions.

In a sign of his commitment to Garryowen, Tom Reid, while on a visit home in 1974, turned out for Garryowen against an Army Select team from the Curragh. The game was played at Dooradoyle.

Tom Reid

*The victorious Garryowen team of 1951/52
Tom Reid is standing back left. Richard Harris is standing back right and Gordon Wood who is standing middle row five from left*

*The victorious Garryowen team of 1953/54 which Tom Reid captained to the Munster Senior Cup and Munster Senior League. Also on the team was Gordon Wood who is sitting next to Tom Reid in the centre of the photo*

**London Irish**

In September 1954, work commitments meant that Tom Reid had to move to the UK. He moved to London Irish and played his first game with them against United Services on 20th September. For the next three years he would be a mainstay of the London Irish team who at the time were playing at Rectory Field south east of London.

### Town of Mount Royal Rugby Club

After the 1957 Barbarians tour, Tom moved to Montreal, Canada. Niall Quaid who had played for Garryowen with Reid had moved there a few years earlier and was one of the founders of Town of Mount Royal RFC. Tom joined and continued to find success with his new club. TMR were crowned Quebec Champions in 1960 and in 1961. In 1968 they again won the Quebec championship and the following year they won the Standard Life Cup.

*Tom Reid (standing third from the left) with the 1960 Quebec Champions Town of Mount Royal team*

Ron Chiasson, a friend of Tom's in Montreal, when asked about any stories there might be about Tom's time there responded that there were many *"like the time one of them snuck Tom into his house through a window so he could crash for the night....a window that was the bedroom's......crawling right passed the guy's not sleeping wife....because there is nothing louder than drunk rugby players trying to be quiet."*

Ron also gave an insight into Tom's training. At the time the skill of dribbling the ball was more prevalent in rugby than it is today. Ron says, *"As a general rule Tom liked to train alone. Did a lot of road work to keep in shape. When he went for a run, he used to keep pebbles in his pocket. As he ran, he would drop one after the other, kicking them with his left foot as a means to practice kicking with his weaker foot."*

## Montreal All-Stars (Montreal Selects)

The Montreal All-Stars were an invitational side that were put together from the best players at the various clubs in the city of Montreal. They played regularly against touring teams and against teams from other Canadian Provinces. Tom first represented them against Ontario in 1958 and would play for them on well over a dozen occasions during the next ten years.

## Quebec Representative Side

*Tom Reid (crouching third from the left) with the Quebec Provincial team in 1958*

As well as turning out for the Montreal Select team, Tom was a regular fixture in the Quebec provincial side. Playing against the other Canadian provinces and visiting team, Tom played many times for this side.

## Eastern Canada All-Stars

Tom had played for the 1955 British and Irish Lions team that toured South Africa. By the time the next tour came around in 1959, Tom was living in Canada and out of contention for selection.

The 1959 Lions toured Australia and New Zealand and had three Limerickmen amongst their ranks, **Gordon Wood, Bill Mulcahy** and **Mick English**. The tourists won their test series against the Australians but lost three games to one against the New Zealand All-Blacks. Enroute home, the Lions flew via Honolulu to Vancouver where they played a team representing British Columbia. Two days later they were in Toronto to play the Eastern Canada All-Stars.

| Eastern Canada | | British Lions | |
|---|---|---|---|
| R. | Parsons | T.J. | Davies |
| I.W. | Nicoll (captain) | W.M. | Patterson |
| C. | Megennaty | K.J.F. | Scotland |
| P. | Froneman | D. | Hewitt |
| J.L.F. | Allan | A.J.F. | O'Reilly |
| R. | Bernard | J.P. | Horrocks-Taylor |
| A. | Whylock | R.E.G. | Jeeps |
| G.H.E. | Denton | T.R. | Prosser |
| G. | Rheeder | A.R. | Dawson (captain) |
| C. | Fagan | H.F. | McLeod |
| I.B. | McK. Greig | R.H. | Williams |
| J.L. | Adam | W.A. | Mulcahy |
| N.S. | Donaldson | N.A.A. | Murphy |
| D. | Allan | H.J. | Morgan |
| T.E. | Reid | J. | Faull |

The Team Sheet for the Eastern Canada v British and Irish Lions game in 1959

On 29$^{th}$ September 1959, Tom Reid turned out for the Eastern Canada All-Stars becoming the first person to play both for and against the British and Irish Lions. The Eastern Canada team were hammered 70-6.

Among the Lions that played that day was Tom's friend from Limerick Bill Mulcahy. Gordon Wood had already returned home so missed the game, as had Mick English. Also playing for the Lions that day were Dickie Jeeps, Tony O'Reilly, Hugh McLeod and Rhys Williams each of whom had toured with Tom on the Lions' 1955 tour. There was no doubt a great sing-song was had after the game.

## Munster Rugby

While playing for Garryowen, Tom received his first Munster cap. His first call up came in November 1947. While still winning, Munster had under performed in their two earlier games but would still be Interprovincial Champions if they beat Leinster. Reid was one of five changes Munster made for the game. He came in at wing forward in place of F. Dineen from Bohs. Munster won the final game on 22$^{nd}$ November, beating Leinster 14-11 and became Interpro Champions.

*Tom Reid (on the right) playing the Australian team at the Mardyke in 1947*

Tom played with Munster for the next ten years. From 1948 to 1951 Munster had little success in the Interprovincial Championship but Tom was on the team when they returned to the top of the table in 1952 and in 1954. By the time Munster won again in 1957, Tom had moved to Canada.

During his time with Munster Tom played in three famous games against inbound touring teams. In December 1947, in only his second appearance for Munster, he played against the Wallabies alongside Tom Clifford. Tom wasn't named in the team when it was first announced but London Irish player John Daly had to drop out of the game through injury ten days out from the game and Tom was named as his replacement. Munster were beaten 6-5 at the Mardyke in Cork.

On 11$^{th}$ December 1951, the Springboks tour of Europe came to Thomond Park, Limerick. The Springboks had defeated the Irish team four days earlier, were on a Grand Slam tour and ended up winning thirty of their thirty-one games on the tour. Tom was on the Munster team who were defeated in the last few minutes at Thomond Park. The teams were deadlocked 6-6 when, with just a few minutes to go the

Springboks scored a late try to win the game 11-6. Munster had also had a try disallowed earlier in the game for a forward pass.

Tom was also on the Munster team beaten by the visiting All Black team in January 1954. Munster went down 6-3 at the Mardyke in Cork.

## International Rugby

Despite his great form for Garryowen and Munster, Tom Reid struggled initially to get selected for the Irish national side. For four straight years (1948-1952), he was called for the annual "Probables" v "Possibles" trial game, each time being selected in the "Possibles" ranks. Finally, in January 1953, the trial teams were announced for that year and he was selected on the "Probables" side.

*Tom Reid (standing far right) with the 1953 Ireland team*

Tom made his debut for the Irish national rugby team at Lansdowne Road on 14th February 1953. Ireland drew with England that day 9-9. England would go on to win the 1953 championship. Tom also played in the win away at Murrayfield (26-8) and the loss against Wales in Swansea.

On 7th January 1954, Tom lined out with the Irish team to play the touring All-Blacks side at Lansdowne Road. Ireland lost the game 14-3. Just a few days later he would play them again with Munster.

*Tom Reid during the National Anthem at Lansdowne Road – against New Zealand*

*Tom Reid with scrum cap in action with Ireland*

Tom played the first game of the 1954 Five Nations away in France where Ireland lost 8-0 but he missed the remaining games of the championship through injury.

Tom Reid

*Tom Reid in action with Ireland*

In 1955 he played in two of the four championship games. He played in the 6-6 draw against England at Lansdowne Road and the loss away at Murrayfield. Again in 1956 he played in two of Ireland's games. Losses away in France and Twickenham.

In his final year with the Irish national team, he played in all four of Ireland's Five Nations championship games. A win at home to France and away at Murrayfield but losses in Wales and at home to England who won a Grand Slam that year. Had he not moved to Canada, Tom

Reid would very likely have continued in the Irish ranks for a few more years.

It was after the 20-0 drubbing at Twickenham in 1956 that one of the best anecdotes about Tom materialised. Tony O'Reilly recounted it.

> "Having seen Tom in action on tour when he was the 'cement' of the side, the 'mortar' that pulled us all together, I had not realised he was not noted for the avidity with which he trained. I'd last seen him in Pretoria as we boarded the plane to fly home and the following February we met again in London for the match against England.
>
> I noted in the dressing room that Tom was extremely vigorous in the pre-match warm-up and I said, 'for God's sake you'll exhaust yourself.' His reply was, 'Jesus, Reilly, this is the first run I've had since Pretoria'. He went out and, like all of us, proceeded to prove it was the first run since Pretoria, for we were hammered 20-0. Coming off the pitch pursued by every hospital orderly, fly-over constructor and trench-digger in the greater London area, I said to him, 'Wasn't that awful?'. Back came the reply: 'Yes, Reilly, and weren't we lucky to get nil?'".

## The Barbarians

Perhaps the team that would have the most profound impact on Tom Reid's life was the Barbarians.

Tom was called up to play for the Barbarians Easter 'tours" in 1954, 1955 and 1956. In 1954 he played against Cardiff and Newport. In 1955 he played against Leicester Tigers and in 1956 he played Penarth, Newport and East Midlands.

In 1957 the Barbarians went on an international tour for the first time, to Canada. Tom was a late replacement but went with them as they flew out on a six-game tour.

On the field the tour went to plan and Tom played in all six of the wins against Ontario (twice), British Columbia (three times) and Quebec. It was the final game of the tour against Quebec that things got interesting for Tom. On the Quebec team that day was his old Garryowen friend Niall Quaid. Quaid was an accountant with Price Waterhouse and had moved to Montreal for work a few years earlier. There, he had established a rugby club (Town of Mount Royal) and had settled in to Canadian life.

*Tom Reid (left) and the Barbarians land in Canada*

There are variations on what happened after the game but the upshot was that 'what goes on tour, stays on tour' and Tom Reid didn't return home with the team. One version of the story is there was a party and he missed the bus. Another story is that he met a girl and when the call went to get up and board the bus to go home, he said *'I'm staying. I'm in love"*.

In an interview with the Montreal Gazette in 1975 Reid said, "*You see we were travellin' across the land, Vancouver, Victoria, Toronto and all those places, I was with the Barbarians, and our last game was in Montreal. We played it and there was a good party afterwards. Well, we were supposed to fly back to England that night, but I fastened my eye on a cute little blonde. I was down to my last two bucks, so I took up a collection from the lads and I wound up with twelve bucks. The next morning when I should've been back* in London, I woke up in the Queen's Hotel. Oh, what a dreadful scene. Everything including the empty whiskey bottle on the dresser".

Whatever the truth, Tom Reid stayed in Canada for the rest of his life. He visited Ireland regularly but Canada became his home. His friend Niall Quaid also stayed in Canada.

Tom Reid joins a Barbarian sing song with Cliff Morgan (Wales) on piano

## The British and Irish Lions

Tom was called up for the 1955 British and Irish Lions team for their tour of South Africa in 1955. He would play in thirteen games during the tour including two test matches. He would also score two tries.

To read more about his Lions tour – Refer chapter South Africa & Kenya (1955)

Reid would become the first man to play for and against the Lions when he played against them during the 1959 tour.

*Tom Reid (standing 2nd right) in July 1994 at Garryowen
Photo courtesy of Garryowen Rugby*

## Post Rugby Career

Tom played with his rugby club in Montreal up until the 1970s. He also coached youth teams and led tours to the UK for the club.

Tom worked as a warehouseman for Anglo Photo in St. Laurent but said *"I always thought of a job as secondary. Anyway, work is too popular. There are too many people who want to do it"*.

## Personal Life

Tom met his future wife Linda Burbach while on tour with the Barbarians to Canada in 1957. They lived in Montreal for the rest of their lives.

In 1994, Tom was invited back to Garryowen for a ceremonial cap presentation alongside other Garryowen internationals.

Tom Reid died in Montreal on 22$^{nd}$ November 1996. He is buried at Notre Dame des Neiges Cemetery.

*Tom Reid (1926-1996)*

# South Africa & Kenya (1955)

Ahead of the previous tour in 1950, Ireland had been doing well in the Five Nations competition with a Grand Slam in 1948 and a triple crown in 1949. That led to a large contingent of Irish players (nine) being invited on the tour. Ahead of the 1955 tour, Ireland had not been doing as well. After winning the 1951 championship Ireland fell out of contention as Wales won a Grand Slam in 1952 and England won a triple crown in 1954. Ireland finished at the bottom of the table in 1954 with just one win at home to Scotland and in 1955 we only managed a home draw with England as we finished last again. It was unlikely that Ireland would have a large number of tourists this time around.

On the domestic front, the Munster Senior Cup had been won by Cork clubs in three of the five years since the last tour. The other two, in 1951/52 and in 1953/54 were won by Garryowen.

The 1955 tour was led by Jack Siggins. Jack had played twenty-four times for Ireland. He had been the chairman of the eight-person selection committee and he put himself forward to manage the tour. Alongside him Irishman Robin Thompson was selected to be the tour captain. Ahead of them a tour and test series against South Africa who were undisputedly world champions at the time. The had not been beaten in a test series by any country in 59 years. When the squad was announced, Ireland as expected had a small contingent. Eleven Welshmen, nine English, six Scots and just five Irishmen would go on the tour. Among the five Irish was Limerickman, Tom Reid. He would be accompanied by Tony O'Reilly who was going on his first tour, Cecil Pedlow who had thirty Irish caps, Robin Roe who had twenty-one caps, and tour captain Robin Thompson who was the least experienced and was aged just twenty-four. Another Irishman, prop Fuzzy Anderson was also originally selected but had to drop out because of injury. His spot was taken by Tom Elliot from Scotland.

One of the criteria set for qualification to be selected was that players had to be under thirty. Because of that, none of the tourists from 1950 were selected, including Jack Kyle which was a shock to everyone. Scot Angus Cameron was appointed as vice-captain. He had an injured knee and probably shouldn't have been on the tour at all. In the second test, the Springboks noticed his weakness and went after him.

1955 South Africa and Kenya

Amongst those selected were Dickie Jeeps who at the time had not yet been capped by England. He would go on to be a Lions legend, travelling on three tours. Also on their first of three tours was Bryn Meredith and Jeff Butterfield. Tony O'Reilly was another with a huge future. He would go on two tours and score a record thirty-eight tries for the Lions before becoming a major player in Irish business and being knighted.

Scottish prop forward Tom Elliot was the first of his family to be selected. In 2025, his grandson Fin Smith was selected for the Lions.

Tom Reid (standing 2$^{nd}$ row, 4$^{th}$ from right) and the 1955 British Lions

## Touring party

The following was the tour party selected for the tour:

**Management**
Manager: J. A. E. Siggins (Ireland)
Assistant Manager: D. E. Davies (Wales)

**Backs**
Doug Baker (Old Merchant Taylors and England), Jeff Butterfield (Northampton and England), Angus Cameron (Glasgow HSFP and Scotland), Phil Davies (Harlequins and England), Gareth Griffiths (Cardiff and Wales), Dickie Jeeps (Northampton and England)

(Uncapped at the time), Trevor Lloyd (Maesteg and Wales), Cliff Morgan (Cardiff and Wales), Haydn Morris (Cardiff and Wales), Tony O'Reilly (Old Belvedere and Ireland), Cecil Pedlow (Queen's University RFC and Ireland), Pat Quinn (New Brighton and England), Arthur Smith (Cambridge University and Scotland), Frank Sykes (Northampton and England), Alun Thomas (Llanelli and Wales), Johnny Williams (Old Millhillians and England)

**Forwards**
Tom Elliot (Gala and Scotland), Jim Greenwood (Dunfermline and Scotland), Reg Higgins (Liverpool and England), Hugh McLeod (Hawick and Scotland), Bryn Meredith (Newport and Wales), Courtney Meredith (Neath and Wales), Ernie Michie (Aberdeen University and Scotland), **Tom Reid (Garryowen and Ireland)**, Russell Robins (Pontypridd and Wales), Robin Roe (Lansdowne and Ireland), Clem Thomas (Swansea and Wales), Robin Thompson (Instonians and Ireland) (Captain), Rhys Williams (Llanelli and Wales), Billy Williams (Swansea and Wales), Dyson Wilson (Metropolitan Police and England)

## The Tour

The squad met up at Eastbourne, south of London on $4^{th}$ June. They had a few days together for some training and formalities before they were to depart on $10^{th}$.

The players each had to have fifty pounds to go on the tour. This money was given into a kitty. Each player was then given one pound and ten shillings a week pocket money. Against the amateur rules of the game at the time, some of the players were given the money by their clubs and national unions but no one asked the question.

At Eastbourne the team were given their gear for the four-month trip. Each was issued with two pair of boots – newly developed ones with rubber studs, tour blazers, shirts and ties. Things had progressed from the previous tour when the players were only issued a blazer and a jersey to play in. By all accounts, the sizes were all wrong and so a tailor spent the few days adjusting everyone's attire.

As training began at Eastbourne it was clear immediately that half of the players weren't fit enough. Rhys Williams commented *"Some of* *these lads wouldn't get into Llanelli 2<sup>nd</sup> team"*. English centre Jeff Butterfield, a PE teacher, assumed responsibility of fitness coach and ran training sessions. Six rugby balls had to be flown in from South Africa so that the players could get used to the subtleties of their ball standards.

During that week at Eastbourne, all of the players were on their best behaviour. No one had a drink and fitness improved. The team were also given briefings by the foreign office on what to expect in the newly formed Republic of South Africa. They were warned by the foreign office to be careful of non-whites in the new apartheid country. Not to invite "these people" into their hotels or to have sexual encounters as that could lead to their imprisonment.

Rules were also set. Players must be well dressed at all times, particularly at official functions. They were reminded that they were adults and should keep their own hours, the only stipulation being on the two nights before a game they had to be in bed at the team hotel before midnight.

In those initial days a good sense of fun emerged. At one team meeting at Eastbourne before the tour, scrum-half Trevor Lloyd spoke up *"Hey, Jack! (not Mr Siggins) what if a player has a girl and somebody tries to muscle in? Now, that could cause a great deal of trouble on a tour. I think that we should have a rule that nobody interferes with another player's girl"*. They all laughed and Lloyds Law was added to the rules for the tour. Another tour favourite came from Reg Higgins (from Lancashire). At Heathrow, they were passed by a lovely looking hostess. As she passed, they all admired and Reg blurted out *"Hey Dad. Buy me that?"*.

The team set off from Eastbourne on 9<sup>th</sup> June. They had a night in London where they were hosted at a farewell reception by the South African Ambassador. Then the following day they were off to London North Airport where they jetted off on their adventure. Ahead of them three and a half months, twenty-five-thousand miles, twenty-one provincial games and four test matches.

The 1955 team were the first British and Irish Lions team to travel by air. This would take a month off the duration of previous tours. They flew on a Lougheed Constellation and it took them thirty-six hours to get from London to Johannesburg. They stopped at Zurich, Rome, Cairo, Khartoum, Nairobi, Entebbe and finally Jan Smuts airport.

1955 South Africa and Kenya

Tom Reid (left) with the Irish contingent of Tony O'Reilly, Cecil Pedlow, Robin Roe and tour captain Robin Thompson

A party broke out at the back of the plane between Khartoum and Nairobi. This was the first time they let their hair down and reports are that they drank the plane dry. So many of the team were at the back of the plane that the captain thought there was a problem. It took him an hour to work out what the problem was.

A huge crowd turned out to meet the team when they arrived in Johannesburg. The team surprised and impressed them by singing

'Sarie Marais' in Afrikaans. Welshman Cliff Morgan had taught the team the words and acted as choir-master.

*Tom Reid (peeking from the back) – The Lions on the move*

This was the first time most of the team had been to Africa. They were taken by coach from the airport, thirty-six miles to the town of Vereeniging. There they would have ten days to acclimatise ahead of the first game. It wasn't lost on the historians amongst the group that Vereeniging was where the treaty that ended the second Anglo Boer war was signed in 1902. This was a significant event in Anglo - South African relations.

In an easy first few days the team settled in. They played a round of golf and were followed by crowds with one player saying afterwards, *"It was like the British Open"*. During the week they also got the opportunity to travel by dirt road to Pretoria where they watched two of their opponents Northern Transvaal and Western Province play. They noted how powerful the players were, how the ball travelled further in the thin air and how high it bounced on the hard dry pitch.

1955 South Africa and Kenya

Tony O'Reilly whispered to his team mates, *"When does the next plane leave for home and couldn't we be on it?"*

In those first few days in South Africa the team bonded. As is the case on most Lions tours, a sing-song was always used to break down the inter nation barriers. Tom Reid, like his uncle Jack Ryan and cousins the Ryan brothers (Gerry, Des and Pat), was musical and had a fine singing voice and was the most popular singer amongst the group. The group first christened him 'The Major' but he was later promoted to 'The Colonel' and throughout the tour he was the go-to singer to get a sing-song going.

## The Games

*Game One*
*v Western Transvaal*
*Olen Park, Potchefstroom, South Africa 22/6/1955*
*6 – 9 - Loss*

**Lions Team** –Thomas (Wales), Smith (Scotland), Butterfield (England), Davies (England), Pedlow (England), Morgan (Wales), Lloyd (Wales), Wilson (England), Greenwood (England), Higgins (England), Williams (Wales), Thompson (Ireland) Captain, Meredith (Wales), Meredith (Wales), Williams (Wales)

Eight days after they arrived in South Africa, the 1955 British and Irish Lions played their first game against Western Transvaal in Potchefstroom. Tom Reid wasn't selected to play because he was carrying a back injury. It would be the third game before he was fit enough to play.

On the day of the game there were five warm up games beginning at 10.30am to give the crowd value for money. 18,000 showed up to watch. The Lions had a lot of support as the coloured Africans were supporting the Lions throughout the tour.

The Lions lost the first game. They were up two tries to nil after Morgan and Pedlow got over but lack of match fitness cost them and a strong Transvaal team came back into the game. Drop goal from Peters and a huge drop goal from Van Der Schyff followed by a penalty from

Van Der Schyff gave them the win. To make matters worse, Arthur Smith broke a bone in his hand and was out for a number of weeks.

Each day a member of the team was designated "duty officer" their duty to ensure the team kept on time. Tom Reid was duty officer after the first game and shepherded them onto the team busses from the after-match party. They had a train to catch to their next destination.

**Game Two**
*v Giqualand West*
*De Beers Stadium, Kimberley, South Africa 25/6/1955*
*24 – 14 - Win*

**Lions Team** – Thomas (Wales), Sykes (England), Quinn (England), Davies (England), Morris (Wales), Morgan (Wales), Jeeps (England), Robins (Wales), Wilson (England), Williams (Wales), Thompson (Ireland) Captain, Higgins (England), Meredith (Wales), Roe (Ireland), McLeod (Scotland)

For the second game in Kimberley, Tom Reid was again not selected. Clem Thomas, who was, was rushed to hospital before the game to have an emergency appendectomy. The president of Griqualand West Rugby, Norman Weinberg was a surgeon. He diagnosed it and sent Thomas to hospital. That evening, after the players dinner, Weinberg went to the hospital and performed the operation. Thomas missed the next ten matches of the tour and returned to play against Rhodesia five weeks later.

The Lions got their tour back on track with a good win. Tries to Morris (3), Jeeps, Davies and Roe was enough to see off Griqualand's try and three penalty goals.

The team left Kimberley the day after the game leaving Clem Thomas in hospital. That night Sailor Malan (a fighter pilot) and Sam Armstrong (local business man) arrived at the hospital with a crate of beer and told Thomas that they wouldn't leave until he finished it all. He did and they visited him for the next five days before Thomas went to Malan's farm for a week to recover, he re-joined the team at Cape Town twelve days later.

1955 South Africa and Kenya

*Game Three*
*v Northern Universities*
*Ellis Park, Johannesburg, South Africa 29/6/1955*
**32 – 6 - Win**

Lions Team – Cameron (Scotland), Sykes (England), Pedlow (England), O'Reilly (Ireland), Morris (England), Baker (England), Williams (Wales), Higgins (England), **Reid (Ireland)**, Greenwood (England), Michie (Scotland), Robins (Wales), McLeod (Scotland), Roe (Ireland), Elliot (England)

Tom Reid made his first appearance for the British and Irish Lions in the third game of their tour in a game against Northern Universities at Ellis Park in Johannesburg. He was one of seven changes to the team from the previous game. Tony O'Reilly would also make his first start in what was an easy win, with the Lions winning 16-0 at half time. Tries to Tony O'Reilly (2), Morris (2), Williams and Baker were more than enough to see them home.

*Tom Reid (far right) cooling off at the pool*

1955 South Africa and Kenya

*Game Four*
*v Orange Free State*
*Loubser Park, Kroonstad, South Africa 2/7/1955*
*31 – 3 – Win*

**Lions Team** – Cameron (Scotland), O'Reilly (Ireland), Davies (England), Butterfield (England), Morris (England), Morgan (Wales), Wilson (England), Robins (Wales), Williams (Wales), Thompson (England) Captain, Greenwood (England), Meredith (Wales), Meredith (Wales), Williams (Wales)

Having come through the previous match unscathed, Tom Reid was given the chance to rest in the game against Orange Free State. While the scoreboard suggests it was an easy game for the Lions, Tom might have been happy to be in the stands for a brutal contest in which an Orange Free State player knocked out the two front teeth of Rhys Williams. The Lions played sublime rugby scoring freely. Butterfield (3), Davies (2), O'Reilly and Thompson, all ran in tries. The Lions were up 8-0 at half time and never looked in danger.

In the first four matches of the tour, the Lions had scored twenty-one tries. The press was starting to take note and the prospect of an amazing test series was beginning to excite the local rugby crowd.

*Game Five*
*v South West Africa*
*Mable Volk Stadium, Windhoek, Namibia 5/7/1955*
*9 – 0 – Win*

**Lions Team** – Cameron (Scotland) Captain, Sykes (England), O'Reilly (Ireland), Quinn (England), Morris (England), Morgan (Wales), Lloyd (England), Robins (Wales), Higgins (England), Michie (Scotland), **Reid (Ireland)**, Wilson (England), Elliot (England), Roe (Ireland), Williams (Scotland)

The next game was played in Windhoek which is now the capital of Namibia. The team flew in a couple of days ahead of the game. They were met at the airport by the mayor. The game itself was viewed by the Lions afterwards as a poor performance. They had won easily with tries to Sykes, O'Reilly and Morris but they were disappointed that they

1955 South Africa and Kenya

hadn't put in a better performance for the spectators. The mayor was there again to see the team off at the airport the following day.

*Game Six*
*v Western Province*
*Newlands, Cape Town, South Africa 9/7/1955*
*11 – 3 - Win*

**Lions Team** – Cameron (Scotland), Sykes (England), Davies (England), O'Reilly (Ireland), Quinn (England), Baker (England), Jeeps (England), **Reid (Ireland)**, Wilson (England), Williams (Wales), Thompson (England) Captain, Greenwood (England), Meredith (Wales), Meredith (Wales), McLeod (Scotland)

This was to be a big test with four Springboks in the ranks of Western Province. Newlands stadium is in a most beautiful setting but back then, it wasn't as well developed as it is today. About 35,000 spectators crammed in with high expectations because of the Lions previous performances.

The game was an excellent, open game and the spectators left saying it had been one of the best games that had been played at the ground. Western Province scored a penalty in the first half but despite the quality of the rugby, the Lions were kept scoreless. In the second half Welsh hooker Meredith scored twice and Thomas got a third in a good win for the Lions.

*Game Seven*
*v South West Districts*
*Recreation Ground, George, South Africa 13/7/1955*
*22 – 3 -Win*

**Lions Team** – Baker (England), Sykes (England), Butterfield (England), Quinn (England), Morris (Wales), Pedlow (Ireland), Williams (Wales), **Reid (Ireland)**, Robins (Wales), Michie (Scotland), Thompson (England) Captain, Higgins (England), Williams (Wales), McLeod (Scotland), Meredith (Wales)

From Cape Town the team had a three-hundred-and-fifty-mile bus journey to get to their next appointment. On the way the team stopped at an ostrich farm where prop Courtney Meredith took the opportunity to go for a ride on an ostrich's back.

Now fully recovered from his back strain, Tom Reid played his fourth successive game against South West Districts. The game was never expected to be a difficult one and so it turned out with the Lions leading 8-3 at half time. Despite Williams having to retire injured, the Lions still scored five tries. Sykes scored three, Morris scored one and **Tom Reid** scored his first Lions try in the game.

*Game Eight*
*v Eastern Province*
*Crusaders Ground, Port Elizabeth, South Africa 16/7/1955*
*0 – 20 - Loss*

**Lions Team** – O'Reilly (Ireland), Sykes (England), Butterfield (England), Davies (England), Morris (Wales), Baker (England), Jeeps (England), Wilson (England), Williams (Wales), Thompson (England), Greenwood (England), Higgins (England), Williams (Wales), Roe (Wales), Meredith (Wales)

The Lions were forced to shuffle their deck for this game due to the number of injuries in their ranks. Only seventeen of the thirty-one players in the squad were fit. Tony O'Reilly was moved to full back and with Bryn Meredith injured, Robin Roe who had two cracked ribs had to stand in as hooker for the game. His inexperience and injury showed as the Lions lost thirty-five of the forty-one scrums in the game. Eastern Province used their scrum domination to good effect. That coupled with the Lions having an awful day at kicking penalties, gave the home team a 9-0 half time lead and a 20-0 win.

Their visit to Port Elizabeth had also been picketed by The Black Sash Women who protested against apartheid outside the team's hotel.

*Game Nine*
*v North Eastern District*
*Aliwal North, South Africa 20/7/1955*
*34 – 6 – Win*

1955 South Africa and Kenya

**Lions team** – Baker (England), Pedlow (Ireland), Quinn (England), Davies (England), O'Reilly (Ireland), Morgan (Wales), Lloyd (England), Greenwood (England), Robins (Wales), **Reid (Ireland)**, Michie (Scotland), Wilson (England), McLeod (Scotland), Meredith (Wales), Williams (Wales)

When the team arrived at their hotel in Aliwal, the found that the Vienna Boys' Choir were also staying there. They were in town for a concert which many of the team went along to.

Tom Reid got his fifth Lions appearance in the game against North Eastern Province. The opposition weren't up to much and the Lions won easily. They were up 16-0 at half time. Tony O'Reilly (3), Morgan (2), Pedlow (2), and Meredith each scoring before the game was out. They could have scored more but eased off.

*Tom Reid (centre 3rd from right) with the 1955 Lions Squad*

*Game Ten*
*v Transvaal*
*Ellis Park, Johannesburg, South Africa 23/7/1955*
*36 – 13 - Win*

**Lions Team** – Cameron (Scotland), O'Reilly (Ireland), Griffiths (Wales), Butterfield (England), Morris (Wales), Baker (England), Jeeps

(England), Robins (Wales), Higgins (England), Thompson (England) Captain, Williams (Wales), Greenwood (England), Meredith (Wales), Meredith (Wales), McLeod (Scotland)

Tom Reid sat out the next game. Two weeks out from the first test which would also be played at this ground, 45,000 spectators turned out for what was expected to be a real test for the Lions. As it turned out, it wasn't. In a masterclass, conducted by Jeeps the Lions scored seven tries in a display that completely outclassed their opposition. Tony O'Reilly was the star of the show scoring three. Butterfield got two and both Griffiths and Higgins also scored.

*Game Eleven*
*v Rhodesia*
*Rokhana Ground, Kitwe, Rhodesia 27/7/1955*
*27 – 14 – Win*

**Lions Team** – Baker (England), Griffiths (Wales), Davies (England), Pedlow (Ireland), Sykes (England), Morgan (Wales), Jeeps (England), **Reid (Ireland)**, Higgins (England), Williams (Wales), Elliot (England), Wilson (England), Meredith (Wales), Meredith (Wales), Williams (Wales)

Kitwe, a mining town, was over a thousand miles from Johannesburg up close to the border of the Congo. No one in the party knew what to expect when they went there. They were pleasantly surprised. Rather than staying in a hotel, the players were distributed out amongst private houses.

This wasn't going to be a walk over. Rhodesia had beaten the All-Blacks just six years earlier. A small crowd of just 5,000 turned out for the game. Those 5,000 were all white. The coloured population was not allowed to attend the game. The game proved to be a difficult one. Tom Reid had to leave the field with a thigh strain in the middle of the second half. The Lions were ahead at half time 8-9 and with just twelve minutes to go as Tom reluctantly walked off, they were only two points ahead. The Lions kicked into another gear though and ran out comfortable winners.

1955 South Africa and Kenya

*Game Twelve*
*v Rhodesia*
*Police Ground, Salisbury, Zimbabwe 30/7/1955*
*16 – 12 - Win*

**Lions Team** – Baker (England), O'Reilly (Ireland), Quinn (England), Griffiths (Wales), Sykes (England), Morgan (Wales), Williams (Wales), Robins (Wales), Thomas (Wales), Williams (Wales), Michie (Scotland), Greenwood (England), McLeod (Scotland), Roe (Ireland), Williams (Wales)

Three days after the game at Kitwe, the Lions and Rhodesia played again in the capital Salisbury (now Harare). Tom Reid missed the game with a thigh strain. Like the previous game it was a tight game but the Lions again came out on top. To celebrate the victory, the team got the opportunity to visit Victoria Falls for a few days rest and recovery.

*Game Thirteen*
*v South Africa (First Test)*
*Ellis Park, Johannesburg, South Africa 6/8/1955*
*23 – 22 - Win*

**Lions Team** – Cameron (Scotland), O'Reilly (Ireland), Butterfield (England), Davies (England), Pedlow (Ireland), Morgan (Wales), Jeeps (England), Meredith (Wales), Meredith (Wales), Williams (Wales), Thompson (England), Williams (Wales), Higgins (England), Robins (Wales), Greenwood (England)

**South Africa** - Ven Der Schyff, Briers, Sinclair, Van Vollenhoven, Swart, Ulyate, Gentles, du Plooy, Kroon, Koch, du Rand, Classens, van Wyk, Retief, Fry (Captain)

Still carrying his injury, Tom Reid wasn't available for selection for the first test against South Africa in Johannesburg.

Over 100,000 people attended the game, including the then anonymous **Nelson Mandela**. This was the biggest ever attendance at a rugby game at that point. Coloured fans were segregated into small sections behind the goals and mostly supported the Lions in protest against apartheid. Demand for tickets was huge. They were changing hands on the black

1955 South Africa and Kenya

market at a hundred pounds each. The Lions even sold their surplus tickets to the hotel barber at fifty pounds each.

This was the first Lions team to play against the Springboks for seventeen years. Anticipation was massive and the excitement came to a crescendo as Scottish Lion Ernie Michie led the team out dressed in his kilt and playing the bagpipes. He was followed by Robin Thompson who was carrying tour mascot Elmer the Lion.

The Lions were the first to score when Jeff Butterfield collected a poor pass and broke on the outside. He drew in the springbok full back before passing out to Pedlow who went over in the corner.

The Springboks then came back and van der Schyff kicked two penalties before Springbok scrum-half Tommy Gentles broke from a scrum and passed to the Springbok captain Stephen Fry who put Briers in for a try. After van der Schyff's conversion the home side were 11-3 up.

*Ernie Michie leads the Lions out playing the bagpipes*

1955 South Africa and Kenya

*Overhead shot of Ellis Park during the first test with over 100,000 people*

Before the break, Jeff Butterfield scored a try under the posts after deceiving his opposite number with some swift footwork. Cameron converted and the teams went into the break at 11-8.

Early in the second half, Reg Higgins tore knee ligaments and had to leave the field. The Lions would then play the second half with a man down. Higgins missed the rest of the tour. Spurred on by this, the Lions scored fifteen points in ten mins. First, Bryn Meredith won against the head in a scrum. Cliff Morgan picked it up and made a break to score. Then an upfield kick took an odd bounce that deceived van der Schyff and Greenwood took advantage and scored. Another speculative kick had the same outcome and O'Reilly scored. All three tries were converted by Angus Cameron.

It was inspiring stuff but playing a man down, the seven Lions forwards began to tire as the game wore on. They clung on but in the dying minutes Chris Koch scored from a break twenty yards out and

1955 South Africa and Kenya

then late in injury time, Fry picked up a loose ball, passed to Briers who beat both Pedlow and Cameron to score. 23-22 to the Lions. The Springboks had the conversion kick to win the game ..... and missed by van der Schyff. When asked after the game what he was thinking during the kick, Tony O'Reilly said he *"was merely in direct communication with the Vatican"*.

The Lions had won by the narrowest possible margin. A sensational finish to a game in which the combined forty-five points was the highest ever point tally for an international test at the time.

*Game Fourteen*
*v Central University*
*Kingsmead, Durban, South Africa 10/8/1955*
*21 – 14 - Win*

**Lions Team** – Cameron (Scotland), Sykes (England), Griffiths (Wales), Quinn (England), Morris (Wales), Baker (England), Williams (Wales), Roe (Ireland), Meredith (Wales), McLeod (Scotland), Michie (Scotland), Thompson (England), Greenwood (England), Robins (Wales), Thomas (Wales)

1955 South Africa and Kenya

After the drama of the first test, the Lions moved to the seaside city of Durban to continue the tour with a game against Central University. Tom Reid was still not available for selection. Many of the test team were also given a break. The Lions got off to a slow start and were behind 10-8 at the break but they lifted the intensity in the second half and won.

*Game Fifteen*
*v Boland*
*Wellington, South Africa 13/8/1955*
*11 – 0 - Win*

**Lions Team** – Cameron (Scotland), O'Reilly (Ireland), Davies (England), Butterfield (England), Griffiths (Wales), Morgan (Wales), Jeeps (England), McLeod (Scotland), Meredith (Wales), Williams (Wales), Thompson (England), Williams (Wales), Wilson (England), Robins (Wales), Thomas (Wales)

The Lions had been warned that this would be a tough game. It was a battle but the Lions were 8-0 up at half time and won 11-0 thanks to tries from O'Reilly, Davies and Wilson.

*Game Sixteen*
*v Western Province Universities*
*Newlands, Cape Town, South Africa 16/8/1955*
*20 – 17 - Win*

**Lions Team** – Griffiths (Wales), Smith (Scotland), Pedlow (Ireland), Quinn (England), Sykes (England), Baker (England), Lloyd (England), McLeod (Scotland), Roe (Ireland), Meredith (Wales), Elliot (England), Michie (Scotland), Wilson (England), **Reid (Ireland)**, Thomas (Wales)

Tom Reid had recovered from his injury and was re-introduced to the team with four days to go until the second test.

35,000 spectators turned out for what was to be one of the best games of the tour. The combination of Cape Town and Stellenbosch Universities were determined to match the Lions running game and the game was played at a high pace.

The superior fitness of the Lions showed in the final fifteen minutes. They were losing 17-12 when Tug Wilson scored and Pedlow's conversion levelled the score. Then, at the very death, **Tom Reid** jumped in a lineout near the African line, secured the ball and managed to get over the line to score the winner. Reid had an outstanding game and effectively played his way into the test side for four days later.

*Game Seventeen*
*v South Africa (Second Test)*
*Newlands, Cape Town, South Africa 20/8/1955*
*9 – 25 - Loss*

**Lions Team** – Cameron (Scotland), O'Reilly (Ireland), Davies (England), Butterfield (England), Griffiths (Wales), Morgan (Wales), Jeeps (England), Meredith (Wales), Meredith (Wales), Williams (Wales), Thompson (England), Williams (Wales), Robins (Wales), **Reid (Ireland),** Greenwood (England)

**South Africa** – Dryburgh, Briers, Sinclair, Rosenberg, Van Vollenhoven, Ulyate, Gentles, Bekker, van der Merwe, Koch, du Rand, Classens, Ackermann, Retief, Fry

Tom Reid was a very popular member of the touring side and there was a lot of joy for him within the group when he was selected for the test team. Having recovered from injury, he wasn't expected to play but his determination showed. Over the course of the tour Tom had worked on his fitness and actually put on weight. Not fat but muscle. At sixteen stone three pounds he was one of the heaviest players on the team.

The Springboks dropped five of their team from the first test. Van der Schyff who missed the decisive kick was dropped and was replayed Dryburgh who came in at full back. The Lions only made two changes. Gareth Griffiths who had flown in as a replacement after Ian Smith had broken his thumb in the first game played and Russell Robins was moved to flanker to allow room for Reid to come in at number eight.

Just like the first test, there was huge demand for tickets for this game. 52,000 eventually crammed into the stadium and there was an electric atmosphere when the teams took the field.

1955 South Africa and Kenya

*The second test at Newlands in Cape Town*

*Lions team for the 2nd Test in Cape Town – Reid back row 2nd left*

1955 South Africa and Kenya

Reid was hit by a heavy early tackle early in the game. He reached high to catch a Springbok drop out and won a penalty for the knock he took. He was down for quite a while recovering his breath and composure.

Things were cagy for the first twenty minutes. The Lions took a lead from a Cameron penalty. Then, three minutes before half time, van Vollenhoven scored a try to level it. Three all at the break.

During the first half the Springboks had realised that full back Cameron was slow because of a bad knee that he had been carrying all tour and took advantage. The Lions took the lead again at the start of the second half but then van Vollenhoven scored twice. His hattrick came on the nineth minute of the second half after which the Lions fell apart. The Springboks scored seven tries which was a record for a test in South Africa. The series was level and all eyes turned to the third test in Pretoria two weeks later.

Colin Johnson recounted a story regarding Tom Reid at the after-game function for this game.

> *"At the time there was a large and famous chemist chain in South Africa with a branch in Cape Town and another in Durban, run by a pair of brothers as proprietors, one in each outlet. They were very successful and sponsored the Boks and attended the function after the match.*
> 
> *The reception dinner dance after the Cape Town game was held in a large room from which the tables were cleared away to make room for dancing after the meal. The teams and chief guests were on a large table sat on a stage. Before the dinner, Clem (Clem Thomas) and several other Lions were talking to the brothers, whom they had previously met in Durban.*
> 
> *Tom Reid, the big Irish second row, sidled up and whispered to Clem, 'You wouldn't have a johnnie about your person, would you?'. Clem explained the need to the brother from Durban, who in turn spoke to the Cape Town man, who contacted his local manager and a carefully wrapped gross carton of Durex arrived shortly after, some of which were distributed immediately.*
> 
> *After the meal and between dances when the floor was cleared, the double doors at the far end of the room were pushed open and Tom with a blushing young lady in hand, emerged in full view of all on the top table.*

1955 South Africa and Kenya

*The Cape Town brother exclaimed, "Jesus, that's my daughter!" And his brother responded, "Well, at least we know it was safe sex.""*

**Game Eighteen**
***v Eastern Transvaal***
***PAM Brink, Springs, South Africa 24/8/1955***
***17 – 17 - Draw***

**Lions Team** – Griffiths (Wales), Sykes (England), Pedlow (Ireland), Quinn (England), Smith (Scotland), Baker (English), Williams (Wales), McLeod (Scotland), Roe (Ireland), Elliot (England), Thompson (England), Michie (Scotland), Wilson (England), **Reid (Ireland)**, Thomas (Wales)

For the next two weeks the Lions were based in Pretoria. They were happy to have a solid base and no travel of note to do. The High Commissioner to South Africa, Sir Percivale Liesching, spent a lot of time with the team in Pretoria and there are reports of a great party in which he and Tom Reid did some great singing, accompanied by Cliff Morgan on piano.

Despite the heavy knock he took in the test game, Tom Reid was one of three test players who played again four days later in the game against Eastern Transvaal which was played at Springs, outside of Pretoria.

The Lions took control in the first half and had a 12 – 0 half time lead. At the start of the second half, Doug Baker who was playing without his contact lenses after losing them on the way to the ground, pulled a muscle in the second half and the Lions played most of the half down a man. Baker had to have replacement lenses flown in from Germany.

With the extra man advantage, the African team had a great spell in which they scored two penalties and two tries in seven minutes to take the lead. Johnny Williams scored a great individual try for the Lions but a drop goal from Forman meant the game finished in a draw.

**Game Nineteen**
***v Northern Transvaal***
***Loftus Versfeld, Pretoria, South Africa 27/8/1955***
***14 – 11 - Win***

1955 South Africa and Kenya

**Lions Team** – Griffiths (Wales), O'Reilly (Ireland), Davies (England), Butterfield (England), Pedlow (Ireland), Morgan (Wales), Williams (Wales), Meredith (Wales), Roe (Ireland), Williams (Wales), Thompson (England), Wilson (England), Robins (Wales), Thomas (Wales), Greenwood (England)

The next game was against Northern Transvaal back in Pretoria. This game and the next were viewed as being like playing back-to-back tests. The Lions put out a strong team but Tom Reid was given a rest.

Robin Thompson had to leave the field after twenty minutes with a twisted knee. Down a man, the Lions put on a brave show. O'Reilly, Davies and Greenwood scored tries. The score with three minutes to go was 11-11 but then Jeff Butterfield took a pass behind his back and juggled it around before running eighty yards to score for a Lions win.

*Game Twenty*
*v South Africa (Third Test)*
*Loftus Versfeld, Pretoria, South Africa 3/9/1955*
*9 – 6 - Win*

**Lions Team** – Baker (England), Griffiths (Wales), Butterfield (England), Davies (England), O'Reilly (Ireland), Morgan (Wales) Captain, Jeeps (England), Williams (Wales), Meredith (Wales), Meredith (Wales), Greenwood (England), Williams (Wales), **Reid (Ireland)**, Thomas (Wales), Robins (Wales)

**South Africa** - Dryburgh, van Vollenhoven, Sinclair, Rosenberg, Briers, Ulyate, Strydom, Koch, Van der Merwe, Bekker, Fry, du Rand, Classens, Ackermann, Lochner.

With the series tied one all and the Lions having just won what was views as a pseudo test against Northern Transvaal, the excitement for the first ever test match to be played in Pretoria was massive.

Tom Reid was again selected for the test team. With Robin Thompson injured, Reid was moved from number eight, where he had played the first test, to the second row. Russell Robins came in at number eight.

In the lead up to the game there was controversy when Springbok coach Danie Craven accused the Lions of spying on the Springbok

1955 South Africa and Kenya

training camp. He took his players off the training pitch only to bring them back that night to train under the moonlight.

The Lions needed to win the game so they parked their free-flowing rugby style and adopted the tactic of attacking the Springboks through the pack. There would be sixty-three lineouts during the game and lots of kicking.

Excitement was high when Ernie Michie, as he had done in previous tests, led the Lions onto the field in his kilt and blowing his bagpipes.

The Lions forwards had struggled in the previous test but in this one they were titanic. Tom Reid and Rees Williams were called out in the Sunday Times for being "giants". It was a real forward tussle with forty-five scrums in all. The only score in the first half came from a drop goal from Jeff Butterfield and the Lions went into the break 3- 0 up.

At the break, Courtney Meredith had blood streaming from his mouth. Teams stayed on the pitch for half time in those days and when the doctors examined him, his tongue almost severed. He played on. After the game he went to hospital have it stitched and he was out until the final test.

Twelve minutes into the second half, Baker scored a penalty to extend the Lions' lead. Then Dryburgh scored a fifty-yard drop goal. Jeff Butterfield scored another try after a pass from Clem Thomas. Dryburgh scored a late penalty but the game was won. The Lions could not now lose the test series.

"If I was to present a metaphorical trophy for the outstanding men of the match, I would award it jointly, and without hesitation to the two second row men, Reid and Williams. It is here that matches against South Africa are won and lost, and the scoreboard is its own tribute to the labours of the two players concerned. They can rest content in the memory of an effort beyond praise". Sunday Times.

171

1955 South Africa and Kenya

After their test victory, the team took a four-day break and went to the Kruger National Park and from there the moved back to the seaside city of Durban.

*Reid in action*

*Game Twenty-One*
*v Natal*
*Kingsmead, Durban, South Africa 10/9/1955*
*11 – 8 - Win*

**Lions Team** – Thomas (Wales), Smith (Scotland), Davies (England), Pedlow (Ireland), Sykes (England), Baker (England), Williams (Wales), Roe (Ireland), Meredith (Wales), McLeod (Scotland), Michie (Scotland), Elliot (England), Thomas (Wales), **Reid (Ireland)**, Wilson (England)

Next game up was Natal, the twentieth game of the tour. The team had been away from home for three months. Tom Reid had played ten of the games so far and this would be his eleventh appearance in a Lions shirt.

1955 South Africa and Kenya

In a performance that disappointed the Lions, they were level at 5-5 at half time with Pedlow having scored a try. In the second half Smith kept the Lions in touch with the Natal side and it was only in the closing second that the Lions won the game when Tom Reid picked up a loose ball, passed to Clem Thomas who in turn passed to Wilson who scored.

*Game Twenty-Two*
*v Junior Springboks*
*Free State Stadium, Bloemfontein, South Africa 14/9/1955*
*15 – 12 - Win*

**Lions Team** – Thomas (Wales), Sykes (England), Butterfield (England), Quinn (England), O'Reilly (Ireland), Morgan (Wales), Lloyd (England), Williams (Wales), Roe (Ireland), McLeod (Scotland), **Reid (Ireland)**, Williams (Wales), Greenwood (England), Robins (Wales), Wilson (England)

The Lions were getting a little tour weary. The poor performance against Natal was followed up with another close game against the Junior Springboks. In eighty-degree heat the Lions scored three tries by Quinn, Sykes and O'Reilly, to scratch out a win against a team of players who were trying to break into the Springboks team.

From Bloemfontein the team flew down to the coastal town of East London where the next game was to be held. While there they enjoyed some down time during which Tom Reid was the target of a practical joke. While he was swimming, a joker in the squad buried his clothes in the sand. He nonchalantly tried to hide his stress when he came out of the water, much to the amusement of his teammates.

*Game Twenty-Three*
*v Border*
*East London, South Africa 17/9/1955*
*12 – 14 – Loss*

**Lions Team** – Thomas (Wales), Sykes (England), Davies (England), Quinn (England), Pedlow (Ireland), Baker (England), Jeeps (England), Williams (Wales), Meredith (Wales), Elliot (England), Michie (Scotland), **Reid (Ireland)**, Wilson (England), Robins (Wales), Greenwood (England)

Tom Reid played his fourth game in succession at East London and the Lions poor performances continued with a loss. After this game there were only two games left and perhaps the team had one eye on the flight home.

The Lions played the bulk of the game down a man. After ten minutes Tom Reid was taken out in a lineout and had to leave the field for fifteen minutes to recover. No sooner had he re-taken the field than Thomas injured his foot and had to leave the field.

Sykes, Davies and Meredith each scored a try for the Lions but a man of the match performance from Border's fullback Marais kicked the Border team to victory. He scored three penalties and converted Bahlmann's try. He also made two huge tackles in the dying stages to keep the Lions out.

*Game Twenty-Four*
*v South Africa (Fourth Test)*
*Crusaders Ground, Port Elizabeth, South Africa 24/9/1955*
*8 – 22 - Loss*

**Lions Team** – Baker (England), Griffiths (Wales), Butterfield (England), O'Reilly (Ireland), Pedlow (Ireland), Morgan (Wales), Jeeps (England), Williams (Wales), Meredith (Wales), Meredith (Wales), Williams (Wales), Thompson (England), Greenwood (England), Robins (Wales), Thomas (Wales)

**South Africa** – Dryburgh, Briers, Sinclair, Rosenberg, Van Vollenhoven, Ulyate, Gentles, Bekker, Van Der Merwe, Koch, Du Rand, Classens, Ackerman, Retief, Fry

Amid much consternation, Tom Reid was left out of the team named for the fourth test in Port Elizabeth. He played so well in the previous test that everyone considered him a certain starter. However, Robin Thompson - tour captain - had recovered from injury and so was brought in to replace Tom Reid.

The Lions were in with a shot of being the first team to win a test series against South Africa in over fifty years but the stubborn Springboks defied defeat and ran out easy winners.

1955 South Africa and Kenya

The Lions had a big opening twenty minutes and scored first. Griffiths kicked ahead, Greenwood picked it up and passed to Pedlow who scored. The Springboks had targeted Cameron in the previous test. This time it was Pedlow who was in their sights. Ulyate began kicking high balls to him, knowing he had poor eyesight. He fumbled one and Briers went over to score.

The Springboks keep up that tactic in the second half and a mirror image try was scored with the same player fumbling and the same player scoring. Then a Gentles break put Ulyate over for a try. With the Lions getting tired van Vollenhoven scored in the corner followed by an Ulyate drop goal to make it 17 – 5 to the home team. O'Reilly pulled a try back for the Lions but broke his shoulder in the process. Then, with a minute to go Retief, scored under the posts. The game was lost and the series drawn 2-2.

After a party to celebrate the end of the South African part of the tour, the Lions left Port Elizabeth the morning after the test to fly to Nairobi for a game against East Africa.

*Game Twenty-Six*
*v East Africa*
*Ngong Road Ground, Nairobi, Kenya 27/9/1955*
*39 – 12 – Win*

**Lions Team** – Baker (England), Pedlow (Ireland), Quinn (England), Griffiths (Wales), Smith (Scotland), Morgan (Wales), Lloyd (England),

Williams (Wales), Meredith (Wales), Elliot (England), Michie (Scotland), Williams (Wales), Wilson (England), Thompson (England), Thomas (Wales)

Tom Reid sat out the game against East Africa. It was more of an exhibition game than a real tour match. Smith (5), Pedlow (2), Griffiths, Morgan, Quinn and Michie all scored in a one-sided game.

*Idi Amin*

There is an African legend, that Idi Amin, came on as a replacement for the East African team during this game. Amin who would later become President of Uganda and become nicknamed the Butcher of Africa, was a rugby player and boxer. He was six foot four inches tall and played first for Nile R.F.C and later Kobs R.F.C.

*"As you know I am a rugby player. I am second row, so I know how to push. I am very big. You don't want to push against me. And I also play wing three-quarter and am very fast. I can run one hundred metres in nine point five seconds. If you tackle me, you will try and you will hurt only yourself. So, to everyone who is a boxer, I say this, do what you have to do to knock out your opponent".*

Amin's exaggeration is most likely the source of this myth. At the time the rules of Rugby did not allow for replacements and there is no sign of Amin in any photographs.

## Post Tour Games

While the 1955 British and Irish Lions Team officially ceased to exist as an entity on their return from South Africa, there were a series of one-off games played after their return. Not sanctioned or counted towards Lions appearances, they were to celebrate the Welsh Rugby Football

1955 South Africa and Kenya

Union's 75th Anniversary. Tom Reid played in three of these games.

*22/10/1955 - A Selected Welsh XV*
*Cardiff Arms Park, Wales*

**Lions Team** – Griffiths (Scotland), Morris (Wales), Quinn (England), Thomas (Wales), Morgan (Wales), Williams (England), McLeod (Scotland), Roe (Ireland), Elliot (Scotland), Michie (Scotland), Williams (Wales), Robins (Wales), **Reid (Ireland)**, Stevens (Wales)

**Wales Team** – P.M Davies, H. Morgan, M, Davies, T.J Brewer, C. Aston, T. Lloyd, R. Prosser, B. Meredith, C. Meredith, E.J Jenkins, G. Hughes, B. Sparks, L. Jenkins


*24/10/1955 - Llanelli*
*Stradey Park, Llanelli, Wales*

**Lions Team** - Davies (Wales), Morris (Wales), Baker (England), Thomas (Wales), Collins, Morgan (Wales), Lloyd (Wales), McLeod (Scotland), Roe (Ireland), Meredith (Wales), Williams (Wales), Michie (Scotland), Thomas (Wales), **Reid (Ireland),** Robins (Wales).

**Llanelli Team** - Peter Davies, J.H Daniels, Ray Williams, Wynford Phillips, Geoff Howells, Caerwyn James, Wynne Evans, H Morgan, D Hopkins, E Foligno, G Hughes, B.J Lewis, I McGregor, G. Jenkins, Peter Evans


*29/10/1955 - Jack Siggins VX*
*Ravenhill, Belfast*
*19 -3 - Loss*

**R. Thompson XV (Lions)** – Baker (England), Sykes (England), Butterfield (England), Quinn (England), Morris (Wales), Morgan (Wales), Jeeps (England), Elliot (Scotland), Thompson (Ireland), Williams (Wales), Thomas (Wales), **Reid (Ireland),** Robins (Wales)

**Siggins XV** – Gilpin (Instonians), Kyle (Civil Service), Pedlow (Queen's), Maguire (Collegians), Lindsay (Queen's), Evans (Sales), Slater (Collegians), Michie (Scotland), Brady (Civil Service), Martin (Instonians), Ross (C.I.Y.M.S), Kennedy (Collegians)

## Tour Reflections

The 1955 Lions tour had been a successful one. 678,000 spectators had turned out to see the games. The Lions had played twenty-five games and won nineteen and drawn one. They had scored 105 tries and 457 points. The test series was a draw but the Lions had played beautiful rugby. Unusually, the Lions had won the two test matches that were played at altitude and lost the two that were at sea level.

Tom Reid had played thirteen of twenty-five games. Had it not been for injury, he would probably have played more. He had scored two tries and played in two test matches. Were it not for his personal decision to move to Canada, there is no knowing what else Tom Reid might have achieved. Would he have been selected in 1959 and 1962?

*"I should think the 1955 tour was the first time in his life that Reid was really fully fit and he played a major role in the success of the tour. We had won one and lost another in the first two tests and then we went 2-1 up in the series with a 9-6 win in the third game. In my opinion, Tom Reid effectively won that game for us because of his dominance at the back of the lineout. He proved more than once that he was something other than a quick tongue and a golden voice and was one of the major successes of the tour, doing superbly in the two tests in which he played."*
Sir Tony O'Reilly

# 1959

# Australia, New Zealand and Canada

Gordon Wood
Bill Mulcahy
Mick English

# Gordon Wood
# Lion #396

**Gordon Wood**
Born - 20 June 1931, Limerick

School – Crescent College
Club – Old Crescent, Garryowen, Lansdowne
Ireland Caps - 29
Lions Tour(s) - 1959
Lions Appearances – 15
Lions Tests – 2
Position - Prop

**Gordon Wood** (Benjamin Gordon Malison Wood), was a five-foot, ten inches, sixteen stone powerhouse prop forward who achieved almost every ambition a rugby player could have. He won Munster Schools and Munster Senior Cups. He captained the Munster team. He won twenty-nine caps for Ireland. He played in one of the most iconic Barbarians games in history and he represented the British and Irish Lions on fifteen occasions including two tests.

> *"There was never a more unlikely figure as a winged god of football than Wood. He had thighs like Ionic columns – or perhaps they were Corinthian – he was as squat in build as an Eskimo, and the last thing, so it seemed, that you could ever accuse him of was an ability to get from point A to point B at a sufficient speed. Tony O'Reilly put the point nicely when he remarked, after viewing a film of one match: 'they took pictures of Gordon in slow-motion. There he was, standing still'. But even Wood, when wound up, moved at quite a remarkable pace."*
> Gordon Wood described in the book Kings of Rugby

Gordon Wood was the first in what has become a Limerick rugby dynasty, with first his son Keith and now his grandsons also achieving success in the game.

## Early Life

Gordon Wood's grandfather, Benjamin Wood, was an English Baptist clothes cutter who came to Limerick from Cork in 1900. His son, Joseph Wood, was a clerk from St Joseph's Street when he married Eileen Downes in 1927. The young couple lived on New Street at Punches Cross and had four daughters and two sons. Benjamin Gordon Malison Wood, born in 1931.

Joseph, who served as Secretary of Young Munster from 1939 to 1944 and was president of the Munster Branch in 1944/45, died at aged just forty-eight in 1948 when Gordon was seventeen.

*Joseph Wood*

## School

Wood was educated by the Jesuits at Crescent College in Limerick. Under the guidance of Fr Gerry Guinane, he played rugby with the school and won the Munster Senior Schools Cup in 1949, beating Rockwell 8-nil in the final. Also on the team, and a school friend of Wood, was future Oscar nominee Richard Harris.

*The 1949 Crescent team with Gordon Wood sitting third from the left Richard Harris is at the very back on the left*

### Munster Schools XV

THE following is the Munster Schools' Rugby team to play Leinster schools at the Mardyke, Cork, on April 13:—
M. Brosnan (Rockwell); G. Murphy (Crescent), M. O'Donnell (do.), G. Kenny (Rockwell), D. Bennett (P.B.C.); N. Harris (Crescent), D. McCarthy (C.B.C.); G. Wood (Crescent), F. O'Sullivan (P.B.C.), J. O'Riordan (do.), S. Foley (C.B.C.), J. Burke (Rockwell), J. Healy (C.B.C.), G. Spillane (Crescent) (capt.), J. Keane (Mungret).

*Wood selected for the Munster Senior Schools team in 1949*

Wood was a standout player in the Crescent team and was selected for the Munster Schools team in 1949. Unfortunately, Munster lost to the Leinster Schools team at the Mardyke in Cork that year.

As well as rugby, Wood was an accomplished swimmer. He was a member of the Limerick Lifesaving Club who won the National Championships in 1949 and 1953.

## Club Rugby

### Old Crescent

While Wood and his son Keith are synonymous with Garryowen rugby club, Wood Snr started his club career with Old Crescent. The success of the Crescent College teams of 1947 and 1949 was the launchpad for a new club, Old Crescent, and Gordon Wood was a member of their team in their inaugural year. The team also included his school pal, Richard Harris.

In their first few years, Old Crescent were a junior rugby club and so any player with aspirations for big rugby success had to move to a senior club. Wood moved to Garryowen in 1951.

*The 1949 Old Crescent team with Wood (front second from the right) Richard Harris (standing third from the left)*

## Garryowen

His schoolboy success followed Wood to Garryowen where he teamed up with another future British and Irish Lion, **Tom Reid**. Together they won the Munster Senior Cup in 1951/52 beating U.C.C in the final and again in 1953/54 when they beat Sundays Well. They had been beaten in the final by Sundays Well in the intervening year.

With Garryowen, Wood also went to play internationally playing against French Champions Lourdes at home in 1951 and away in France in 1952.

*The Garryowen Munster Senior Cup winning team of 1951/52. Gordon Wood (standing fourth from left) and Tom Reid (with ball)*

On St Stephens Day 1951, Wood played in a Garryowen/Shannon select XV team that played the first Italian team to come to Ireland, Roma-Rugby. Roma where four times Italian champions and had been unbeaten that season. The Garryowen/Shannon select team featured four future Limerick British and Irish Lions; Gordon Wood, Tom Reid, Mick English and Tom Clifford. They beat the Italians easily.

*The Garryowen team embarking on their trip to Lourdes in 1951 (Wood is at the top of the stairs)*

*Wood (centre of picture kneeling) at the opening of the Garryowen ground at Dooradoyle in 1958*

## Lansdowne

Gordon Wood worked as an insurance inspector for Hibernian Insurance. In February 1959, he moved to Dublin with his job. Newspaper speculation was that he would move to Blackrock but he elected to move to Lansdowne RFC and played with them for three years. He captained them in the 1960/61 and 1962/63 seasons. Lansdowne won no notable cups during that period.

*Wood standing second from the left, with the Lansdowne team in 1959*

## Munster Rugby

In 1951, Wood was given the opportunity to play a trial game for the Munster side. He lined out on the "possibles" team against the "probables". He wasn't selected. The following year, he again played in the Munster trial game but by then he had progressed and lined out on the "probables" side. When the team was announced for an interprovincial game against Connacht the following week, Wood was not on the team sheet only because he was travelling with the Garryowen team in Lourdes, France.

Wood made his Munster debut on November 22nd 1952 in a win over Leinster at Lansdowne Road. Limerick Lions **Tom Reid** and **Tom Clifford** both played that day too. In his first season with the province, Munster were crowned Interprovincial Champions. He would go on to win this competition four times in his career. He won it again in 1957, again in his year as Munster Captain in 1959, and he was on the team that won it in 1962.

Wood was a regular in the Munster team from 1952 until 1963. During that time, he played in three notable games against international touring sides.

In 1954, Wood turned out alongside future fellow British and Irish Lions, Tom Reid and Tom Clifford in a game against the New Zealand All-Blacks at the Mardyke in Cork. Munster narrowly lost 6-3.

In 1958, he again played for Munster at Thomond Park against the Australian Wallaby team. Also playing that day was his great friend and future Lion Mick English. In a great performance Munster drew with the Wallabies 3-3.

On 21st December 1960, Wood and English teamed up again in the Munster team that played the all-conquering South African team that came to Musgrave Park. Wood had played them just four days earlier with the Irish team at Lansdowne Road. The Springboks won all but one of their games on this tour and they beat Munster 9-3. Wood did however get a victory over that Springbok side when he played with the Barbarians in the team that defeated them later on in their tour.

Wood's last appearance in a Munster jersey came in December 1962 when Munster beat Connacht 6-0 to win the Interprovincial Championship at Thomond Park. A fitting end to a champion Munster career.

Gordon Wood

*Gordon Wood standing 2<sup>nd</sup> left with Munster
Mick English sitting in front of him*

## International Rugby

Gordon Wood won his first Irish Cap in the 1954 Five Nations championship. After Ireland had lost their first game away to France, Wood was called into the team for the second game, away to England. The Irish team were soundly beaten 14-3. Two weeks later Wood was again on the team that played Scotland at home. This would be the last international played at Ravenhill for over fifty years. Ireland was victorious on the occasion, winning 6-0.

Wood played in all of the games during the 1956 Five Nations. Ireland lost away to France and England but won their two home fixtures and finished second from bottom in the championship.

In 1957 Wood again played in all four games. England won a Grand Slam with Ireland winning at home to France and away in Scotland, while losing to Wales away. On the flight to

189

Wales, one of the engines of their propeller plane ran out of petrol causing a mid-air crisis. The plane landed safely.

1958 saw Ireland finish last in the Five Nations, winning only our home game to Scotland. Ireland also played the touring Wallaby side that year, winning 9-6 at Lansdowne Road.

Wood again played all of the games in the 1959 Five Nations. Ireland finished second in the championship, losing at home to England and away in Wales but beating Scotland at Murrayfield and France 9-5 in Dublin.

*Wood, seated on the right, with the Irish team*

In 1960 Ireland had another disastrous season. Ireland lost all four games in the Five Nations. Wood did score his one and only Irish try that season. He got over the line against Scotland at Lansdowne Road in what was Scotland's first victory in Dublin for twenty-seven years.

In December 1960, Wood was on the Ireland team that played the touring Springboks at Lansdowne Road. Ireland lost 8-3. Four days later he played them again with the Munster team and lost again but was victorious over them with the Barbarians.

Wood's last season with Ireland was also a difficult one. In the 1961 Five Nations Ireland again finished last in the table with only a victory over England at Lansdowne Road to their credit.

*Wood shakes off a tackle from Wales's Cliff Morgan in the 1961 Five Nations*

With the 1962 British and Irish Lions tour looming, Wood went on Ireland's tour of South Africa in May 1961. Because of the politics of the time the team played under the title of Shamrocks and the games were not officially recognised. The team left Dublin on 7th May for a five-game tour. The tour opened with a test match against South Africa at Newlands in Cape Town a week after they had arrived. Wood played in a 24-8 loss with all of Ireland's points scored by Tom Kiernan.

Wood was also selected to play against South West Districts in Kings Park, Mossel Bay. Ireland won 11-8 and then three days later he again played when Ireland faced West Transvaal at De Beers Stadium at Olen Park in Potchefstroom. Again, Ireland won 16-6. This was Wood's final appearance in an Ireland jersey.

In the next game of the tour against Rhodesia in Salisbury (now Harare), Wood lost his place to Jim Thomas. Ireland won the game 24-

0. Wood would also miss the final game of the series against Boland in Wellington which Ireland won 16-0.

## The Barbarians

Wood was invited to play for the Barbarians on their April 1957 Welsh tour. He played in the victories over Penarth at the Recreation Ground (28-15) and Newport a few days later at Rodney Parade (8-5). Newspaper reports say that he was again invited to play for them in December 1959 but he didn't play. No reason was reported.

*The 1957 Barbarians Team with Gordon Wood (back row fourth from the right) Tom Reid (Middle of photo with glasses)*

In 1961 he was again invited to play for the Barbarians and turned out in what was to become one of the most famous Barbarian games off all time. The Springboks had beaten the Barbarians on their first encounter in 1952. When the opportunity came for them to lock horns again the Barbarians took their moment and defeated the all-conquering Springboks six nil at the National Stadium in Cardiff. This was the only loss that Springbok team experienced in their entire tour of England, Ireland, Scotland, Wales and France a total of thirty-four matches.

Gordon Wood

*The 1961 Barbarians that defeated the Springboks with Gordon Wood (extreme left)*

*The 1961 v Springboks game*

## The British and Irish Lions

Along with fellow Limerick Lions, **Bill Mulcahy** and **Mick English**, Wood was called up for the 1959 British and Irish Lions tour of South

Africa. On that tour he played in fifteen games including two test matches and scored two tries.

To read more about his Lions tour – Refer chapter Australia, New Zealand and Canada (1959)

## Wolfhounds and Charity Games

Wood was picked for the first Wolfhounds tour in 1956 and played in two of the games that year, against Vigilantes at Windsor Park and Tom Clifford's XV in Limerick. In 1957 he played in all four Wolfhounds games. He missed the 1959 tour as he was touring with the Lions but in 1960, he was back in the select XV team. He played the opening game of the tour at Twickenham against Harlequins and he also turned out in the last game of the tour. In that game he played for his old club Old Crescent against the Wolfhounds.

## Post Rugby Career

After finished playing Gordon focused on coaching rugby with Ballina Killaloe Rugby Club where he was living. He coached the senior team there for a number of years alongside his friend Brendan Foley.

## Personal Life

Gordon Wood married Pauline Dwane from Charleville in December 1958. Their first child, Pauline, was born in 1960 and they went on to have seven children, the youngest being future Limerick Lion **Keith Wood**.

In November 1954, Wood made the press for something other than his rugby skills. He was awarded a bravery certificate by the Mayor of Limerick. Wood saved the life of a woman who was drowning in the Shannon at Corbally the previous May.

Gordon Wood died following a short illness on 18th May 1982. He was just fifty years old. He is buried at Punchbowl Church Cemetery just outside Meelick Village in County Clare.

Gordon Wood's legacy lives on. His sons and grandsons have followed in his footsteps. His youngest son Keith became an Irish rugby legend and is in the IRB Rugby Hall of Fame. His grandsons Gordon and Tom are also now Munster and Ireland players with a bright future ahead of them.

*Gordon Wood (1931-1982)*

# Bill Mulcahy
# Lion #403

**Bill Mulcahy**
Born - 7 January 1935, Rathkeale, Co. Limerick

School – St Munchin's College
Club – Bohemians, U.C.D., Bective
Ireland Caps - 35
Lions Tour(s) – 1959, 1962
Lions Appearances - 32
Lions Tests – 6
Position – 2nd Row/Flanker

Bill Mulcahy had success at all levels of the game, winning with his school and multiple clubs before going on to represent Munster, Leinster, Ireland, the Barbarians and the British and Irish Lions. He was the first Limerick Lion to go on two Lions tours (1959 and 1962) and made thirty-two appearances in all across the tours including six tests. He was for a time the President of the Leinster Branch of the IRFU and was inducted into the Irish Rugby Hall of Fame.

## Early Life

Sixty years after the first game of rugby to be played in Limerick was played there, William (Bill) Mulcahy was born in Rathkeale, County Limerick on 7th January 1935. His father William was the local physician. His mother Ellen Liston was the daughter of a farmer from Mulgrave Street in the city. The couple had met while William Snr was working at the Limerick County Infirmary.

## School

*Bill Mulcahy (standing 2nd from the left) and the St Munchin's team that won the 1949/50 Limerick City Cup*

Bill Mulcahy was educated at St Munchin's College. During his life he was affectionately referred to as 'wigs'. One theory is that he was given that name because he would doodle pictures of wigwams on his copybook in class. His family's theory is that it comes from his initials WAM (wigwam). Whatever its origin was, the nickname stuck and he would be referred to by that name throughout his life both on and off the rugby field.

While at St Munchin's, Bill took up rugby and he was on the St Munchin's team that won the Limerick City Cup in 1949/50. At the time of his senior years in school, Crescent College won the Munster Schools Senior Cup and so he would have come up against Gordon Wood. St Munchin's didn't win their first Munster Senior Schools Cup until 1968.

## Club Rugby

### Bohemians

*Mulcahy standing second left with the 1962 Bohs team
Mick English (seated on ground front left)*

Bill first played his club rugby with Bohemians in Limerick. He had moved on to university in at U.C.D by the time Bohs won the Munster Senior Cup for the first time in thirty years in 1958.

After his time at U.C.D, he returned to Bohs for a season and was on the team, alongside Mick English, in 1962 when they again won the title. However, because of his success in being selected for the British and Irish Lions tour that year, he had to miss the final.

*Munster Cup 1962 v U.C.C*

## U.C.D Rugby

After school, Bill went to U.C.D to study medicine and played rugby for U.C.D from 1953/54. He would play for them right through his college days. In 1961 they reached the final of the Leinster Senior Cup but after a replay they lost narrowly to Blackrock College.

His education completed, Bill returned to play for Bohemians for a season in 1962 and in that year lifted the Munster Senior Cup.

Bill Mulcahy

*Mulcahy putting in a tackle against Old Belvedere in January 1960*

*Bill Mulcahy (centre holding the ball) with the U.C.D team*

## Bective Rangers

After the 1961/62 season playing back in Limerick with Bohemians, Bill Mulcahy joined Bective Rangers in Dublin in 1963. They had won the Leinster Senior Cup the previous year. In his first year with the club, they again got to the Leinster Senior Cup final but that year they were beaten by his alma mater U.C.D. Bective haven't won the title since. Bill went on and captained Bective Rangers in the 1964/65 season.

## St Vincent's Hospital

Bill Mulcahy was a doctor and played in the Dublin Hospitals Cup with St Vincent's Hospital. The Hospitals Cup, which is still going today, is a challenge competition played annually since 1881. The Hospitals Cup it is an institution in Dublin rugby. With Bill on board, St Vincent's won the competition in 1956, 1961 and 1962.

*Bill Mulcahy (standing third from the right) with a St Vincent's Hospital team*

## Skerries RFC

Bill had a long association with Skerries RFC where he and his family lived. He played for them towards the end of his career and went on to be a coach and the president of the club.

## Leinster Rugby

Despite his successful performances with Bohemians in Limerick, Bill Mulcahy didn't get called for Munster's annual trial for the provincial side. In the autumn of 1955, after he moved to Dublin and was established on the U.C.D team, Mulcahy was called into the white (possibles) team for the Leinster provincial trial. Against the odds he was selected for the game against Connacht a few weeks later. The Irish Independent saying *"Perhaps the only unexpected feature of the pack is the preference for W Mulcahy over L Lynch, in the second row, but the younger college man has been showing marked improvement since the start of the season"*.

Bill played in Leinster's first game of the season at Lansdowne Road on 9th November 1955. In that game, Connacht made history by winning against Leinster for the first time at the venue by 6-8. Bill was dropped for the second game of the season against Munster at the Mardyke a week later with Lansdowne's L. Lynch picked ahead of him. The Irish Independent saying, *"Goff is a neat clever centre if rather light and Lynch and Fahy were obvious choices after the Connacht debacle"*. However, Lynch had to drop out and Bill regained his place. In his second game for Leinster, Bill came up against three other Limerick Lions, Gordon Wood, Mick English and Tom Reid, and came out on the winning side as Leinster beat Munster 9-12 in Cork. Bill kept his place after that.

In his first season Leinster won the Interprovincial Championship. Bill would go on to play for Leinster until 1967. With him in the team Leinster won the Interprovincial Championship in 1955, 1957, 1959, 1961, 1962, 1964, 1965.

During his time with Leinster Bill played in some games of note against incoming international touring teams.

At the end of November 1957, Bill played on the Leinster team, captained by Paddy O'Donoghue, who lost to the Australian team. In an exciting game, Leinster lost to a late Australian score four minutes from the end to lose the game 8-10.

*Mulcahy captaining the Leinster team*

In February 1961, Bill played in the Leinster team that played the inbound Springbok team. The Irish Independent reported that *"Cuddy, Mulcahy and Costello were about the best of a rather disorganised Leinster Pack"* as they went down by 5-12. This was the Springbok team that won all but one of their thirty-one games on tour. Bill had already played them a few weeks earlier with the Irish team and also lost.

In January 1964, the All-Blacks tour arrived in Leinster. Bill played in another close game; this time Leinster lost by 8-11. As with the Springboks in 1961, Bill had played the All-Blacks the previous December with the Irish team and lost 5-6.

Bill had his last chance to beat an inbound touring team with Leinster in December 1966. This time it was the Australians and again Leinster came up short, losing 3-9.

## International Rugby

In December 1957, Bill was edging towards a place on the Irish team. He played in two trial games that won him his place. First, he turned out for a 'Combined Universities' team that played a 'Rest of Ireland' team at Lansdowne Road. While he was on the losing side (17-11), he did enough to be invited to play in the final Irish trial on January 4th. In that trial he would play alongside Gordon Wood and against Mick English. After that game, Bill Mulcahy was one of six new caps announced for the first game of the season against Australia. The Independent saying *"Second row berths were wide open, and one cannot cavil at the choice of Mulcahy"*.

*Bill Mulcahy leading the Irish team out at Lansdowne Road*

Bill Mulcahy made his Irish debut at Lansdowne Road on January 18th 1958. Gordon Wood was also in the team that won 9-6. The newspapers sang his praises the following day, *"Mulcahy controlled an early tendency to wildness and, as the game progressed, gained in stature to an extent that he rivalled Stevenson's greatness"*.

Bill Mulcahy would go on to win thirty-five Irish caps with his last coming against South Africa in 1965. He also captained Ireland in the 1962, 1963 and 1964 Five Nations championships and on eight occasions in total. Unfortunately, his time in the Irish shirt was not a very successful time for Ireland.

*Bill Mulcahy with the Ireland team in 1960*
*Nine of these players would be Lions at some point in their careers*

In 1961, Bill was also on the Irish "Shamrocks" touring party that played a five-game series in South Africa. He played in the test match against the Springboks in Cape Town which Ireland lost. He also played against South Western Districts, West Transvaal, and he played the game against Rhodesia in Salisbury (Harare).

## The Barbarians

Bill Mulcahy twice played for the Barbarians. He was invited to the annual Easter event in 1958.

Bill, along with Irish colleagues Mick English, Andy Mulligan and Cecil Pedlow, played in the game against Penarth at the Recreation Ground on 4$^{th}$ April which the Barbarians won 6-5. Mick English scored a second half try for the Barbarians in that game.

Bill also played four days later against Newport at Rodney Parade. While the Barbarians lost an exciting match the newspaper report said

*"Both sides must be congratulated for their ready approach, and in the forwards Evans, McLeod, Mulcahy and Wilcock were great for the Barbarians".*

## The British and Irish Lions

Along with fellow Limerick Lions, **Gordon Wood** and **Mick English**, Bill Mulcahy was called up for the 1959 British and Irish Lions tour of South Africa. On that tour he played in fifteen games including two test matches and scored two tries.

To read more about his 1959 Lions tour – Refer chapter Australia, New Zealand and Canada (1959)

*Bill Mulcahy's Lions Cap issued in 2018*
*Photo courtesy of the Mulcahy family*

Bill Mulcahy went on to become the first Limerick Lion to go on two Lions tours and one of the greatest ever Lions when he was again selected to travel on the 1962 tour to South Africa, Rhodesia & Kenya. On his second tour he played in seventeen games including four test matches and scored one try.

To read more about his 1962 Lions tour – Refer chapter South Africa, Rhodesia & Kenya (1962)

## Wolfhounds and Charity Games

During his career, Bill Mulcahy played in a number of charity games and represented numerous select XV teams. He played for the Wolfhounds in their inaugural year, 1956, featuring in the game against a Galwegians' XV. He continued to play both for and against the select XV during their early years. He missed the 1959 Wolfhounds tour as he was with the Lions but played again for them in their opening game of 1960 against Harlequins at Twickenham.

For over sixty years, from 1905 to 1971, the GAA had Rule 27 in force which read *"Any member of the Association who plays or encourages in any way rugby, football, hockey or any imported game which is calculated to injuriously affect our National Pastimes, is suspended from the Association"*. When that rule was abolished at the GAA Annual Congress on 10th April 1971, it opened the door for the big sports to interact. One of the first such examples took place at Anglesea Road on 1st May 1971, when a Rugby XV captained by Bill Mulcahy took on an Inter-County Gaelic Football XV captained by Kevin Heffernan. The code they played was Gaelic Football. Played for charity, the game ended in a 2-4 to 2-4 draw with Mick English scoring one of the rugby goals.

Under the headline Gaelic No Problem for Rugby Stars, the Irish Independent reported on the game.

> *"Only a late point by Kevin Behan enabled the former Inter-County Gaelic Stars to draw with a former International Rugby selection in an extremely entertaining Gaelic match which was played at Anglesea Road yesterday.*
> 
> *Surprisingly, most of the rugby players seemed to be well versed in the Gaelic code. However, although they were helped as much as possible by the referee, they failed to get the winning point in the final few minutes.*

*Ronnie Kavanagh, Bill Mulcahy, Kevin Flynn and Mick English adapted themselves well enough to give their opponents an extremely tough time and none of the others let the team down in any way".*

## Post Rugby Career

Bill Mulcahy was a physician and worked as the Chief Medical Officer for Aer Lingus at Dublin Airport.

He was actively involved in Skerries Rugby Club with whom his son Billy played Billy was capped by Leinster and went on to have a distinguished career with Connacht. He was inducted into the Connacht Hall of Fame.

Bill also stayed involved with Bective and became President of the Leinster Branch of the IRFU in the 1995/96 season.

He was inducted into Leinster Rugby Hall of Fame in 2009.

*Bill Mulcahy on the cover of Rugby World magazine in December 1962*

In 2025, a new cup was dedicated in Bill Mulcahy's honour. The Bill Mulcahy Cup pits the best under fourteen from North Munster against the best of South Munster. Christian Brothers Cork were the inaugural winners.

## Personal Life

Bill Mulcahy and his wife Christine had four children; Billy, Cara, Fiona and Michael.

Dr Bill Mulcahy passed away on 28th February 2025 aged ninety. He was recognised with a standing ovation at the next Ireland game played at Lansdowne Road.

Bill Mulcahy

Bill's son Billy and grandson Mark presenting the inaugural Bill Mulcahy Cup at St Munchins in 2025
Photo courtesy of the Mulcahy family

Bill Mulcahy being acknowledged at Lansdowne Road 2025

# Bill Mulcahy

*Bill Mulcahy (1935 -2025)*

Bill Mulcahy

# Mick English
# Lion #408

**Mick English**
Born - 2 June 1933, Limerick

School – Rockwell College
Club – Bohemians, Lansdowne
Ireland Caps - 16
Lions Tour(s) - 1959
Lions Appearances - 2
Lions Tests – n/a
Position – Out-half

Michael Anthony Francis English (aka Mick English and Mick the Kick) had phenomenal success at schools and club rugby. One of the few who can claim to have won the Munster Senior Cup and the Leinster Senior Cup, Mick went on to play for Munster and was capped sixteen times for Ireland. He played for the Barbarians on four occasions and only for injury could have had a huge impact on the 1959 Lions tour. As it was, he played for them on two occasions.

> *"Mick English might have stepped out of the pages of Experiences of an Irish R.M for there was a look in his eye which suggested that he was about to buy a spavined horse for $25 and sell it for $50. This droll expression was accentuated by his incessant rendition on bus or train journeys of a boxful of republican ballads among which "Kevin Barry" was comparatively milk-and-water. Mick had one particular song, "The Irish Volunteer" which according to Tony O'Reilly "could never be sung in England", and a side-splitting affair he made of it with the wild look in his eye, the dramatic scream in his voice at the juicy bits, and other unexpected note or gestures. He came of course from Limerick, where the English are not loved, and perhaps this accounted for his queer affection for these songs which to the disinterested listener made the revolution sound such a dreadfully dull affair".*
> Mick English - Described in the book Kings of Rugby

## Early Life

Michael Anthony Francis English was born in Limerick on 2nd June 1933. He was the fourth of six children born to Patrick, an inspector for the Dept. of Agriculture from Tipperary and his wife Bridget Moloney from Lisnagry. They had married in 1927.

The family lived at Rosehill on O'Callaghan Strand in the city. Amongst his siblings was Chris who would play rugby alongside his brother at Bohemians. Mick's father died of cancer aged fifty-two when Mick was just eleven years old.

The English family home in O'Callaghan Strand was just a few hundred metres from Richard Harris lived on the Ennis Road. The two were childhood friends. In an interview for a Lansdowne RFC event years later, Richard Harris recounted how the English family were the reason he got into acting.

*"There was a great Irish Shakespearian thespian named Anu McMaster and Anu McMaster used to come to Limerick once or twice a year with his very sparce productions, and they used to stay at your (English's) mother's house. You, myself and Teddy Curtain used to go there night after night by the fire in your kitchen, and Anu McMaster used to regale us with stories about Shakespeare, with stories about the theatre which began to ignite me, spark my imagination and made me become an actor".*

Richard Harris

## School

Mick English originally went to Christian Brothers in Limerick but moved to Rockwell College in County Tipperary in 1946. With Rockwell he had incredible schoolboy success. He was on the team that won the Munster Schools Junior Cup in 1949, scoring two drop-goals in the final. That same year, he also played on the school's senior rugby team that were defeated in the Senior Cup final by Crescent College. On the Crescent team that day was **Gordon Wood**.

Mick English (sitting on floor left) with the Rockwell Senior Cup winning team 1950

The following year 1950, English was on the team that won the Munster Schools Senior Cup, the first time Rockwell had won it since 1942. They beat Mungret in the final. The senior rugby team also won the Bowen Shield in 1950 beating Pres in the final.

A remarkable sportsman, Mick also turned out on the team's athletics team (as a javelin thrower and a member of the relay team), the hurling team and the cricket team.

*Mick English (standing 2nd from right) with the Rockwell Cricket team 1950*

*Mick English (seated 2nd from right) with the Rockwell Athletics team 1950*

He was invited to play in the Munster Schools trial in December 1949 as was his brother Christopher two years later in 1951. Again, Richard Harris had a story to tell on Mick's Munster Schools career.

> "My brother Noel Harris played out-half for the Munster Schools Senior team for three seasons in a row. He had eight caps for Munster schools. You (Mick English) were the substitute for two of those occasions. My brother Noel was playing a Munster schools cup match against Presentation Brothers Cork down in the Mardyke and he broke his shoulder and because he broke his shoulder, he couldn't play and you (Mick English) as a reserve got on the team. So, therefore I claim that one of my family put you where you are today".
>
> Richard Harris

Whether that is true or not, Mick English played for Munster Schools in 1949, beating their Leinster equivalent 3-0 at Donnybrook.

## Club Rugby

### Shannon

After finishing school, Mick English played junior club rugby initially with Shannon. With them he won the City Cup in 1952 but was a beaten finalist in the Junior Cup and the Transfield Cup.

*Mick English (standing 3rd left) with the 1952 Shannon team*

## Bohemians

After just one seasons with Shannon, Mick moved to Bohemians. His time at Bohs was the most successful in their history, with three wins in the Munster Senior Cup, first in 1958 when they beat Highfield, then again, the following year 1959 when they beat Shannon. The third win was in 1962 when Bohs beat Old Crescent.

In the aftermath of their first win in 1958, the Munster Cup trophy went missing during the celebrations. The press got wind of it and there were newspaper reports wondering about its whereabouts for a few days. It was eventually and mysteriously found in Mick English's front garden. There has never been any explanation as to who had taken the cup or if Mick English had any role in its disappearance.

*Mick English (Seated on left) wearing his Irish cap with the 1959 Bohs team*

While at Bohs in September 1955, Mick played on a Limerick Select XV, alongside Tom Clifford, Gordon Wood and his brother Christy, in an exhibition game at Thomond Park against an Auvergne side from France.

*Three Limerick Lions - Limerick v Auvergne 1955*

**Lansdowne**

After his three successes with Bohemians, in Autumn 1962 Mick English moved to Dublin to pursue business interests and switched to Lansdowne RFC where his good friend Gordon Wood was already playing. With Lansdowne he went on to win the Leinster Senior Cup in 1965. In that year they were lucky to beat Clontarf in the final after a replay.

One of the many anecdotes about Mick English is related to his lack of interest in training. Having arrived at Lansdowne, then captain Caleb Powell 'invited' Mick and the team out to their junior ground at Templeogue with the intention that they would run back to Lansdowne Road which didn't have lights to enable night training. All went swimmingly until Mick saw a passing bus and decided to jump on. When the rest of the team arrived back to the clubhouse, Mick was already there, refreshed and ready to greet them. Criticised by his captain, Mick replied, "when they start playing rugby on the roads, I will train on the roads".

Mick retired from playing senior at Lansdowne in 1968. He was thirty-five. He played on in various other teams until he was forty-four. His final game of rugby was played in Maynooth on a Gaelic Football pitch – *"Gaelic pitches are much wider so I kept missing touch"*. The pitch was surrounded by barbed wire to keep out the sheep in the next field. *"Clambering through the barbed wire after the game, I cut myself and had to go straight to hospital for an anti-tetanus shot. So, I couldn't even have a jar with the lads to mark my last rugby match"*.

*Mick English (Seated 2nd from right) with the 1965 Leinster Cup Lansdowne Team*

## Munster Rugby

Mick English was invited to play for North Munster against South Munster in a trial for the Munster team in October 1955. He did well enough to earn his first cap at the end of that month against Connacht. He lost his first game at the Sportsground in Galway but went on to win the Interprovincial title with Munster in 1957, 1959 and 1962.

During his time with Munster, Mick English played the three big inbound international touring sides. He played Australia in January

1958 at Thomond Park when Munster held the Wallabies to a 3-3 draw, South Africa in 3-9 loss in December 1960 at Musgrave Park. He completed the set in December 1963 when he played the All-Blacks at Thomond Park and narrowly lost 3-6. That game also proved to be his last game for Munster. He had played twenty-eight times for his province.

English (seated 3rd from left) with the 1963 Munster team that played New Zealand

## International Rugby

Mick English had the unenviable task of taking over the Irish number 10 shirt from Jack Kyle, who many believe was the best of all time. His first cap came in the 1958 Five Nations. He played in the games against Wales at Lansdowne Road and France at Stade Colombes that year both of which Ireland lost.

In the 1959 championship he played in three of the games, a home loss against England, an away win in Scotland and a home win over France. He scored his first Irish points in the third of these with a drop goal against France. Ireland won that game 9-5. He was fond of drop goals and, in fact, all of his international points (9) were scored from drop goals.

Mick's nickname "Mick the Kick" came about because of his excellent kicking. Some people felt he kicked too often but he didn't care what others thought. In one of the games he played for Ireland, he received the ball close to the opposition try line. The crowd rose in anticipation of him scoring but English opted instead to kick for touch. When asked about it after the game, he gave one of his witty answers. *"Yes, I know I was only a couple of yards from the goal line. But I was only a couple of feet from the touchline, so I considered my options and kicked for touch."*

The 1960 season saw English play in two of the Five Nations games, against England away (8-5 loss) and Scotland at home (5-6 loss). Seamus Kelly took over at out-half for the other games in the championship.

In 1961 he missed the first game of the championship against England but then played in the remaining three games, losses in Scotland and Wales and another loss at home to France.

Ireland started the 1962 championship poorly losing the first two game and English was called up for the two remaining ones. He played in a loss in France and then scored a drop goal that secured a 3-3 draw at home against Wales.

In 1963 Ireland were hammered 5-24 in the opening game against France which led to English being called up for the remaining three games of the championship. He played in a 3-0 loss in Scotland, a scoreless draw against England at Lansdowne Road and then he scored another of his drop goals in Cardiff with Ireland winning 6-14. It is interesting to note Ireland never lost when Mick English scored.

Mick English's last appearance in the Ireland shirt was against New Zealand at Lansdowne Road in December 1963. Ireland lost a thrilling game 5-6.

Having started his international career taking over from an Irish rugby legend in Jack Kyle, English handed over the shirt to another incoming legend, Mike Gibson.

## The Barbarians

Mick English was invited to play for the Barbarians on two occasions. First at Easter 1958 when he played in the games against Penarth on 4th April at the Recreation Ground and then against four days later against Newport at Rodney Parade.

English was again invited to play for the Barbarians in 1960. He played two games in the space of three days, first against a Cardiff side at the National Stadium and then on 18$^{th}$ April, against Swansea at the St Helen's ground.

## The British and Irish Lions

Along with fellow Limerick Lions, **Gordon Wood** and **Bill Mulcahy**, Mick English was called up for the 1959 British and Irish Lions tour of South Africa. On that tour he played in just twice because of injury.

To read more about his 1959 Lions tour – Refer chapter Australia, New Zealand and Canada (1959)

## Wolfhounds and Charity Games

Mick English was known as an entertainer both on and off the pitch and so was a popular selection for one off charity games. In 1956, he turned out for Tom Clifford's XV that played against the Wolfhounds in their first year. The following year he was selected by both Dolphin and Clanwilliam for their games against the "Irish Barbarians".

English was selected to play for the Wolfhounds for the first time in September 1958. He played for them against a combined Oxford and Cambridge University selection at Lansdowne Road. He missed the 1959 Wolfhounds season as he was with the Lions but in 1960, he played for Young Munster's Select XV against them and in 1961, he played for a Killarney XV that played them.

## Post Rugby Career

After he retired from playing at Lansdowne, he stayed on as an active club member for the rest of his life, becoming Club President in 1989-1990. Mick was an entertaining and much sought after after-dinner speaker where he would regale audiences with slightly exaggerated stories from his playing days.

The Rugby Writers of Ireland inducted him to the Hall of Fame in 2008 in celebration of his contribution to Irish rugby.

While he was still in Limerick, English worked for ICI Insurance. When he moved to Dublin, he worked for Reeds International but then in 1978 he set up his own Insurance company.

## Personal Life

Mick married Pauline in 1965. Together they had three children; Michele, Conor and John.

Mick English died on April 27th 2010. He was seventy-seven years old. He is buried at Shanganagh Cemetery in Bray, Co. Wicklow.

# Australia, New Zealand & Canada (1959)

It was anyone's guess how many Irish would be selected for the 1959 Lions tour. Ireland's performances in the Five Nations had been patchy. Ireland had finished second to France in 1959 but had finished bottom of the table the year previous. England had won the championship in 1957 and 1958.

Two selectors were appointed from each home union and Alf Wilson, *"a cantankerous old bugger"* and *"a gruff military type"* from Scotland was appointed as manager for the tour.

Irish hooker Ronnie Dawson was named tour captain becoming the fourth Irish captain of a Lions tour in a row. There was some contention about this as Welsh hooker Bryn Meredith who had done so well on the 1955 tour, didn't get a test game even though he was viewed by some as being a better player.

## Touring party

When the tour squad was announced in March 1959, there were three Limerick men amongst ten Irish, nine English, nine Welsh and five Scots. **Gordon Wood** from Garryowen, **Bill Mulcahy** who was playing with U.C.D and **Mick English** from Munster champions Bohemians.

Also among the party were six players from the 1955 tour – Jeff Butterfield, Dickie Jeeps, Hugh McLeod, Bryn Meredith, Tony O'Reilly, and Rhys Williams. Malcolm Thomas who had toured with Tom Clifford in 1950 but had missed the 1955 tour, was also in the tour party.

Englishman Phil Horrocks-Taylor was also selected and would give Mick English one of his famous after dinner anecdotes. *"Every time I went to tackle him, Horrocks went one way, Taylor went the other, and all I got was the bloody hyphen."*

Limerick's contribution to the tour would be substantial. Gordon Wood would play in fifteen games including two test matches. Bill Mulcahy would play in fifteen games including two test and Mick English, dogged by injury, would play in two games.

1959 Australia, New Zealand and Canada

*The 1959 British and Irish Lions*
*Gordon Wood (back row, extreme right), Bill Mulcahy (middle row, extreme left).*
*Mick English (front row, extreme right)*

The following was the squad selected for the 1959 tour:

**Management**
Manager A. W. Wilson (Scotland)
Assistant Manager O. B. Glasgow (Ireland)

**Backs**
Niall Brophy (U.C.D. and Ireland), J. Butterfield (Northampton and England), S. Coughtrie (Edinburgh Academicals and Scotland), Terry Davies (Llanelli and Wales), **Mick English (Bohemians and Ireland)**, David Hewitt (Queen's University RFC and Ireland), J. P. Horrocks-Taylor (Leicester and England), Peter Jackson (Coventry and England), Dickie Jeeps (Northampton and England), Tony O'Reilly (Old Belvedere and Ireland), Andy Mulligan (Wanderers and Ireland), William "Bill" Michael Patterson (Sale), Malcolm Price (Pontypool and Wales), Bev Risman (Manchester and England), Ken Scotland (Cambridge University and Scotland), Malcolm Thomas (Newport and

1959 Australia, New Zealand and Canada

Wales), G. H. Waddell (Cambridge University and Scotland), J. R. C. Young (Harlequins and England)

**Forwards**
Alan Ashcroft (Waterloo and England), Ronnie Dawson (Wanderers and Ireland), Roddy Evans (Cardiff and Wales), John Faull (Swansea and Wales), Hugh McLeod (Hawick and Scotland), David Marques (Harlequins and England), Bryn Meredith (Newport and Wales), Syd Millar (Ballymena and Ireland), Haydn Morgan (Abertillery and Wales), **Bill Mulcahy (U.C.D. and Ireland)**, Noel Murphy (Cork Constitution and Ireland), Ray Prosser (Pontypool and Wales), Ken Smith (Kelso and Scotland), Rhys Williams (Llanelli and Wales), **Gordon Wood (Garryowen and Ireland)**

## The Tour

The 1959 tour began in the first week of May and finished in the first week of October. In that time the team would play thirty-three games, six in Australia, followed by twenty-five in New Zealand and then two on the return journey in Canada.

As with previous tours, the squad assembled at Eastbourne ahead of the journey to Australia. Tour veteran Jeff Butterfield, a PE teacher, was appointed coach of the training sessions to get them all fit. He ran the team really hard which was later put forward as one of the possible reasons there were so many injuries on the tour.

Mick English had to miss the Munster Senior Cup Final because he was with the Lions. He was however, injured anyway. He had developed a groin strain during Ireland game against France in the Five Nations. By the time the team arrived in Australia, it was clear he was in trouble and that he would have a limited role.

Bill Mulcahy brought his medical books with him as the tour clashed with his finals at U.C.D.

*"I had to put off my final medical examinations much to the distress of my mother, who was widowed. She wanted me to get my exams and get the hell out. I had an elderly uncle who was a parish priest in Kilmallock, County Limerick, and he was a sort of father figure because my old man had passed on and he said I should go, so she pulled back her objections and*

*I travelled. He was 89 at the time and wrote her a nice letter. The finals were put off but I had a big medical book with me on the tour".*
Bill Mulcahy

The squad left London on May 16th. Their exhausting journey took them four days before they reached Melbourne. They flew London – Zurich – Beirut – Bombay – Calcutta – Singapore – Darwin – Sydney – Melbourne. Having arrived in Melbourne, they stayed at the Temperance Hotel in St Kilda and trained at St Kilda Oval, home of the St Kilda Aussie Rules team.

The 1959 Lions set out to play open, attacking rugby and over the tour they delivered against that. They scored 842 points in total on the tour. They scored 105 tries, with Tony O'Reilly beating his own record from the previous tour scoring 22 tries.

Richard Harris retold a story about Mick English on the tour, which he had heard from Llanelli, Wales and Lions player Ray Gravell.

*"Mick English came down one morning when you were on the tour and you ordered breakfast and you said 'I want two eggs - swamped with grease,*

1959 Australia, New Zealand and Canada

and I want some bacon – burnt to a cinder, and I want sausages burnt to a cinder. I want toast that you can't eat and I want a pot of cold tea'. The waitress looked at him and said, 'Sir, we don't serve food like that' to which English replied, 'Well you did yesterday fuckin mornin'."

## The Games

*Game One*
*v Victoria*
*Melbourne, Australia 23/5/1959*
*53–18 – Win*

**Lions Team** – Scotland (Scotland), Jackson (England), Butterfield (England), Hewitt (Ireland), Young (England), Risman (England), Jeeps (England), **Wood (Ireland)**, Dawson (Ireland), McLeod (Scotland), Marques (England), Williams (Wales), Smith (Scotland), Ashcroft (England), Morgan (Wales)

Gordon Wood got a run out in the first outing. Despite the jet-lag, the Lions were rampant in their opening game at Olympic Park in front of 7,000 people. Olympic Park had been built for the 1956 Olympic Games. Victoria had some "imported" players in their team in an attempt to make their standards higher but it didn't work. Melbourne and the Victorian state are hotbeds for Aussie Rules. Rugby tends to be played more in New South Wales and Queensland so it was expected to be an easy start.

A little rusty after the journey, the Lions were slow to start. Gilroy kicked Victoria into the lead after nine minutes. He kicked another one after 16 minutes. Then the lions kicked into action and scored thirteen points in six minutes. Bev Risman scored two tries, a penalty and hit five conversions. Jackson scored three tries, Hewitt and Smith got two apiece and Ashcroft, Young and Scotland each scored one.

*Game Two*
*v New South Wales*
*Sydney, Australia 30/5/1959*
*14–18 – Loss*

**Lions Team** – Davies (Wales), Brophy (Ireland), Thomas (Wales), Price (Wales), Young (England), Risman (England), Jeeps (England), Prosser (Wales), Meredith (Wales), Millar (Ireland), Murphy (Ireland), **Mulcahy (Ireland)**, Evans (Wales), Ashcroft (England), Faull (Wales)

Bill Mulcahy played in the second match of the tour, a disappointing loss to New South Wales. The Lions had made ten changes from the previous game, giving everyone a chance to stretch their legs.

Irishman Niall Brophy went off after three minutes with a sprained ankle meaning the Lions played virtually the entire game down a man. Welshman Faull moved from the pack to the wing to cover the gap and scored two tries and the Lions were up 9-11 at half time. The Lions played into the sun in the second half and some passes were dropped as a result. The extra man proved vital. The Lions pack tired as the game went on and New South Wales pulled ahead to win the game.

*Game Three*
*v Queensland*
*Brisbane, Australia 2/6/1959*
*39–11 - Win*

**Lions Team** – Scotland (Scotland), O'Reilly (Ireland), Butterfield (England), Hewitt (Ireland), Jackson (England), **English (Ireland)**, Coughtrie (Scotland), Millar (Ireland), Dawson (Ireland), McLeod (Scotland), Evans (Wales), Williams (Wales), Faull (Wales), Marques (England), Morgan (Wales)

Mick English made his Lions debut in the first game the British and Irish Lions had ever played under floodlights.

The Lions lost the toss and kicked off to the Queensland team. During a slow and cagy start, both English and Dawson were booed by the crowd for minor infringements. Queensland were the first to score after fourteen minutes with a penalty from twenty-five yards. After that the Lions put on a magnificent display of attacking rugby with Mick English controlling the game directing the attacks. English's Irish colleague, Tony O'Reilly scored two tries during the game as the Lions turned on the style. So impressive was English in the game that the question was later asked, 'what if he hadn't been carrying an injury?'

1959 Australia, New Zealand and Canada

Both teams finished with fourteen men. The Queensland hooker broke his collar bone and Lions wing forward, Morgan, had to retire with an ankle injury in the second half.

*Game Four*
*v Australia (First Test)*
*Brisbane, Australia 6/6/1959*
*17–6 – Win*

**Lions Team** – Scotland (Scotland), Jackson (England), Price (Wales), Hewitt (Ireland), O'Reilly (Ireland), Risman (England), Jeeps (England), McLeod (Scotland) Dawson (Ireland) Captain, Millar (Ireland), Smith (Scotland), **Mulcahy (Ireland),** Williams (Wales), Ashcroft (England), Faull (Wales)

**Australia** - Linehan, Morton, Potts, Diett, Donald, Summons, Connor, Dunn, Johnson, Ellis, Carroll, Miller, Fenwicke, Outterside, Thornett

While all three Limerick men had had a run out in the first three games, only Bill Mulcahy was selected for the first test of the tour. The game against Australia was played at the Exhibition Ground in Brisbane in front of 20,000 spectators. It was a remarkable choice of venue as Australia hadn't won in Brisbane for thirty years.

In over seventy-degree heat, there was lots of pageantry ahead of the game. Princess Alice, mother of the Governor of Queensland was in attendance and the crowd were entertained by a military band before the game.

Lions lost the toss and kicked off. Australia missed an early thirty-yard penalty before Tony O'Reilly opened the scoring with a try in the corner after six minutes. He received the ball from Ken Scotland about twenty-five yards out, dodged a tackle and danced along the touchline to score. Hewitt missed the conversion. With eight minutes remaining in the half, Hewitt kicked a penalty to put the Lions 6-0 up. Having missed five previous penalties, Donald scored one for Australia and shortly after he scored again to make it 6-6 at the break.

In the second half the Lions took an early lead with a Hewitt penalty. Ken Scotland scored a dropped goal and in the last few minutes of the game the Lions pulled away when Risman scored a try. The Lions had won the first of the two-test series against Australia.

**17-6 victory to Lions in Union Test**

From STAN BAXTER

BRISBANE, Sat.—Scrappy, jolted play marred the first Rugby Union Test in which the British Isles beat Australia 17-6 at the Exhibition Ground today.

*Game Five*
*v New South Wales Country Districts*
*Tamworth, Australia 9/6/1959*
*27–14 – Win*

**Lions Team** – Davies (Wales), O'Reilly (Ireland), Price (Wales), Butterfield (England), Young (England), Coughtrie (Scotland), McLeod (Scotland), Dawson (Ireland), **Wood (Ireland)**, Meredith (Wales), Marques (England), Evans (Wales), **Mulcahy (Ireland)**, Murphy (Ireland)

After the test, the Lions moved about eight hundred miles south to the New South Wales country town of Tamworth. There the team was split up and in groups of three or four were invited out to private homes around Tamworth for tea with a local family.

Having missed the test a few days earlier, Gordon Wood got another run out and Bill Mulcahy backed up his test appearance. This was a

1959 Australia, New Zealand and Canada

midweek game and it was played in the afternoon but all the schools closed so that everyone could get to the ground to see the event.

NSW Country scored a try after fourteen minutes to go ahead. Young equalised for the Lions but tore a hamstring in the process. Shortly after, the Lions were chasing a ball upfield when Meredith pulled up and dropped to the ground like he had been shot. He had also pulled a hamstring. Both forwards had to leave the field and the Lions played the game down two men.

The remaining six men in the Lions pack put in a huge performance for the rest of the game and more than matched the eight Australians they were up against. Bill Mulcahy even scored a push-over try in the second half before he too had to leave the field with an arm injury reducing the Lions pack to just five. To make the even more impressive, Gordon Wood broke a finger in this game but played on. He would miss the next three weeks of the tour while he recovered.

Welshman Terry Davies playing at full back scored fifteen points to go along with tries scored by Mulcahy, Young, Evans and Price.

After this game, twelve of the Lions squad were either injured or ill and the tour was only five games old. Mulcahy had torn muscles in his shoulder in the dying minutes of the game. He was in excruciating pain for a few days and had to take sleeping pills to get sleep. He was out for six weeks which really impacted his tour. While he recovered, he trained every day with his arm in a sling running laps of the field to ensure he didn't lose fitness.

*Game Six*
*v Australia (Second Test)*
*Sydney, Australia 13/6/1959*
*24-3 - Win*

**Lions Team** - Scotland (Scotland), Jackson (England), Hewitt (Ireland), Price (Wales), O'Reilly (Ireland), Risman (England), Jeeps (England), McLeod (Scotland), Dawson (Ireland) Captain, Millar (Ireland), Evans (Wales), Williams (Wales), Murphy (Ireland), Marques (England), Smith (Scotland).

1959 Australia, New Zealand and Canada

**Australia** - Linehan, Morton, Kay, Diett, Donald, AJ Summons, Connor, Ellis, Johnson, Dunn, Carroll, Miller, Thornett, Outterside, Fenwicke

With all three Limerick men injured, none were available for the second test against Australia which was played at the Sydney Sports Ground in Sydney.

In front of an attendance of 20,000, the Lions won in a very one-sided game that was played in poor conditions as it had been raining in the lead up to the game. Malcolm Price scored two tries and O'Reilly, Risman and Dawson got one each. The test series against Australia had been an easy 2-0 win.

After this game the Lions moved over to the New Zealand leg of the tour. A huge crowd greeted the Lions in Auckland when they arrived. An estimated 40,000 people were at the airport and more turned out as they were transported in open top cars to their hotel.

*Game Seven*
*v Hawke's Bay*
*Napier, New Zealand 20/6/1959*
*52-12 – Win*

**Lions Team** – Scotland (Scotland), Jackson (England), Butterfield (England), Hewitt (Ireland), Thomas (Wales), Waddell (England), Jeeps (England), Millar (Ireland), Dawson (Ireland), McLeod (Scotland), Williams (Wales), Evans (Wales), Faull (Wales), Ashcroft (England), Morgan (Wales)

A week on from the second test in Sydney, all three of the Limerick Lions were still nursing injuries and missed the first game in New Zealand.

The Lions set a new point scoring record for a visiting international rugby team in the first game of the New Zealand tour. David Hewitt was the star of the show scoring four tries, one penalty and three conversions (twenty-one points in total). Jeff Butterfield injured his foot midway through the second half and had to leave the field but the game was well won at that point. When the Lions reached the fifty-point mark, the crowd gave them a huge standing ovation in appreciation the flowing running rugby.

1959 Australia, New Zealand and Canada

*Game Eight*
*v Poverty Bay / East Coast*
*Gisborne, New Zealand 24/6/1959*
*23-14 – Win*

**Lions Team** – Davies (Wales), O'Reilly (Ireland), Price (Wales), Waddell (England), Thomas (Wales), **English (Ireland)**, Mulligan (Ireland), McLeod (Scotland), Dawson (Ireland), Millar (Ireland), Williams (Wales), Marques (England), Faull (Wales), Ashcroft (England), Murphy (Ireland)

Mick English was the first of the trio to recover from injury enough to play and was one of six Irish players who played in front of 15,000 spectators in Gisborne. One of them, Andy Mulligan had only arrived in New Zealand the day before the game as cover for the injured Dickie Jeeps who was out with a shoulder injury.

The Lions scored one goal, four tries and two penalties to Poverty Bay's one goal, two tries and a penalty.

The Lions scored a penalty in the first minute. Terry Davies kicking from thirty yards to settle the nerves. For the next twenty minutes Mick English orchestrated as the Lions played scintillating running rugby. They ran out to a 17-0 lead which they held until half time.

After nine minutes of the second half the Lions had moved out to 23-6. From that point, the Poverty Bay pack targeted English. They felt that if they could disrupt him, the Lions would struggle. English was repeatedly hammered but the Lions still won the game.

This game had been refereed by Alan Fleury who would cause debate later in the tour. Despite the heavy-handed treatment of Mick English during the game, the Lions had no concern about his performance in this game.

This game proved to be Mick English's last game for the Lions. He had played twice and in both games the Lions played exceptionally. English never lost in a Lions jersey but left everyone thinking about what could have been.

1959 Australia, New Zealand and Canada

*Game Nine*
*v Auckland*
*Auckland, New Zealand 27/6/1959*
*15–10 - Win*

**Lions Team** – Scotland (Scotland), Jackson (England), Hewitt (Ireland), Price (Wales), O'Reilly (Ireland), Risman (England), Mulligan (Ireland), Prosser (Wales), Dawson (Ireland), Millar (Ireland), Williams (Wales), Evans (Wales), Smith (Scotland), Marques (England), Morgan (Wales)

None of the Limerick men were selected for what was to prove to be the toughest game of the tour to that point. Auckland were one of the strongest New Zealand provincial sides.

This was a very tight game that could have gone either way. The Lions were trailing 10-6 at half time. It was a very tough battle and Ken Scotland was knocked unconscious during a tackle. It was only in the last minutes of the game when Dawson scored for the Lions that the Lions got on top. In the end they won by three tries and two penalties to two goals.

*Game Ten*
*v New Zealand Universities*
*Christchurch, New Zealand 1/7/1959*
*25–13 - Win*

**Lions Team** – Scotland (Scotland), O'Reilly (Ireland), Price (Wales), Thomas (Wales), Murphy (Ireland), Risman (England), Mulligan (Ireland), Prosser (Wales), McLeod (Scotland), **Wood (Ireland)**, Marques (England), Williams (Wales), Ashcroft (England), Faull (Wales), Smith (Scotland)

Gordon Wood's broken finger had recovered enough for him to play in this, the Lions' ninth win of the tour. With no concussion protocols, Ken Scotland who had been knocked unconscious in the previous game recovered and captained the side.

40,000 spectators watched as the Lions won well scoring six tries. The Lions looked strong out on the right wing with Price and O'Reilly standing out. O'Reilly scored two tries and Price scored three.

1959 Australia, New Zealand and Canada

Midway through the first half, Thomas went on a run and beat several university tacklers before he kicked ahead. Leary for the student team caught it about ten yards out but was tackled heavily by O'Reilly. The ball bobbled free and Gordon Wood picked it up. Most of the Universities pack were on the goal line in defence but Wood drove through them to score his first try for the British and Irish Lions.

The Lions were ahead by nineteen points at half time but Risman and Malcolm Thomas got injured in the second half and the numerical advantage let the Universities team off what could have been a real beating.

*Game Eleven*
*v Otago*
*Dunedin, New Zealand 4/7/1959*
*8–26 – Loss*

**Lions Team** – Scotland (Scotland), O'Reilly (Ireland), Price (Wales), Morgan (Wales), Murphy (Ireland), Thomas (Wales), Mulligan (Ireland), Millar (Ireland), McLeod (Scotland), **Wood (Ireland)**, Evans (Wales), Marques (England), Ashcroft (England), Faull (Wales), Smith (Scotland)

Gordon Wood backed up three days after the previous game to play Otago. Injuries meant that there were two forwards playing in the Lions backline for this game. Not ideal and nor were the conditions. Heavy rain had left a slippery pitch for the teams to navigate.

Otago had beaten the Lions team in 1950 and did so again in this game. The Lions got out to an 8-6 half time lead but Otago crushed the Lions pack in the second half. The Otago forwards were much faster in the loose and managed the conditions better. Ken Scotland missed five penalty kicks for the Lions as the Lions performed poorly all around the field.

*Game Twelve*
*v South Canterbury / Mid Canterbury / North Otago*
*Timaru, New Zealand 8/7/1959*
*21–11 - Win*

1959 Australia, New Zealand and Canada

**Lions Team** – Davies (Wales), O'Reilly (Ireland), Thomas (Wales), Hewitt (Ireland), Faull (Wales), Waddell (Scotland), Mulligan (Ireland), **Wood (Ireland)**, Meredith (Wales), Prosser (Wales), Evans (Wales), Williams (Wales), Morgan (Wales), Ashcroft (England), Murphy (Ireland).

Bill Mulcahy and Mick English were still injured for this game as Gordon Wood played his third game in a week in Timaru. Welsh hooker Bryn Meredith got his first game of the tour under his belt alongside him in the front row.

Six of the combined team arrived onto the field wearing shoulder padding. While it was common for a player recovering from injury to wear protective padding, this was another level and the Lions manager Alf Wilson went mad at the referee but nothing was done. There was a lot of press coverage on the subject after the game.

While the Lions won the game comfortably in the end, this was a sluggish performance until the back end of the game and message was *"must do better"* after the game. The Lions' pack was well beaten in the loose but were far superior in the lineout. The backs were stronger with O'Reilly (2), Faull and Hewett scoring tries.

There was a little bit of high-jinx at the after-game meal. A number of the Lions players got into a food fight to the consternation of their hosts. The following day they received a formal warning from the NZRFU. The press got wind of this and there were some embarrassing stories in the papers for the Lions for a few days.

*Game Thirteen*
*v Southland*
*Invercargill, New Zealand 11/7/1959*
*11–6 - Win*

**Lions Team** – Scotland (Scotland), Jackson (England), Price (Wales), Patterson (England), Thomas (Wales), Waddell (Scotland), Jeeps (England), McLeod (Scotland), Dawson (Ireland), Millar (Ireland), Evans (Wales), Williams (Wales), Smith (Scotland), Marques (England), Faull (Wales)

1959 Australia, New Zealand and Canada

Invercargill is as far south as you can get in New Zealand. Next stop is the Antarctic. This was southern hemisphere winter, mid-winter and the game, played at Rugby Park, took place in awful sleety conditions. The three Limerick men were probably happy to be in the stand, not that it was much warmer.

Despite the weather, 20,000 spectators showed up for a dull first half. The two pack beat each other up in a game for the purists. Ken Scotland scored a penalty for the Lions and then on the stroke of half-time, Southland scored an unconverted try to make it 3-3 at the break.

There was plenty of opportunity for the Southland side. Ashby missed six kicks which proved costly. Another try for the Lions scored by Jackson was enough to win it for the touring side.

*Game Fourteen*
*v New Zealand (First Test)*
*Dunedin, New Zealand 18/7/1959*
**17–18 - Loss**

Lions Team – Scotland (Scotland), Jackson (England), Price (Wales), Hewitt (Ireland), O'Reilly (Ireland), Risman (England), Jeep (England), McLeod (Scotland), Dawson (Ireland) Captain, **Wood (Ireland),** Evans (Wales), Williams (Wales), Smith, Faull (Scotland), Murphy (Ireland)

New Zealand: Clarke, Walsh, McMullen, Lineen, McPhail, Brown, Urbahn; Whineray, Hemi, Clarke, Hill, Finlay, Jones, Pickering, MacEwan

A week after he played Southland, Gordon Wood was selected to play for the Lions in the first test against the All-Blacks in Dunedin. The game was refereed by Alan Fleury who had previously covered the game in Poverty Bay on the stop of the New Zealand leg of the tour.

There was huge controversy after the game about the performance of the referee. This was particularly because of an incident in the dying seconds. The Lions were down by a point and had worked their way down the field and are within reach of the All-Black's line. With just seconds to go. Welshman Roddy Evans was penalised for picking the ball up in the scrum when he was certain to score. The Lions were down 1-0 in the test series.

*"Fleury from Otago. Lovely man, God Bless him."*
Bill Mulcahy

*"In that first test every time they got in our half it seemed like a penalty would result. Even when we went 18-17 behind, we scored another try and he found reason to disallow it, whereupon Roddy Evans threw the ball at him with a few expletives".*
Bill Mulcahy

*Game Fifteen*
*v West Coast-Buller*
*Greymouth, New Zealand 22/7/1959*
*58–3 - Win*

Lions Team – Davies (Wales), Young (England), Thomas (Wales), Patterson (England), Jackson (England), Waddell (Scotland), Mulligan (Ireland), **Wood (Ireland)**, Meredith (Wales), **Mulcahy (Ireland)**, Marques (England), Morgan (Wales), Ashcroft (England), Smith (Scotland)

Bill Mulcahy made his return from injury in this game which was played a few days after the first test. Gordon Wood also played again, his seventh appearance for the Lions.

1959 Australia, New Zealand and Canada

Greymouth's population is 9,000 but 11,000 spectators showed up for the game. They were rewarded when the Lions scored fourteen tries.

Unfortunately for the home team, they lost one of their forwards Gardner to injury after twenty-six minutes. To that point the Lions had just a 5-3 lead. Once their pack was down a man, the Lions took complete control and the game was effectively over. They had stretched their lead to 18-3 at half time and by the end Young had scored four tries, Jackson had scored four, Waddell had scored two and Smith and Meredith had also scored.

*Game Sixteen*
*v Canterbury*
*Christchurch, New Zealand 25/7/1959*
*14–20 - Loss*

Lions Team – Scotland (Scotland), Young (England), Hewitt (Ireland), Price (Wales), O'Reilly (Ireland), Risman (England), Mulligan (Ireland), Millar (Ireland, Dawson (Ireland), McLeod (Scotland), Evans (Wales), **Mulcahy (Ireland)**, Smith (England), Ashcroft (England), Murphy (Ireland)

Bill Mulcahy played a second game back from injury in this disappointing game for the Lions. Lions wing forward Ken Smith left the field after seventeen minutes with a torn stomach muscle and then six minutes into the second half Ken Scotland was carried off in a stretcher. The Lions played bravely and the newspapers suggested afterwards that with a bit of luck they might have actually won the game.

*Game Seventeen*
*v Marlborough / Nelson / Golden Bay – Motueka*
*Blenheim, New Zealand 29/7/1959*
*64–5 - Win*

**Lions Team** – Thomas (Wales), Jackson (England), Butterfield (England), Patterson (England), Young (England), Waddell (Scotland), Jeeps (England), Millar (Ireland), Meredith (Wales), **Wood (Ireland)**, Marques (England), Williams (Wales), Morgan (Wales), Faull (Wales), Ashcroft (England)

1959 Australia, New Zealand and Canada

Smarting from the loss in the previous game, the Lions were rampant in this game. In front of 7,000 spectators, they set the highest score of the tour to days, which also set the record for the highest score by a touring team in New Zealand history. Malcolm Thomas' contribution from full back was twenty-five points. It could have been more had he not missed a penalty kick and a conversion. Jackson scored four tries, Young scored three, Patterson scored two and Waddell, Faull, Morgan and Gordon Wood also scored tries. Their five points came from an intercept and an eighty-yard dash from Māori Johnny Green

After this game it was clear that Mick English and Niall Brophy, who was also injured, would not be able to take part in any more games on the tour. The New Zealand RFU invited them to stay on as guests for the remainder of the tour, however, the Home-Nations committee ordered that they return home. The rest of the Lions tour party even wrote a petition requesting that they be allowed to accept the NZRFU's offer. The petition was declined and the two injured players returned home.

The Evening News reported that *"Considerable distress was felt in the team when it was announced at a meeting that Brophy and English were to return. Subsequently it is understood that an approach was to be made to Mr Wilson. Before this could be done, Mr Wilson faced a series of questions at a press conference at which he said 'I agree with the decision'."*

To make life interesting, the duo decided to return home by sea and so set off from New Zealand on 31st July. They were at sea for six weeks. Their adventure took them to Singapore, Egypt, up the Suez Canal and Greece amongst other stops. They only arrived in Dublin the day before the Lions team themselves returned from the tour.

*"When myself and Brophy arrived back in Dublin, we went straight to the Wicklow Hotel. We hadn't had a pint of Guinness for three months, can you imagine?*

*On the way to the bar, I spotted Donogh O'Malley who I knew well, he was aa Bohs fella, and he offered me a lift back to Limerick in the state merc. He gave me the keys to put my stuff in the boot, and to cut a long story short, he couldn't be found after that.*

*I searched all the pubs but there was no sign. So, I drove back to Limerick in the merc, where my own little ford Anglia was waiting for me, and then went out to Corbally where Donogh lived to drop off the keys".*
Mick English

An interesting aside of Mick English's odyssey is that he and his co-sailor Niall Brophy remained firm friends after the tour and the English and Brophy families remained close. So much so that Mick's son John English, married Niall's daughter Marie-Elana. Their children have the unusual distinction of having two Lions as their grandfathers.

*Game Eighteen*
*v Wellington*
***Wellington, New Zealand 1/8/1959***
*21-6 - Win*

**Lions Team** – Scotland (Scotland), Young (England), Hewitt (Ireland), Price (Wales), Thomas (Wales), Risman (England), Jeeps (England), McLeod (Scotland), Dawson (Ireland), Millar (Ireland), Marques (England), Williams (Wales), Murphy (Ireland), Evans (Wales), Morgan (Wales)

After the relatively easy game in Blenheim, the Lions were expecting a much sterner test against one of the strongest provincial sides in Wellington.

Ahead of kick-off the 48,000 crowd were entertained by a performance from City of Wellington Highland Pipe Band. To the crowd's delight, their choreographed march first took the shape of a 'V' for Victory and then formed a 'W' for Wellington.

Wellington had much of the early play and Russell Walt kicked two penalties to give the home team a 6-3 half time lead. The Lions were not playing well but in the second half they turned it around.

The Lions' pivots of Jeeps and Risman upped the pace and the Lions scored five tries, two for Price and one each for Young, Millar and Risman. Jeeps took a heavy blow in the second half but refused to leave the field and limped to the end of the game.

1959 Australia, New Zealand and Canada

The Wellington captain said after the game that the Lions were *"the finest pack I have ever scrummaged against"*.

**Game Nineteen**
**v Wanganui**
**Wanganui, New Zealand 5/8/1959**
**9–6 -Win**

**Lions Team** – Waddell (Scotland), Young (England0, Hewitt (Ireland), Patterson (England), O'Reilly (Ireland), Risman (England), Mulligan (Ireland), Prosser (Wale), Dawson (Ireland), **Wood (Ireland), Mulcahy (Ireland)**, Evans (Wales), Faull (Wales), Ashcroft (England), Murphy (Ireland).

Wood and Mulcahy both played in this game which was remembered more for the punch ups than the rugby.

Soon after the game started, Mulcahy went down injured after a ruck. Unbelievably, the referee ran up to him and said *"Serves you bloody well right. You should get off the ball"*. Wood was warned twice for pulling a Wanganui player out of the Lions' side of the ruck and Mulcahy was also spoken to for punching. A penalty each, scored by Risman and Boswell had the score level at half time.

The game remained scrappy in the second half but two tries, one scored by Mulcahy, won it for the Lions. Wanganui almost scored again at the death but the Lions' defence held firm.

> *"Some matches were very tough and of their time. I think it was my first game back after a long period out injured. Wanganui -a game we were expected to waltz through. We won 9-6 and I scored a try. I remember being the recipient of a lot of hospitality on the ground in that match. We had a situation where they awarded us a penalty and Bev Risman was lining up when a policeman, who was walking up and down, tapped the ref on the shoulder to point out to him that the touch judge on the far side of the field had his flag up. The ref told Risman to go ahead. He kicked the goal, then the ref went over and discussed it with the touch judge and they gave New Zealand a lineout instead".*
>
> Bill Mulcahy

1959 Australia, New Zealand and Canada

*Bill Mulcahy and Gordon Wood in the thick of it against Wanganui*

**Game Twenty**
*v Taranaki*
*New Plymouth, New Zealand 8/8/1959*
*15–3 - Win*

**Lions Team** – Scotland (Scotland), Jackson (England), Price (Wales), Thomas (Wales), O'Reilly (Ireland), Waddell (Scotland), Jeeps (England), McLeod (Scotland), Dawson (Ireland), Millar (Ireland), Williams (Wales), Evans (Wales), Faull (Wales), Marques (England), Morgan (Wales)

There were none of the Limerick men on the field when the Lions scored one of the best wins on the tour. Taranaki were reigning provincial champions and the press were calling this the fifth test.

Taranaki scored in the first minute with a penalty kicked Bayley. Thomas levelled with a penalty and the score remained level until half time. Taranaki were getting the better of the game.

In the second half though, Ken Scotland dropped a goal from forty yards and then a minute later he scored a penalty. A try to Price who ran twenty yards to score and a further Thomas penalty secured the win for the Lions.

*Game Twenty-One*
*v Manawatu / Horowhenua*
*Palmerston, New Zealand 11/8/1959*
*26–6 - Win*

**Lions Team** – Scotland (Scotland), O'Reilly (Ireland), Paterson (England), Price (Wales), Young (England), Risman (England), Mulligan (Ireland), Prosser (Wales), Meredith (Wales), **Wood (Ireland)**, Marques (England), **Mulcahy (Ireland)**, Murphy (Ireland), Faull (Wales), Morgan (Wales)

Both Wood and Mulcahy played in the game in Palmerston. The Lions scored an impressive win scoring six tries, two to Patterson and one each to O'Reilly, Price and Mulcahy. Mulcahy's try came after a nice sidestep from Risman who passed to O'Reilly, to Morgan and then to Mulcahy. Mulcahy had little to do and appeared to drop the ball as he touched it down but the try was awarded.

Bev Risman got an ankle injury midway through the second half and had to leave the field. It was later confirmed that he had a chipped bone at the bottom of this tibia and he would miss the test.

*Game Twenty-Two*
*v New Zealand (Second Test)*
*Wellington, New Zealand 15/8/1959*
*8–11 - Loss*

**Lions Team** – Davies (Wales), Young (England), Thomas (Wales), Patterson (England), O'Reilly (Ireland), Price (Wales), Jeeps (England), Millar (Ireland), Dawson (Ireland) Captain, McLeod (Scotland),

## 1959 Australia, New Zealand and Canada

Williams (Wales), Evans (Wales), Ashcroft (England), Marques (England), Murphy (Ireland)

**New Zealand** - Clarke, Diack, McMullen, Lineen, Caulton, McCullough, Briscoe, Whineray, Webb, Clarke, Hill, MacEwan, Meads, Conway, Tremain

Having lost the first test, the Lions were determined to get level. They were devastated by injuries though. In addition to Mick English and Niall Brophy who were gone home, Risman was out, Hewitt was out, Scotland was out, Mulligan was out and Jackson had the flu. Hugh McLeod was picked to play at Hooker where he had never played before.

None of the remaining Limerick men were selected to play. Without them, the Lions put up a brave and spirited performance.

The Lions lost the toss and played into a light breeze in the first half. Davies missed a penalty in the first few minutes. Clarke who had kicked New Zealand to success in the first test also missed early penalties. After fourteen minutes, New Zealand went ahead after Ralph Caulton, on his All-Blacks debut, picked up a wonderful through kick from Lineen and scored in the left corner. The same pair combined shortly afterwards to score an almost identical try. The Lions were down six nil at the break. The All-Blacks had the best of the first half and the score was a fair reflection of the game.

Ten minutes into the second half, Don Clarke blatantly obstructed O'Reilly after he had chipped him and Clarke

*Clarke breaks Lions' hearts*

NEW ZEALAND .......... 11
LIONS ..................... 8

A TRY two minutes from time by full back Don Clarke, which he converted himself, gave New Zealand victory over the Lions Rugby team by one goal and two tries (11 pts.) to one goal and one

247

1959 Australia, New Zealand and Canada

dropped his shoulder. Instead of awarding a penalty try, as he ought to have done, the referee merely awarded a penalty, which Terry Davies kicked. 6-3.

The Lions then took the lead with a try by Young, after a marvellous run by Price and a lovely scissors with Thomas. Davies converted to make it 8-6 to the Lions. The score remained that way until the final minute when New Zealand's McCullogh, broke down the blind side and passed to Clarke, who scored the winning try with a massive dive over the line. Clarke also converted it himself, to make the score 11-8 and to give the All-Blacks a two-nil lead in the series.

*Game Twenty-Three*
*19/8/1959 - King Country / Counties*
*Taumarunui, New Zealand*
*25–5 - Win*

Lions Team – Thomas (Wales), Jackson (England), Butterfield (England), Patterson (England), O'Reilly (Ireland), Waddell (Scotland), Jeeps (England), Prosser (Wales), Meredith (Wales), **Wood (Ireland)**, Williams (Wales), **Mulcahy (Ireland)**, Smith (Scotland), Morgan (Wales), Faull (Wales)

Just a few days after the loss in the second test, Wood and Mulcahy were back in action at Taumarunui. 12,500 spectators showed up for a difficult game for the Lions.

Both teams eager to get going and in a scrum in the first minute, the front rows engaged without letting the referee get out of the way. There were cheers from the crowd as the referee was trapped in the middle of them.

Welshman Faull missed some early penalty chances but scored the first from twenty yards. A try from Tony O'Reilly followed, after a kick through from Patterson. Then three more Faull penalties gave the Lions a 17-0 lead at the break.

The first half is remembered for Colin Meads grabbing Tony O'Reilly's hair so forcefully that O'Reilly, who was punched in the ribs at the same time, went down needing treatment. The Taranaki Daily News called his reaction *"a theatrical fainting fit"*.

1959 Australia, New Zealand and Canada

Early in the second half, the game saw the first ever penalty try awarded to a visiting team in NZ. Patterson kicked through and O'Reilly ran through having recovered from his hair pulling incident. As O'Reilly went for the ball on the goal line, he was impeded by the hip and shoulder of a New Zealander. The Lions couldn't believe they had been given what was a clear penalty try.

O'Reilly was in sparkling form and scored again after the Lions created an overlap. There was a late consolation try for the home team. Colin Meads made a run and was tackled by Mulcahy but Meads got to his feet again and passed to Katterns who scored.

*Game Twenty-Four*
*v Waikato*
*Hamilton, New Zealand 22/8/1959*
*14–0 - Win*

**Lions Team** – Thomas (Wales), Young (England), Price (Wales), Hewitt (Ireland), Jackson (England), Waddell (Scotland), Jeeps (England), **Wood (Ireland)**, Meredith (Wales), Millar (Ireland), Evans (Wales), **Mulcahy (Ireland)**, Morgan (Wales), Faull (Wales), Smith (Scotland)

Mulcahy and Wood were back on the field four days later for the game against Waikato. Don Clarke, New Zealand's kicking machine, was fullback for the Waikato team and he had a nightmare, missing seven kicks.

The game was played on a really poor field. The pitch had been recently re-laid by the Waikato Rugby Union but it didn't have time to set in. Then, rain the day before the game and right through the game, caused it to become a mud bath.

Because of the conditions, the Lions' running game was neutralised and it became a kicking contest. The only score in the first half was a penalty to the Lions, kicked from twenty-five yards by Faull. Clarke missed 4 penalties in the first half and 3 attempted drop goals.

Bill Mulcahy in the second row did trojan work and Gordon Wood was also very prominent in the match reports. A second half try for Young and remarkably a second penalty try in two games gave the Lions the win.

1959 Australia, New Zealand and Canada

*Game Twenty-Five*
*v Wairarapa / Bush*
*Masterton, New Zealand 25/8/1959*
*37–11 - Win*

**Lions Team** – Scotland (Scotland), Jackson (England), Butterfield (England), Hewitt (Ireland), O'Reilly (Ireland), Horrocks-Taylor (England), Mulligan (Ireland), Millar (Ireland), Meredith (Wales), Prosser (Wales), Marques (England), Murphy (Ireland), Ashcroft (England), Smith (Scotland)

With four days to go before the all-important third test, both Wood and Mulcahy were left out of the team that faced Wairarapa. Phil Horrocks-Taylor who had flown in just a few days earlier as a replacement for Mick English got his first run out on the tour and scored a try. It was nineteen-year-old David Hewitt who stole the show though. Playing his first game at centre, he scored twenty points from two tries, four conversions and two penalties. Tony O'Reilly scored two tries as did Peter Jackson.

*Bill Mulcahy in action for the Lions against Wairarapa and Bush*

*Game Twenty-Six*
*v New Zealand (Third Test)*
*Christchurch, New Zealand 29/8/1959*
*8–22 – Loss*

Lions Team - Scotland (Scotland), Jackson (England), Price (Wales), Hewitt (Ireland), O'Reilly (Ireland), Horrocks-Taylor (England), Jeeps (England), McLeod (Scotland), Dawson (Ireland), **Wood (Ireland)**, Evans (Wales), Williams (Wales), Morgan (Wales), Faull (Wales), Smith (Scotland)

New Zealand - Clarke (Waikato), Brown (Taranaki), Lineen (Auckland), Caulton (Wellington), McCullough (Taranaki), Urbahn (Taranaki), Irwin (Otago), Hemi (Waikato), Whineray (Canterbury) Captain, Hill (Canterbury), MacEwan (Wellington), Tremain (Canterbury), Conway (Otago), Meads (Kings Country)

The Lions had to win the third test to keep the series alive. The day before the game, Vivian Jenkins rugby correspondent for the Sunday Times and an ex-Lion, wrote an article in the Christchurch Star newspaper in which he called the All-Blacks "Softies" for wearing padding. True to form, seven of the New Zealand team turned out in shoulder padding for the game. Lions' manager Alf Wilson lodged a formal protest but the referee showed him medical certificates showing that they were 'required'.

Bill Mulcahy wasn't selected for the game. Gordon Wood came in for Syd Millar at prop. Phil Horrocks-Taylor was selected at out-half for what would only his second game in four months.

In response to the "softies" article, the All-Black forwards were fired up and there was a lot of aggression on show in the early stages at Lancaster Park in Christchurch.

Caulton scored the first try for New Zealand, he was put through by Urbahn after they had won a scrum against the head. Faull kicked a penalty from 25 yards to bring the Lions back level. Levelled. Don

Clarke then kicked a penalty from fifty yards after the Lions infringed in the lineout. Soon after Clarke scored again from a drop goal.

With four minutes to half-time, young Hewitt scored a magnificent try for the Lions after a half break by Horrocks-Taylor. Welshman Faull converted and the Lions were within a point of the All-Blacks. They couldn't hold out though and with a minute to go to the interval, Colin Meads swept through for a try which Clarke converted to make it 14-8 at half-time to the blacks.

The 57,000 spectators saw a disappointing second half. There would be no scoring or the first thirty minutes and the Lions didn't score again at all.

With ten minutes to go Urbahn scored after an obvious knock on but the referee gave the home side the advantage and awarded it. Caulton scored again in the final minute. Again, there was questions about the validity of the score as he seemed not to ground it but it didn't matter. New Zealand had won convincingly and the series was lost.

*Gordon Wood emerges from a scrum in the 3rd Test*

*Game Twenty-Seven*
*v New Zealand Juniors*
*Wellington, New Zealand 2/9/1959*
*29–9 - Win*

1959 Australia, New Zealand and Canada

**Lions Team** – Davies (Wales), Young (England), Butterfield (England), Hewitt (Ireland), O'Reilly (Ireland), Waddell (Scotland), Jeeps (England), Prosser (Wales), Meredith (Wales), Millar (Ireland), Marques (England), **Mulcahy (Ireland)**, Smith (Scotland), Ashcroft (England), Murphy (Ireland)

The New Zealand Juniors were the national under twenty-three side and not to be discounted. The young All-Blacks lost Don Davidson after fifteen minutes with a 'dislocated foot'. Even with the extra man, the Lions found it difficult going. The Lions trailed 6-3 at half time with all of the points coming from penalties.

Mulcahy and the Lions took stronger control in the second half. They scored their one-hundredth try of the tour as they ran up the scoreboard. Waddell scored three tries, O'Reilly scored two and Thomas also got over the line.


*Game Twenty-Eight*
*v New Zealand Māori*
*Auckland, New Zealand 5/9/1959*
*12–6 - Win*

**Lions Team** – Davies (Wales), Jackson (England), Price (Wales), Hewitt (Ireland), O'Reilly (Ireland), Horrocks-Taylor (England), Mulligan (Ireland), Prosser (Wales), Meredith (Wales), **Wood (Ireland)**, **Mulcahy (Ireland)**, Evans (Wales), Morgan (Wales), Faull (Wales), Murphy (Ireland)

Both Gordon Wood and Bill Mulcahy were on the field for this game which was the first on the tour in which the Lions didn't score a try.

45,000 spectators showed up to watch a poor game in which the Lions team were starting to look tour weary. The Lions were ahead at half time by 9-6 but the most interesting part of the half was a number of "undignified" incidents. After thirty minutes, Pryor and Mulcahy had a right punch up. The referee called the captains together and told them to talk to their teams but it was to no avail.

Pryor who had played for Auckland against the Lions earlier in the tour, when he was a little aggressive. In this game he was far more interested in the fighting and in one incident, he could have been convicted of assault on English forward Marques.

The game ended in a Lions win but with seventy-two lineouts, thirty-five scrums and forty-two penalties, it wasn't a great game. The New Zealand Herald called it *"a bad game, sour in spirit, and devoid of that imaginative sparkle which was supposed to be the birthright of the two teams"*.

*Game Twenty-Nine*
*v Bay of Plenty / Thames Valley*
*Rotorua, New Zealand 9/9/1959*
*26–24 - Win*

**Lions Team** – Scotland (Scotland), Young (England), Butterfield (England), Patterson (England), Thomas (Wales), Horrocks-Taylor (England), Mulligan (Ireland), Millar (Ireland), Dawson (Ireland), McLeod (Scotland), Williams (Wales), Marques (England), Smith (Scotland), Ashcroft (England), Murphy (Ireland)

Having played against the Māori, Wood and Mulcahy sat out the game in Rotorua against Bay of Plenty.

The Lions lost Jeff Butterfield after fifteen minutes to a leg injury which levelled the playing field for what turned out to be a fantastic game and a real contrast to the brawl in the previous game against the Māori.

The Lions raced out to a twenty-one-point lead after half an hour but the home side worked their way back into the game and were ahead 24-21 with thirteen minutes to go. It was only because of a Ken Scotland try, with two minutes left on the clock, that the Lions won the game.

*Game Thirty*
*v North Auckland*
*Whangārei, New Zealand 12/9/1959*
*35–13 - Win*

**Lions Team** – Davies (Wales), Jackson (England), Scotland (Scotland), Hewitt (Ireland), O'Reilly (Ireland), Risman (England), Mulligan (Ireland), Prosser (Wales), Meredith (Wales), **Wood (Ireland),** Williams

(Wales), **Mulcahy (Ireland)**, Morgan (Wales), Faull (Wales), Murphy (Ireland).

Wood and Mulcahy were back on the field against North Auckland. Up against a strong North Auckland team, the Lions were guilty of responding to aggressive play with some of their own. The newspaper reports included the line - *"A good deal of fighting, much of it, to be candid, begun by Wood"*.

Fists were flying throughout the game and Bill Mulcahy was warned by the referee three times for rough play. Gordon Wood's "activities" were also pointed to the referee by the Auckland players.

On the day after the game, it was ironic that the Lions squad were taken from Whangārei to Maitangi which was where the treaty between the Māori and the colonial whites was signed. From there the team went to Russell where they had a Māori hangi on the beach while they relaxed and began to think about the fourth test.

*Game Thirty-One*
*v New Zealand (Fourth Test)*
*Eden Park, Auckland, New Zealand 19/9/1959*
*9–6 - Win*

1959 Australia, New Zealand and Canada

**Lions Team** - Davies (Wales), Jackson (England), Hewitt (Ireland), Scotland (Scotland), O'Reilly (Ireland), Risman (England), Mulligan (Ireland), Prosser (Wales), Dawson (Ireland) Captain, McLeod (Scotland), Williams (Wales), **Mulcahy (Ireland)**, Murphy (Ireland), Faull (Wales), Morgan (Wales)

**New Zealand** - Clarke, McPhail, Lineen, Clarke, Caulton, McCullough, Urbahn, Irwin, Hemi, Whineray, Hill, Meads, Pickering, Conway, Tremain

The test series had already been lost but the Lions still had their pride to play for at Eden Park in Auckland in front of a capacity crowd of 60,000.

Gordon Wood was nominated to the Lion linesman and so had a role in the test even though he wasn't playing. Ray Prosser took his place on the team.

Bill Mulcahy, however, was selected to play in the game. He took the place of Roddy Evans who had an injured knee.

In a very tight game, Ken Scotland, Peter Jackson and Tony O'Reilly scored tries for the Lions. Don Clarke kicked two penalties and had the chance to tie the game five minutes from time with a twenty-five-yard kick. He missed. This game summed up how the series had gone; the Lions playing open running rugby and scoring tries, the All-Blacks kicking penalties but winning.

The Lions had won a test in New Zealand. It was the first Test won by a British team in New Zealand since the initial Test of the 1930 tour, and only the second Lions victory over New Zealand in sixty years.

*"It was wet and not the sort of day that suited us. Everybody was tired, we had lost the series, but we still managed to get it together to win the Test, and again it was by scoring tries to none. They were proud and determined men, those guys, and it was all about being able to leave with our heads*

1959 Australia, New Zealand and Canada

*held high. Very few people beat the All-Blacks in New Zealand and I still regard it as one of life's great triumphs."*

Ken Scotland

*Gordon Wood (Linesman) watches on as Tony O'Reilly scores in the 4th Test*

On the way from New Zealand to their next game in Vancouver, the Lions' plane had a stop off in Honolulu, Hawaii. Much to the disgust of the team, they were unable to get out to see the delights of Waikiki Beach.

**Game Thirty-Two**
**v British Columbia**
**Vancouver, Canada 27/9/1959**
**16–11   Win**

1959 Australia, New Zealand and Canada

Lions Team – Davies (Wales), O'Reilly (Ireland) Captain, Patterson (England), Price (Wales), Young (England), Mulligan (Ireland), McLeod (Scotland), Meredith (Wales), Millar (Ireland), **Mulcahy (Ireland)**, Marques (England), Smith (Scotland), Ashcroft (England), Morgan (Wales)

Bill Mulcahy was on a strong Lions side that was picked to play against British Columbia in Vancouver. 8,000 Canadians showed up for a game that was much closer than it should have been. The Lions were up 8-3 at half time but the home side stayed in the game and it was only in the last ten minutes that Bev Risman scored the winner.

*Game Thirty-Three*
*v Eastern Canada All-Stars*
*Toronto, Canada 29/9/1959*
*70–6 - Win*

Lions Team – Davies (Wales), Patterson (England), Scotland (Scotland), Hewitt (Ireland), O'Reilly (Ireland), Horrocks-Taylor (England), Jeeps (England), Prosser (Wales), Dawson (Ireland), McLeod (Scotland), **Mulcahy (Ireland)**, Murphy (Ireland), Williams (Wales), Faull (Wales), Morgan (Wales)

The final game of the tour was played in Toronto against a select side of players from across Eastern Canada. Amongst those selected was 1955 British and Irish Lion, Limerick Lion, **Tom Reid**. Reid had moved to live in Canada after he toured there with the Barbarians in 1957 and in this game became the first person to play both for and against the Lions.

In a sign of the popularity of the sport in Canada, less than five thousand people turned out to see the superstar touring team. Those that did saw an exhibition game with fourteen tries. The Lions were out to a 31-0 lead at half time and by the end it was 70-6. Murphy scored three tries, Hewitt and Patterson each got two, Scotland, Morgan, Faull, O'Reilly, McLeod and Williams also scored but the final try of the tour came from Limerickman Bill Mulcahy. There must have been a cheeky wink and a wry smile at his Limerick friend Tom Reid at the finish. In true Lions fashion they would have celebrated Tom's achievement with a beer and a song.

Three days after the final game of the tour in Toronto, the Irish Lions Dawson, Mulcahy, O'Reilly and Murphy arrived home at Dublin Airport on Thursday 1$^{st}$ Oct. They were met by crowds of fans wanting to catch a glimpse of the players. Gordon Wood had already returned home.

## Post Tour Game

*17/10/1959 - Jubilee Game*
**Twickenham, England**

England/Wales Team – Davies (Wales), Jackson (England), Patterson (England), Thomas (Wales), Young (England), Risman (England), Jeeps (England), Prosser (Wales), Meredith (Wales), Benton (England), Williams (Wales), Currie (England), Morgan (Wales), Faull (Wales), Ashcroft (England)

Ireland/Scotland Team – Scotland (Scotland), Smith (Scotland), Flynn (Ireland), Hewitt (Ireland), O'Reilly (Ireland), Sharp (Scotland), Mulligan (Ireland), McLeod (Scotland), Dawson (Ireland), Millar (Ireland), Kemp (Scotland), **Mulcahy (Ireland)**, Murphy (Ireland), Greenwood (Scotland), Smith (Scotland)

Two weeks after they had arrived home, most of the tourists were back in London for a Jubilee Game that was held at Twickenham. Bill Mulcahy turned out as a combined England/Wales team played a combined Ireland/Scotland team. England/Wales won 26 – 17.

## Tour Reflections

The 1959 Lions tour to Australia and New Zealand was a mixed bag in terms of success. An easy test series win in Australia was followed by a 3-1 defeat in New Zealand. The victory in the final test at Eden Park put a slightly positive spin on the New Zealand leg of the tour but ultimately, they had lost the series.

The three Limerick men had performed well. Despite missing games because of a broken finger, Gordon Wood had played in fifteen games including two test matches and scored two tries. Bill Mulcahy, again despite injury, had played in fifteen games including two test matches and scored two tries. Finally, Mick English had shown glimpses of brilliance in the two games he played and left everyone with a feeling of 'what if'. He played twice and won on both occasions.

*"Mulcahy was never less than good and sometimes was superb. He was one of the most courageous footballers I have ever played with."*
Tony O'Reilly

*"My memories of the 1959 tour are that we played good rugby and we had a terrific team spirit. You have to remember in these days when 20,000 people can follow the team to Australia and New Zealand, and when they're talking about 50,000 going to South Africa, that we were very much on our own, and it was definitely an 'us against them' mentality which drew us all very close, no matter where in these islands we came from."*
Syd Millar

# 1962
# South Africa, Rhodesia and Kenya

Bill Mulcahy

# Bill Mulcahy
# Lion #403

Bill Mulcahy was the first Limerickman to go on two British and Irish Lions Tours.

Please see his profile ahead of the 1959 tour.

# South Africa, Rhodesia & Kenya (1962)

At the end of 1960 and the start of 1961, the Springboks toured Britain and Ireland. Across a total of thirty-four games, they only lost one, the final one against the Barbarians. Before that they had completed a comprehensive Grand Slam beating Wales (3-0), Ireland (8-3), England (5-0) and Scotland (12-5). Ireland had gone on an unsanctioned tour of South Africa in May 1961. Under the name of Shamrocks, the Irish team were resoundingly beaten in the test game played at Cape Town 24-8. The Springboks were undoubtedly the best team in the world at that time.

The 1962 Lions tour would take in twenty-five matches across what is now South Africa, Namibia, Zimbabwe and Kenya. Playing the Springboks was a challenge. Travelling all over the southern continent of Africa and playing a tough game of rugby every two days made it a really tough ask.

South Africa was in a tense state when the tour was to take place and there were calls that it should be cancelled for player safety reasons. At that point, apartheid and civil rights for black South Africans wasn't the cause it would later become. There was a lingering threat of violence throughout the tour as the ANC used the tour as an opportunity to gain publicity. That ramped up further on the day after the third test when Nelson Mandela was arrested and imprisoned charged with incitement to strike and with illegally leaving South Africa.

> *"We had some sort of briefing from an embassy individual before we left London about the situation in South Africa. Some of us threw a couple of awkward questions at him which he batted away. I asked him about some South African fella who'd written a book about his mixed-race marriage and how he had to leave the country. I asked him what he thought of the book. He wasn't too pleased with the questions."*
>
> Bill Mulcahy

## Touring party

Coming into the 1962 tour, Ireland had come off the back of two poor Five Nations championships. In 1960 they finished bottom of the table having lost all four games. In 1961, they hadn't done much better. Again, they had finished in last place with a single victory at home over England to their credit. France was the dominant team at the time in the Five Nations. They won four on the trot from 1959 to 1962. The Irish side was captained by Bill Mulcahy in 1962 who, having been on the previous tour, was almost assured of a Lions spot.

The 1962 squad would be managed by England's Brian Vaughan who was assisted by Ireland's Henry McKibbin. The squad selected was very controversial as the selectors failed to pick a specialist blindside flanker which everyone felt was a must against the big Springbok pack.

Selected were ten English, ten Welsh, six Scottish and seven Irishmen. Considering Ireland's poor form in the championship, seven Lions places was an achievement. Bill Mulcahy was indeed amongst those selected and he would go on to play in seventeen of the twenty-four games including all four tests.

Welsh hooker Bryn Meredith was selected for his third tour with the Lions as was England' scrum-half Dickie Jeeps. Scotsman Arthur Smith was to be tour captain.

Also in the squad were two Irishmen who would go on to be legends of the game. Willie John McBride and Tom Kiernan were selected for their first tours with the British and Irish Lions. McBride had broken his leg in the Five Nations game against France just a few weeks earlier. He had been kicked by French prop forward Domenech. With no replacements allowed, McBride played on until the end of the game. It was only afterwards that he found out his leg was badly broken. He was still in a cast when he was selected for the Lions. Against medical advice he took off the cast and went on the tour.

> *"Most people told me I wouldn't be able to go, but I was determined. We all had to produce a medical form signed by a doctor to say we were fit to travel. I went down to see my GP and told him 'Doc, you have to sign this.' He did so, and the last thing I said to him was I won't let you down. 'They took the plaster off four days before we were due to meet up in Eastbourne, and it had wasted away to skin and bone, but I knew we had a few weeks before we had to play and I was sure I could build it up.".*
> Willie John McBride

1962 South Africa, Rhodesia and Kenya

*Bill Mulcahy – sitting 5th from right – with the 1962 Lions*

The following was the squad selected for the 1962 tour:

**Management**
Manager D. B. Vaughan (England)
Coach H. R. McKibbin (Ireland)

**Backs**
Dewi Bebb (Swansea and Wales), Niall Brophy (University College Dublin and Ireland), H. J. C Brown (Blackheath and RAF), John Dee (Hartlepool Rovers and England), Ronnie Cowan (Selkirk and Scotland), David Hewitt (Queen's University RFC and Ireland), Raymond Hunter (CIYMS and Ireland), Dickie Jeeps (Northampton and England), Ken Jones (Llanelli and Wales), Tom Kiernan (University College Cork R.F.C. and Ireland), Tony O'Connor (Aberavon and Wales), Richard Sharp (Oxford University and England), Arthur Smith (Edinburgh Wanderers and Scotland), Gordon Waddell (London Scottish and Scotland), Mike Weston (Durham City and England), John Willcox (Oxford University and England)

**Forwards**
Mike Campbell-Lamerton (London Scottish, Army and Scotland), Glyn Davidge (Newport and Wales), John Douglas (Stewart's College FP and Scotland), Bert Godwin (Coventry and England), Stan Hodgson (Durham City and England), Kingsley Jones (Cardiff and Wales), Willie John McBride (Ballymena and Ireland), Bryn Meredith (Newport and Wales), Syd Millar (Ballymena and Ireland), Haydn Morgan

(Abertillery and Wales), **Bill Mulcahy (Bohemians and Ireland),** David Nash (Ebbw Vale and Wales), Alun Pask (Abertillery and Wales), Budge Rogers (Bedford and England), David Rollo (Howe of Fife and Scotland), Keith Rowlands (Cardiff and Wales), Peter Wright (Blackheath and England)

## The Tour

Mulcahy was the Irish captain and on his second tour. He was now one of the senior players and along with Gordon Waddell (Scotland), Dickie Jeeps (England) and Bryn Meredith (Wales) was part of the team that selected the players for each game. Irishmen Niall Brophy, Syd Millar and David Hewitt were going on their second tour, along with Bill Mulcahy.

As they always did, the team met up at Eastbourne for some travel formalities and to start training together. After a week of training, the team were taken to the Washington Hotel in Mayfair where a send-off had been arranged where family and friends could join the team for tea. Following that the team had two receptions to attend. One was at South Africa House with the South African Ambassador and other dignitaries and then a second one with the Home Unions Tour Committee.

*Training at Eastbourne ahead of the tour*

1962 South Africa, Rhodesia and Kenya

*Training at Eastbourne ahead of the tour*

Finally, on the day of their departure for South Africa, the team were collected from the Washington Hotel in the afternoon and brought to London Airport North where they boarded their flight and took off at 6pm.

## The Games

Ahead of the first game in Harare, the Prime Minister came to visit the Lions at one of their training sessions. On another day, they went on a flyover of Victoria Falls.

*Game One*
*v Rhodesia*
*Hartsfield Ground, Harare, Zimbabwe 26/5/1962*
*38 – 9 - Win*

**Lions Team** – Wilcox (England), Smith (Scotland), Jones (Wales), Weston (England), Brophy (Ireland), Sharp (England), O'Connor (Wales), Jones (Wales), Hodgson (England), Rollo (Scotland), **Mulcahy (Ireland)**, Campbell-Lamerton (Scotland), Pask (Wales), Nash (Wales), Rogers (England)

1962 South Africa, Rhodesia and Kenya

In what was described in the press the next days as "*a most satisfactory start to the tour*", the Lions kicked off with a strong win at Salisbury (now Harare). Mulcahy got a run out in this game which the Lions won well scoring seven tries and conceding none.

10,000 people watched a very one-sided affair. Hodgson was badly injured towards the end of the game and was stretchered off. It was later confirmed that he had a broken leg and his tour was over. Nash also left the field late on, leaving just thirteen Lions to finish the game.

*Syd Millar (left) and Bill Mulcahy (right) at Livingstone during preparation*

Game Two
v Giqualand West
De Beers Diamond Oval, Kimberley, South Africa 31/5/1962
8 – 8 – Draw

**Lions Team** – Kiernan (Ireland), Smith (Scotland), Cowan (Scotland), Dee (England), Hunter (Ireland), Waddell (Scotland), Jeeps (England), Wright (England), Meredith (Wales), Millar (Ireland), Rowlands (Wales), Campbell-Lamerton (Scotland), Rogers (England), Pask (Wales), Morgan (Wales)

1962 South Africa, Rhodesia and Kenya

Mulcahy didn't play in the second game of the tour. Future Ireland legend Tom Kiernan made his Lions debut in front of 15,000 spectators. He scored a penalty that contributed to the Lions going into the break ahead.

In the second half, the Giqualand forwards battered the Lions with up-and-unders. That tactic paid off when Froneman scored for the Springboks. The game however ended in a stalemate.

On the same day that the Lions struggled to get the better of a South African provincial side, the All-Blacks, touring Australia, set an international record by scoring twenty-two tries in a 103-nil win over Northern New South Wales at Quirindi.

On the way from Kimberley to their next destination Potchefstroom, the bus carrying the Lions broke down and they had to squeeze into a bus that was following along with members of the media. It made for an uncomfortable journey in more ways than one. Tour manager Brian Vaughan was cautious about the press getting too much access to the players. Now they were sitting on their laps – literally.

*Game Three*
*v Western Transvaal*
*Olen Park, Potchefstroom, South Africa 2/6/1962*
*11 - 6 - Win*

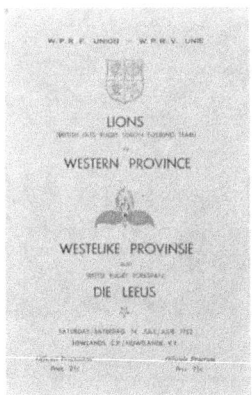

**Lions Team** – Wilcox (England), Hunter (Ireland), Dee (England), Jones (Wales), Cowan (Scotland), Waddell (Scotland), O'Connor (Wales), Millar (Ireland), Meredith (Wales), Rollo (Scotland), **Mulcahy (Ireland) Captain**, Rowlands (Wales), Douglas (Scotland), Nash (Wales), Morgan (Wales)

On a very proud day for Limerick, Bill Mulcahy captained the Lions in the absence of tour captain Arthur Smith.

271

1962 South Africa, Rhodesia and Kenya

*Bill Mulcahy captain of the British and Irish Lions v Western Transvaal Potchefstroom, South Africa 2/6/1962*

1962 South Africa, Rhodesia and Kenya

With 16,000 spectators watching on, Western Transvaal scored first from a line out 25 yards out; a nice passing move put Putter through and he scored in the corner. There was an immediate response from Lions. A deep kick off from Waddell was picked up by Cowan who scored. The sides were level at the break.

As the game progressed, things remained tight. Seventeen minutes into the half Ken Jones completed the best passing move of the game, scoring in the corner. Not long after that Waddell scored a drop goal giving the Lions a good lead. Transvaal got a late penalty but it wasn't enough and Bill Mulcahy had won his first game as Lions captain.

After the game, the team flew down to Cape Town for the next game.

*Game Four*
*v Southern University*
*Newlands, Cape Town, South Africa 6/6/1962*
*14 – 11 – Win*

**Lions Team** – Wilcox (England), Smith (Scotland). Dee (England), Weston (England), Cowan (Scotland), Sharp (England), Jeeps (England), Jones (Wales), Millar (Ireland), Wright (England), **Mulcahy (Ireland)**, Campbell-Lamerton (Scotland), Morgan (Wales), Pask (Wales), Rogers (England)

In a reminder to the squad of where they were travelling, Lions squad member David Nash from Wales was taken to hospital before the game with an infection. He had suffered a toe injury in the previous game and the toe became infected. He developed septicaemia. He was up all night with a fever and his roommate, Sharp had to nurse him through the night. Telegrams were sent to his wife to assure her that he was ok but in fact he had been seriously unwell. He spent a few days in hospital before being sent to a nursing home where he spent four weeks recovering before he was forced to go home early.

1962 South Africa, Rhodesia and Kenya

In front of 25,000 spectators the Lions took time to settle in this game before grinding out a win scoring three tries and a penalty two tries and a penalty.

With regular hooker Meredith out injured, Syd Millar who was normally a prop, filled in at hooker. The big strong forwards of the Southern University team took it to Lions in the first half and forced errors. University scored first. After a poor pass from Sharp the ball came to Gillies who scored for the University. Another poor pass from Sharp led to their second try at thirty-four minutes. This time his pass was intercepted by Slabbert who scored. The Lions were down by eleven points at the break.

After the break, the Lions came into the game. Mulcahy, Campbell-Lamerton and Millar slowly gave the Lions pack the upper hand and the Lions played some dazzling running rugby. It took just four minutes of the second half for Smith to score a try in the corner. A few minutes later, Sharp scored a penalty and the Lions started to settle. It stayed tight for a lot of the second half but with ten minutes to go Dee scored for the Lions and Smith's conversion gave the win to the Lions.

*Game Five*
*v Boland*
*Boland Stadium, Wellington, South Africa 9/6/1962*
*25 – 8 - Win*

**Lions Team** – Kiernan (Ireland), Brophy (Ireland), Hewitt (Ireland), Weston (England), Smith (Scotland), Sharp (England), O'Connor (Wales), Millar (Ireland), Meredith (Wales), Jones (Wales), **Mulcahy (Ireland),** Rowland (Wales), Pask (Wales), Campbell-Lamerton (Scotland), Rogers (England)

On a warm but cloudy day in Wellington the Lions carved out a good win. Early in the game Brophy was awarded a penalty after he was obstructed following a move by Sharp and Hewitt. Smith Kicked the penalty to put the Lions ahead. After twenty-three minutes Du Toi caught from a high kick and Pierre van Der Merwe scored. The score was converted by Koch. Almost immediately from the ensuing kick-off, full back Steenkamp kicked wildly and the kick was caught by Pask who put the Lions back in front with a try. The conversion was missed by Smith though. Late in the first half a penalty against Meredith gave

1962 South Africa, Rhodesia and Kenya

Boland an easy score but just before half time Weston broke and ran thirty yards before passing to Brophy to score in the corner. Half time 11-8.

Hewitt tore a hamstring at the end of the first half. He had previously pulled it during the Five Nations in the game away in Paris. In the second half the Lions played with 14 men because Hewitt was off injured. Wayward kicking could have cost them as the Lions missed five conversions and several penalty kicks. As the half got going the Lions pack took control. Front row of Millar, Meredith and Jones were outstanding and in the second role Rowlands and Mulcahy did well. The experiment of playing Campbell-Lamerton at number eight was also a success. In the end, the Lions ran out comfortable winners despite having fewer men on the field.

*Bill Mulcahy leaps in the line out during the 1962 Lions tour*

*Game Six*
*v South West Africa*
*South West Stadium, Windhoek, Namibia 12/6/1962*
*14 – 6 - Win*

1962 South Africa, Rhodesia and Kenya

Lions Team – Wilcox (England), Brophy (Ireland), Dee (England), Weston (England), Hunter (Ireland), Waddell (Scotland), Jeeps (England), Rollo (Wales), Godwin (England), Wright (England), Pask (Wales), McBride (Ireland), Rowland (Wales), Campbell-Lamerton (Scotland), Morgan (Wales)

It hadn't rained in Windhoek for three years so the Lions were playing on an extremely hard and dry field. Going into this game the Lions were strong favourites but the hard work of the South West African forwards dominated the Lions up front and gave the Lions backs no room to move. Lions were down 6-3 at half time and were fortunate to win. This game was, in hindsight, most notable as it was the first appearance of Willie John McBride, arguably the most famous Lion of all time.

*Game Seven*
*v Northern Transvaal*
*Loftus Versfeld, Pretoria, South Africa 12/6/1962*
*6 - 14 – Loss*

Lions Team – Kiernan (Ireland), Smith (Scotland), Jones (Wales), Weston (England), Brophy (Ireland), Sharp (England), Jeeps (England), Millar (Ireland), Meredith (Wales), Jones (Wales), Rowlands (Wales), **Mulcahy (Ireland),** Rogers (England), Campbell-Lamerton (Scotland), Pask (Wales)

A week out from the first test and the Lions fielded what was viewed as their probable test XV. The game was most notable by an incident that happened in the first five minutes. Sharp at out-half was hammered by Springbok back François du Toit 'Mannetjies' Roux. A clear tactic to weaken the Lions a week later. Sharp left the field on a stretcher unconscious.

Weston moved to fly half, Pask played on the left wing and the Lions played down a man in the pack for almost the entire game which was never an easy task especially against a South African team.

The score was held at six nil at half time. The Lions put up a brave fight but they were up against it as they were down a man. In the end, they succumbed their first defeat of the tour.

1962 South Africa, Rhodesia and Kenya

After the game there was uproar about what had happened to Sharp. Lions' management and the press all heavily criticised Roux for his dangerous play. There was an expectation that he might be dropped from the test team for the following week but in the end the Springboks selected him.

*"We played Northern Transvaal the week before the First Test and there was some debate about whether Richard Sharp should be played or not because he was the golden boy at fly-half; a lot of the South African who were well disposed to us and looked after us said 'Don't play Sharp in this match, don't play him'. We played him. What we said to him was, 'Don't attempt anything for the first 15-20 minutes, just move it on'. We thought their fellas would want to put a stamp on him and, usually, if that kind of thing doesn't get done early it probably doesn't get done at all. The games settled down, but then, unfortunately, Sharp was going openside and then changed his mind and came on the short side and he met Mannetjies Roux who hit him high and caused a depressed fracture to his jaw. That was our golden boy gone for a while."*.

Bill Mulcahy

*Game Eight*
*v South Africa (First Test)*
*Ellis Park, Johannesburg, South Africa 23/6/1962*
*3 – 3 - Draw*

**Lions Team** – Wilcox (England), Brophy (Ireland), Jones (Wales), Weston (England), Smith (Scotland), Waddell (Scotland), Jeeps (England), Millar (Ireland), Meredith (Wales), Jones (Wales), Rowlands (Wales), **Mulcahy (Ireland)**, Pask (Wales), Campbell-Lamerton (Scotland), Rogers (England)

Ahead of the test, Lions Manager Commander Brian Vaughan said *"We're not favoured so if we lose nobody's going to mind very much. But if we win, a lot of people are going to be surprised – so be prepared to be surprised"*.

*"Rugby is a game in which you must play to strengths – be it up front or in backs. I have a sneaking suspicion we have quite some strengths up front and we're not here to play basketball"*, he added.

1962 South Africa, Rhodesia and Kenya

South Africa went into the test as firm favourites. The game had been a sell out for a few weeks with 75,000 attendees on a bright sunny day. In the ninth minute the springboks gave away a penalty on their twenty-five-yard line. Weston took the kick at goal but missed badly. A few minutes before half time the springboks scored. In a slap in the face to the Lions, it was Roux who had inflicted such an injury on Sharp a week earlier, who started a move that ended with Springbok centre Johnny Gainsford decisively run to score in the corner.

At the end of the first half, the Lions trailed 3-nil. There was a huge battle up front through the second half. Neither pack got the better of the other. There was no further score through most of the second half but then with ten minutes to go the Lions scored. Ken Jones, Welsh centre, scored with a run from sixty yards. Arthur Smith missed the conversion which would have won the game for the Lions. The game finished three points each.

In this game, scrum-half Dickie Jeeps became the first player to appear in test matches on three Lions tours.

Ahead of the game, the South African Rugby union arranged for the wives and mothers of each of the players to receive a bouquet of flowers on the Monday after the test. A goodwill gesture they said.

278

1962 South Africa, Rhodesia and Kenya

Despite having drawn the test game, there was a great celebration in the Lions camp after the game. The Springboks had been firm favourites so it was a moral victory for the tourists. The team went first to have some drinks at Ellis Park Glasshouse and from there they went to Wanderers Club for dinner. Mannetjies Roux, the Springbok who had so badly injured Sharp was there and as is the case most of the time with rugby, what happens on the field stayed there. There was great camaraderie and they shared a drink and the party went on into the early hours.

*Game Nine*
*v Natal*
*Kings Park, Durban, South Africa 27/6/1962*
*13 - 3 - Win*

**Lions Team** – Wilcox (England), Smith (Scotland), Jones (Wales), Dee (England), Bebb (Wales), Waddell (Scotland), O'Connor (Wales), Wright (England), Godwin (England), Rollo (Wales), McBride (Ireland), **Mulcahy (Ireland)**, Rogers (England), Douglas (Scotland), Morgan (Wales)

Durban was hot and sticky. Luckily the team's hotel was right on the beach so they had the chance to cool off a few times a day. They also visited a snake park just near the hotel.

Territorially, Natal had the better of this game. The Lions were forced to do some superb defending. The crowd got a little annoyed as they came looking for attacking rugby but were instead met with a Lions team having to kick to touch to relieve pressure.

The Lions went ahead with a try after twenty-five minutes. Weston kicked ahead from a scrum and Jones dove over the line and onto the ball. Weston converted successfully. Half time, 5-nil to the Lions.

In the second half Smith kicked a penalty to put the Lions 8-0 up. Then Bebb, playing his second game of the tour after coming back from a hamstring injury, scored the second try. Natal got a late consolation penalty. The score board flattered the Lions.

At the final whistle the teams were engulfed by fans and were applauded from the field by spectators who were ecstatic with the game they had witnessed. The after-game formalities were held at the Durban Country Club with a reception and dance described as 'the nicest of the tour'.

*Game Ten*
*v Eastern Province*
*Boet Erasmus, Port Elizabeth, South Africa 30/6/1962*
*21 – 6 – Win*

**Lions Team** – Wilcox (England), Dee (England), Jones (Wales), Hunter (Ireland), Waddell (Scotland), O'Connor (Wales), Millar (Ireland), Meredith (Wales), Rollo (Scotland), **Mulcahy (Ireland),** Rowlands (Wales), Douglas (Scotland), Morgan (Wales), Brown (England), Campbell-Lamerton (Scotland)

Bill Mulcahy was not scheduled to play in this game when the teams were announced. Mike Campbell-Lamerton had to pull out of the game with the flu and so at the last minute, Mulcahy was added to the team.

A crowd of 22,000 saw the home side take the lead with Wentzel dropped a goal from the centre of the field in the middle of the Lions' half. They continued to have an advantage for the first twenty minutes. After twenty minutes, Pask scored for the Lions and that turned the tide.

After twenty-six minutes du Toit injured his shoulder and had to leave the field giving the Lions a man advantage for the rest of the game.

After seven minutes of the second half, Eastern Province were penalised at the scrum and Wilcox kicked a penalty. He kicked another shortly afterwards and the Lions started to pull away. Morgan scored a try to make it 16-3. That was followed by a try from Douglas and the Lions were out of reach.

The Lions had enjoyed their stay in Port Elizabeth. The local fruit exporter sent each team member a box of fruit to enjoy and the Eastern Province Rugby Union presented each of them with a Springbok hide.

1962 South Africa, Rhodesia and Kenya

*Game Eleven*
*v Orange Free State*
*Free State Stadium, Bloemfontein, South Africa 4/7/1962*
*14 - 14 - Draw*

**Lions Team** – Wilcox (England), Smith (Scotland), Dee (England), Brown (England), Hunter (Ireland), Waddell (Scotland), Jeeps (England), Wright (England), Godwin (England), Jones (Scotland), McBride (Ireland), Campbell-Lamerton (Scotland), Pask (Wales), Douglas (Scotland), Morgan (Wales).

Ahead of this game Hodgson and Nash were sent home with neither of them recovered enough to have any chance of playing again on the tour.

30,000 attended this game which was one of the most exciting of the tour. The Lions led 6-3 at half time and then moved 9-3 clear with just fifteen minutes to go. Orange Free State then came storming back into the game and took the lead 14-9. It was only a Morgan try in the last seconds of the game that allowed the Lions to snatch a draw.

While in Bloemfontein, some of the players visited the local zoo where a game keeper introduced them to a fourteen-month-old Lion cub. The playful cub gave John Douglas a 'clout' on the arm, ripping his jumper. The Lions made light of it saying that it had been the most dangerous part of the tour so far.

*Game Twelve*
*v Junior Springboks*
*Loftus Versfeld, Pretoria, South Africa 7/7/1962*
*16 - 11 Win*

**Lions Team** – Kiernan (Ireland), Cowan (Scotland), Brown (England), Weston, Bebb (Wales), Jones (Wales), Jeeps (England), Campbell-Lamerton (Scotland), Douglas (Scotland), Rowlands (Wales), **Mulcahy (Ireland) Captain**, Morgan (Wales), Rollo (Wales), Goodwin (England), Millar (Ireland)

At the half way stage of the tour, this was another proud day for Limerick when Bill Mulcahy again captained the British and Irish Lions team as they played the Junior Springboks.

With 35,000 onlooking, the Junior Springboks had the better of the first half. After 17 minutes the Junior Springboks when ahead when Jones mishandled on his own line and Labuschagne was quick to grab the ball and score. Labuschagne scored again ten minutes later from a line out move. Both tries were unconverted.

After twenty-six minutes, Cowen chased an upfield kick and collided with the opposition full back Pretorius. He got up with a clearly broken nose. With no medical staff traveling with the team, it was left to Bill Mulcahy to put his nose back in place. He left the field for a few moments to wash the blood away but he played on. The Lions fought back and won a penalty before half time that Mike Weston put over to make the score 6-3 at half time.

Early in the second half, Kiernan slipped and let the ball loose. Holtzhausen was quick to capitalise and scored a third try for the Springboks. Mulcahy, playing his captain's role, moved Weston to flyhalf and that improved the effectiveness of the Lions attack. Morgan scored for the Lions. That was followed by the try of the game. Jones intercepted a loose pass and ran thirty yards to score under the posts. With eight minutes remaining, Kiernan made amends for his earlier error by scoring a 40-yard drop goal. Bill Mulcahy had again captained the Lions to victory.

On the Friday before the game, the team were at the Pretoria Country Club where a civilised game of bowls was played. Bill Mulcahy was heard to say *"there is less bad language in this game than golf"*.

*Game Thirteen*
*v Combined Services*
*Olen Park, Potchefstroom, South Africa 11/7/1962*
*20 – 6 - Win*

**Lions Team** – Wilcox (England), Bebb (Wales), Weston (England), Hunter (Ireland), Cowan (Scotland), Waddell (Scotland), Jeeps (England), Millar (Ireland), Meredith (Wales), Jones (Wales), Rowlands (Wales), **Mulcahy (Ireland) Captain,** Pask (Wales), Campbell-Lamerton (Scotland), Morgan (Wales)

In the absence of tour captain, Arthur Smith, Bill Mulcahy again had the honour of leading the Lions in this famous match. The game was

1962 South Africa, Rhodesia and Kenya

spoiled by rough tactics from the African side and has since become known as the "Battle of Potchefstroom". There was a flurry of late tackles and fisticuffs throughout the game and the referee should have taken greater care of the spectacle.

15,000 spectators watched as the Lions took a 14-3 lead at half time. Combined Services played most of the second half with a man down after fullback Oliver went off injured after a tackle from Hunter.

The Lions' points came from Weston, Bebb, Waddell and Wilcox.

ROUGH RUGBY — Players scuffle during one of the incidents that marked rugby match between the touring British Lions and the South American Combined Services at gets a blow from J. van der Wall, while in foreground, Mike Campbell-Lamerton of the Lions gets his hands around the neck of J. Swart of the Combined Services. The

*A photo that ran in newspapers around the world after the game*

The headlines the following day say it all:

    *"Lions Slay Punch-Mad Services"* – Daily Express

    *"Rugby Savagery"* – Daily Herald

1962 South Africa, Rhodesia and Kenya

*"The Lions wisely kept their heads under the leadership of Mulcahy and well deserved their victory in the roughest match of the tour"* - Western Mail

The Rand Daily Mail editorial called this match, *"Rugby at its worst and a deplorable display all around. Our own reporter blamed the Combined Services for obviously adopting tactics designed to intimidate and bulldoze their opponents and in this view, he is amply supported by other observers".*

*"We had an infamous game in Potchefstroom against the Combined Services and it was like another test match. It was very nasty. I think Roux played in that one as well. Lots of fisticuffs on either side. The guy coaching them was the same guy who coached Northern Transvaal. He seemed to have a certain ethos about how the opposition should be treated. Mayhem. Fists flying, boots flying. It was dangerous. The crowd were baying for blood".*

Bill Mulcahy

*"The battle of Potchefstroom they called it. They had everyone in a uniform – postmen, army, airforce – they took them into a camp about two weeks before the game and one of them told me they started off saying 'These people (The Lions), their great-great-grandfathers put your people into concentration camps in the Boer War. So, they came on the field and Keith Rowlands was our biggest forward, got the ball from the kick-off and his feet didn't touch the bloody ground until he was about 10 metres from our line. Mad. This went on the whole bloody game and the referee let them get on with it. It was an all-Afrikaans crowd. My opposite number was puling me in the scrum so I smacked him. The referee said to me, 'Millar, you do that again, you're off'. I said, 'Well, if you don't look after me, I'm going to look after me'. I said to Wigs (Bill Mulcahy), 'Next Scrum, you smack him'. I went up and Wigs put his fist through. Bang! Hit me right on the bloody nose. And the referee said, 'Penalty to the Lions!'. There was digging, raking, late tackling. It was an horrendous scene. We never played them again. Our press were terribly critical and the South African press were critical, saying 'This can't happen again'. But at the end of the day, their objective was to win the Test series and they would do these things".*

Syd Millar

*"Rugby football is a game, not organised warfare".*

Bill Mulcahy

The team flew from Potchefstroom down to Cape Town for the next game and on the way were treated to some 'rebel songs' being sung over the plane's speaker system by Bill Mulcahy and Niall Brophy. At this stage in the tour, they were on good terms with the Ulster and English players so could push the boundary a little.

*Game Fourteen*
*v Western Province*
*Newlands, Cape Town, South Africa 14/7/1962*
*21 – 13 - Win*

**Lions Team** – Wilcox (England), Bebb (Wales), Weston (England), Jones (Wales), Smith (Scotland), Waddell (Scotland), Jeeps (England), Millar (Ireland), Meredith (Wales), Jones (Wales), Rowlands (Wales), **Mulcahy (Ireland)**, Pask (Wales), Campbell-Lamerton (Scotland), Morgan (Wales)

*A shot from the stands of the Western Province game*

The Lions went ahead 8-3 at half time but got a fright when Western Province came back into the game and went ahead 13-8 with eight minutes to go. It spurred them into action. Welshman Pask scored and then Jones and Morgan both scored in quick succession. Meredith and

1962 South Africa, Rhodesia and Kenya

Morgan scored late tries as the Lions pulled away. One of the best games of the tour so far.

*Mulcahy (headband) watches on as Rowlands breaks against Western Province*

*Game Fifteen*
*v South West Districts*
*George, Western Cape, South Africa 17/7/1962*
*11 - 3 – Win*

**Lions Team** – Kiernan (Ireland), Dee (England), Brown (England), Hunter (Ireland), Waddell (Scotland), O'Connor (Wales), Wright (England), Godwin (England), Rollo (Wales), McBride (Ireland), Campbell-Lamerton (Scotland), Rogers (England), Douglas (Scotland), Davidge (Wales)

Without Mulcahy and most of the test starters, this game was a lot more difficult than it needed to be. There was no score at all in the first half. In the second half the Lions scored two tries. The first, just after half time, was scored by Dee after a long pass out to him. Brown scored the second late in the game. The South West Districts team missed eight goal kicks and the Lions missed five. The Lions were lucky to come away with a win.

1962 South Africa, Rhodesia and Kenya

*Game Sixteen*
*v South Africa (Second Test)*
*Kings Park, Durban, South Africa 21/7/1962*
*0 – 3 – Loss*

**Lions Team** – Wilcox (England), Smith (Scotland), Jones (Wales), Weston (England), Bebb (Wales), Waddell (Scotland), Jeeps (England), Millar (Ireland), Meredith (Wales), Jones (Wales), **Mulcahy (Ireland)**, Rowlands (Wales), Pask (Wales), Campbell-Lamberton (Scotland), Morgan (Wales)

**South Africa Team** – Wilson, Engelbrecht, Gainsford, Wyness, Roux, Oxlee, de Villiers, Malan, Kuhn, Bezuidenhout, Botha, Claassen, du Preez, Schmidt, Hopwood

High drama at Durban in the second test match. Going into the game the Lions were seen as slight favourites. The game was a bit of a stalemate. Neither team established superiority in the big forward battle.

Both teams missed chances, Lions' Wilcox missed three reasonable penalty chances and both Waddell and Weston missed drop goal attempts. Keith Oxlee scored the only penalty of the game for the Springboks with just five minutes to go.

At the end it looked like the Lions had at least equalised. They were awarded a scrum on the Springbok line. In a move off the training field, Bill Mulcahy called for the Lions to wheel the scrum and Keith Rowlands dove to claim a score. It looked like a perfectly good try.

However, referee Ken Carlsen didn't blow his whistle for a score. Instead, he awarded a five-yard scrum to the Lions, claiming that he was unsighted so couldn't award a try. As soon as the game restarted, he blew the final whistle robbing the Lions of an important result.

*"We had a big heavy pack and, remarkably it might seem to a lot of people, we hooshed them over their own try line. The press photographers with*

1962 South Africa, Rhodesia and Kenya

*their zoom lenses had the clearest picture of the pack and the ball over the white line and then the ref found a reason not to give it."*
Bill Mulcahy

*The Lions celebrate the try that wasn't given in the 2nd Test*

## 'TRY' DECISION SHOCK FOR LIONS

### Referee disallows last-minute effort

**Springboks chairman is 'not satisfied'**

1962 South Africa, Rhodesia and Kenya

After the game there was the usual cocktail party at the Durban Country Club. All thirty-three Lions were there but only three of the Springbok players made an appearance. The Lions had been slighted twice in the space of a few hours.

*Game Seventeen*
*v Northern Universities*
*PAM Brink, Springs, South Africa 25/7/1962*
*6 - 6 – Draw*

**Lions Team** – Kiernan (Ireland), Bebb (Wales), Jones (Wales), Weston (England), Smith (Scotland), Sharp (England), Jeeps (England), Millar (Ireland), Meredith (Wales), Rollo (Wales), **Mulcahy (Ireland)**, McBride (Ireland), Rogers (England), Campbell-Lamerton (Scotland), Pask (Wales)

Controversy reigned over a try awarded to the Lions when Hewitt appeared not to properly ground the ball over the line when he went to score. A try was awarded nonetheless. Richard Sharp scored a penalty in his first game back after he was hammered again by Roux before the First Test a month earlier.

The Lions were slated in the South African press after this game. *"Lions most inept display of tour"*, said the Rand Daily Mail headline. *"You cannot really call the match anything else than inept for the Lions as they missed several sitters. The trouble in the Lions back line started with Richard Sharp, the blond flyhalf playing his first match since he broke a cheekbone a month ago. He was hesitant from the kick-off and his lack of confidence seemed to spark a chain reaction"*.

*Game Eighteen*
*v Transvaal*
*Ellis Park, Johannesburg, South Africa 28/7/1962*
*24 – 3 - Win*

**Lions Team** – Kiernan (Ireland), Bebb (Wales), Jones (Wales), Weston (England), Smith (Scotland), Sharp (England), Jeeps (England), Millar (Ireland), Meredith (Wales), Rollo (Wales), **Mulcahy (Ireland),** McBride (Ireland), Rogers (England), Campbell-Lamerton (Scotland), Pask (Wales)

An important win for the Lions ahead of the third test. 55,000 people turned out in perfect weather to see the Lions trounce a Transvaal team featuring five Springbok players.

Sharp who had played poorly in the previous match (his second since returning from injury) was in fine form scoring fifteen points in an impressive display. He scored a drop-goal, two penalties and he also converted the three tries which came from Bill Mulcahy and two from Smith. The Mulcahy try came after the Transvaal team won a scrum but were spoiled by Jeeps. Pask picked up the ball and threw a pass out the line bypassing Rollo. When it got to Mulcahy, he still had twenty yards to cover to get over the line. He made it over to score his first try of the tour.

The team celebrated the victory and Mulcahy's try with a sing-song into the early morning at the local Wanderers' club.

*Game Nineteen*
*v South Africa (Third Test)*
*Newlands, Cape Town, South Africa 4/8/1962*
*3 – 8 - Loss*

**Lions Team** – Kiernan (Ireland), Smith (Scotland), Jones (Wales), Weston (England), Bebb (Wales), Sharp (England), Jeeps (England), Millar (Ireland), Meredith (Wales), Jones (Wales), **Mulcahy (Ireland)**, McBride (Ireland), Morgan (Wales), Campbell-Lamerton (Scotland), Pask (Wales)

**South Africa** – Wilson, Engelbrecht, Gainsford, Wyness, Roux, Oxlee, De Villiers, Kuhn, Malan, De Bezuidenhoudt, Botha, Claassen, De Preez, Van Zyl, Hopwood

Rain in the build-up was thought to have tilted the balance towards the Lions. The pitch was muddy. The game was a sell out with 55,000 tickets sold. Another 5,000 spectators were unable to get into the ground which led to disturbances outside the ground. Police used batons when 'coloured spectators twice stormed the gate'. In ugly scenes twenty-three spectators were injured.

This was Willie John McBride's Test debut and he was paired in the second row with Bill Mulcahy. McBride's had a recollection of a pre-

1962 South Africa, Rhodesia and Kenya

match encounter with Springbok prop Mof Myburgh. McBride commented on the muddy conditions and the lack of grass on the pitch. *'I didn't come here to fucking graze'* was Myburgh's intimidating reply.

Another forward dominated head-to-head and the two packs battered each other up front. In the loose, springboks had an edge.

Sharp missed a penalty mid-way through the first half but the Lions took the lead after twenty-seven minutes. Sharp drop goal after a line out. This was their first time to be ahead in any of the tests. Welshman Bebb went off in the first half with a busted lip but returned shortly afterwards having received six stitches. Oxlee levelled the scores just before half time and they went into the break locked at 3-3

Over 100 police had to manage the coloured end behind the goal as they were climbing the fence and coming onto the field. On the field, Oxlee missed a penalty early in the second half but scored another after Meredith was caught offside just inside his own half.

Oxlee scored a try eight minutes from the final whistle. He picked up a loose ball after Sharp had tried to run at the Springbok line, and scored an easy try. He also converted it to beat the Lions and wrap up the test series.

## Death Mars Lions Match — Coloured Spectators Hurt

Twenty-three coloured spectators were injured and a white man died of a heart attack during disturbances at Newlands Grounds, Cape Town, to-day, when the British Lions Rugby team met South Africa in the third international game of the series.

Police used batons when coloured spectators twice stormed gates to the packed

Ken Jones made touch inside the Springboks' 25. Jeeps caught De Villiers

and the Lions might have gone ahead following a fine run. But the movement broke down when Bebb failed to pass to Meredith, who was outside him.

**WENT IN FRONT**

1962 South Africa, Rhodesia and Kenya

*Game Twenty*
*v North Eastern Districts*
*Danie Craven, Stellenbosch, South Africa 8/8/1962*
**34 – 8 - Win**

**Lions Team** – Wilcox (England), Brophy (Ireland), Hewitt (Ireland), Brown (England), Cowan (Scotland), Waddell (England), O'Connor (Wales), Jones (Wales), Godwin (England), Rollo (Wales), Rowlands (Wales), McBride (Ireland), Morgan (Wales), Douglas (Scotland), Davidge (Wales)

Most of the test players were rested for this game which was a very one-sided affair. The Lions were up 16-5 at half time and pulled away in the second half. The Lions threw away chances but won easily. The newspapers say they should have scored fifty points.

*Game Twenty-One*
*v Border*
*Buffalo City, East London, South Africa 11/8/1962*
**5 – 0 – Win**

**Lions Team** – Kiernan (Ireland), Smith (Scotland), Hewitt (Ireland), Dee (England), Hunter (Ireland), Sharp (England), Jeeps (England), Wright (England), Meredith (Wales), Millar (Ireland), **Mulcahy (Ireland)**, Rowlands (Wales), Morgan (Wales), Campbell-Lamerton (Scotland), Douglas (Scotland)

18,000 watched in ideal conditions as the Lions ground out a win against Border. Despite the Lions' weight advantage up front, Border had the better of the opening stages.

Millar scored just before half time after a move from a lineout. Campbell-Lamerton and Douglas providing neat passing to get the ball to him. Sharp converted.

*Game Twenty-Three*
*v Central University*
*Boet Erasmus, Port Elizabeth, South Africa 15/8/1962*
**14 – 6 – Win**

1962 South Africa, Rhodesia and Kenya

**Lions Team** – Wilcox (England), Bebb (Wales), Weston (England), Dee (England), Cowan (Scotland), Sharp (England), O'Connor (Wales), Jones (Wales), Rollo (Wales), Rowlands (Wales), McBride (Ireland), Hunter (Ireland), Campbell-Lamerton (Scotland), Millar (Ireland)

Ahead of this game John Douglas left the squad to fly home to be with his seriously ill father. He was the third to go home after Stan Hodgson and David Nash. Douglas was to play in the game against Central University but Millar took his place.

In front of a crowd of 15,000 the Lions took a 6-0 half time lead with two penalty goals. This was one of their better performances of the tour despite the fact that they had only one fit backrow forward (Campbell-Lamerton). Dee left the field in the second half due to injury. Irishman Hunter scored a try midway through the second half.

*Game Twenty-Four*
*v Eastern Transvaal*
*PAM Brink, Springs, South Africa 18/8/1962*
*16 – 19 – Loss*

**Lions Team** – Kiernan (Ireland), Smith (Scotland), Hewitt (Ireland), Jones (Wales), Cowan (Scotland), Waddell (England), Jeeps (England), Jones (Wales), Meredith (Wales), Rollo (Wales), **Mulcahy (Ireland)**, Rowlands (Wales), Morgan (Wales), Campbell-Lamerton (Scotland), Rogers (England)

This was the last game before the final test and a loss did nothing for the Lions' confidence going into that game.

Ken Jones scored five mins into the first half. His try was converted by Jeeps but two minutes later Labuschagne scored a try and then Eastern Transvaal took the lead when Riley scored another. After twenty-six minutes, Ken Jones broke well and passed to Bill Mulcahy. Mulcahy made a run for the line but was tackled just short of it. Somehow, he managed to get the ball to Rogers who crossed to score. Again, Jeeps converted.

Fifteen minutes into the second half Cowan scored and the Lions looked to be in control but the long tour took its toll and they faded as the half went on. Jacobsohn got a try back from Eastern Transvaal.

Buitendag scored a penalty and then in the last minute Labuschagne scored his second try, winning the game.

**Game Twenty-Five**
**v South Africa (Fourth Test)**
**Free State Stadium, Bloemfontein, South Africa 25/8/1962**
**14 – 34 - Loss**

**Lions Team** – Wilcox (England), Brophy (Ireland), Hewitt (Ireland), Weston, Cowan, Sharp, Jeeps (England), Millar (Ireland), Meredith (Wales), Jones (Wales), Rowlands (Wales), McBride (Ireland), Rogers (England), Campbell-Lamerton (Scotland), **Mulcahy (Ireland)**

**South Africa Team** – Wilson, Englebrecht, Wyness, Gainsford, Roux, Oxlee, Uys, Juhn, Hill, Bezuidenhout, Botha, Claassen, du Preez, Van Zyl, Hopwood

The fourth Test in Bloemfontein was an anti-climax, the Lions going down fighting but ultimately well beaten by 34-14. Unlike the other tests this one was more open and freer flowing and the 65,000 spectators got a great show.

The Lions missed two early penalties; one from Wilcox and the other from Hewitt. After sixteen minutes the Lions went ahead with a penalty from Wilcox after the Springboks were penalised in a maul just fifteen yards out. Two minutes later the Springboks took the lead. Wyness scored after a break from Gainsford. Oxlee converted to make it 5-3. They then scored a second try with Roux at the end of the move. In the blink of an eye the Springboks were up 10-3. Scotsman Cowan scored a try for the Lions after twenty-six minutes to pull it back to 10-6 at half time.

With a strong breeze at their backs, the springboks started quickly in the second half and scored after just two minutes with centre Gainsford scoring in the corner. Rowlands got one back for the Lions, picking up a ball and thundering through three springbok tackles. Oxlee scored a penalty after 15 mins. Then in a blitz the Springboks scored thirteen points in six minutes with Classen scored two great tries. Campbell-Lamerton got one back for the Lions but the game was gone.

1962 South Africa, Rhodesia and Kenya

*Game Twenty-Six*
*v East Africa*
*RFUEA Ground, Nairobi, Kenya 28/8/1962*
*50 – 0 - Win*

**Lions Team** – Kiernan (Ireland), Smith (Scotland), Dee (England), Jones (Wales), Bebb (Wales), Waddell (England), O'Connor (Wales), Jones (Wales), Godwin (England), Rollo (Wales), Rowlands (Wales), McBride (Ireland), Morgan (Wales), Campbell-Lamerton (Scotland), Hunter (Ireland)

There was talk that this game should be cancelled because the Lions players were tired and homesick. In the end it went ahead.

## Tour Reflections

Technical trouble with their comet aircraft delayed the squad for twelve hours in Nairobi on their way home.

> *"We didn't have the same depth of talent in the back division that we had three years previously. We had a big heavy pack in 1962 but not the talent of 1959. I ended up on the blindside flank in the last Test because we were running out of players through injury."*
>
> Bill Mulcahy

*"In 1959 the difference between the Lions and the All-Blacks had been Don Clarke's boot. In 1962, it was also a very close series; we had good forwards but we lost Sharp and others in the backs and that determined the way we played afterwards. It was not to our advantage, I would say. The Springbok backs turned out to be more adventurous than ours, and that was not what you would have expected."*
Syd Millar

*"I don't think the 1962 side was particularly good, and certainly not as good as the 1955 team. We had some good forwards and a couple of good backs, but it wasn't a side that stamped its authority at all. You have got to have a couple of really hard forwards who take some responsibility when they go on the field, and we didn't have that in 1962."*
Bryn Meredith

*"We played good, clean rugby and so did South Africa. I am very pleased with the tour. As for the tests, I don't think south Africa fielded a team that was any better than us. They were on their home grounds with their home crowds and that is worth five points in any match."*
Brian Vaughan – Tour Manager

# 1980
# South Africa

## Colm Tucker
## Tony Ward

# Colm Tucker
# Lion #568

**Colm Tucker**
Born - 22 September 1952, Limerick

School – St Munchin's College
Club – Shannon
Ireland Caps - 4
Lions Tour(s) - 1980
Lions Appearances - 9
Lions Tests – 2
Position - Flanker

If club rugby is a barometer of success, then Colm Tucker was a champion amongst champions. For forty years he was a Shannon RFC man and in an astonishing eleven-year spell, he won five Munster Senior Cups and was runner up three times. Tucker was also one of the greats of '78 that beat the All-Blacks at Thomond Park and he took down a second major touring side when he was on the Munster team that defeated Australia in 1981. Despite this, his Irish opportunity was limited by rugby politics but the Lions saw enough to pick him for the 1980 tour to South Africa. On that tour he made nine appearances, including in two of the test matches.

## Early Life

Colm Tucker was born on 22$^{nd}$ September 1952. He was one of seven children born to Christopher Tucker, a dock worker, and his wife Bridget Bennis. Colm was the youngest of the family and had five older brothers and a sister. Christopher Tucker's father Patrick was also a dock worker and the family came from Curry Lane in Limerick city, close to the docks.

## School

Colm Tucker was educated at St Munchin's College, Corbally. While he played rugby with the school, St Munchin's had no notable success during the years he attended.

## Club Rugby

### Richmond

Colm Tucker's first club was Richmond with whom he played the Enright Cup (Under sixteen) in 1968/69. His Richmond team won the cup that year, beating Thomond in the final 8-0. In the final itself, Tucker scored a try and converted it himself. The other Richmond try was scored by their captain Paul McNamara.

Colm Tucker

## St Mary's

After one season at Richmond, Colm moved to St Mary's for the 1969/70 season and won the Juvenile Cup and the Juvenile League (Under eighteen) that year.

*Tucker (standing 5th from right) on the 1969/70 St Mary's Team*

## Shannon

Colm Tucker joined Shannon in 1971 and, despite still being a teenager, he quickly forced his way into their senior team.

Alongside Brendan Foley and **Gerry McLoughlin**, Tucker was instrumental in transforming Shannon's reputation from an also-ran into one of Munster's strongest rugby clubs. Shannon had won just one Munster Senior Cup in its ninety-year history when Tucker started playing for them. That one had been won in the 1959/60 season.

*A Decade of Success in the Munster Senior Cup*

Over an astounding ten-year period, Shannon won six Munster Senior Cups and were runners up on three other occasions. Colm played on five of those teams and would have played more if it weren't for a serious knee injury that kept him off the field for almost three years.

       1976-77 Winners - Shannon beat Garryowen
       1977-78 Winners - Shannon beat Garryowen

Colm Tucker

1978-79 – Lost to Garryowen in Semi-Final
1979-80 – Lost to Bohs in 2nd Round
1980-81 Runners Up - Shannon lose to UCC
1981-82 Winners - Shannon beat Young Munster
1982-83 Runners Up - Shannon lose to Cork Con
1983-84 – Lost to Young Munster in Semi-Final
1984-85 Runners Up - Shannon lose to Cork Con
1985-86 Winners - Shannon beat Garryowen
1986-87 Winners - Shannon beat Highfield
1987-88 Winners - Shannon beat Garryowen

Colm Tucker was also on the Shannon team that won the Munster Senior League in 1981, Munster Charity Cup in 1974 and 1979 and the Castle Trophy in 1981. He was also the captain of the Shannon in 1983/83 when they reached the final of both the Munster Senior Cup and the Munster Senior League.

*Tucker (seated 2nd left) on the 1973/74 Shannon team that won the Limerick Charity Cup and the Sean O'Carroll Memorial Trophy*
*Gerry McLoughlin is standing 2nd from the right*

After he finished playing in the late eighties, Colm stayed deeply involved with the Shannon club. He was a coach, selector and manager at various stages and was instrumental in the success that Shannon had through the 1990s and 2000s. Shannon would win four Munster Senior Cups in the 1990s and eight in the 2000s (including a record equalling eight in a row). The also won none All Ireland Leagues, including a famous four in a row during the nineties.

Colm Tucker became President of his beloved Shannon in 1999, a year in which they won the Munster Senior Cup again.

*Tucker (standing 2nd right) on the 1977 Munster Cup winning Shannon team Gerry McLoughlin is standing 3rd left*

## Munster Rugby

In August 1974, before Shannon had gone on their amazing run in the Munster Senior Cup, Colm Tucker was called up to the Munster team. His first game was against the Wolfhounds in Waterford on September 8th 1974. Also playing that day were other names that would become legendary in Munster Rugby; Donal Spring, Seamus Dennison, Donal Canniffe, and Moss Keane.

With Colm Tucker on board, Munster would win the Interprovincial Championship in 1975 and again in 1978. 1978 would also, of course, be the year in which Colm Tucker became an immortal of Munster Rugby. On 31st October, the All-Blacks came to Thomond Park and were beaten 12-0. It was no fluke. That day Munster out-played their international adversaries.

Alongside Tucker were Shannon teammates **Gerry McLoughlin** and Brendan Foley, Larry Moloney (Garryowen), Moss Finn (U.C.C.), Seamus Dennison (Garryowen), Greg Barrett (Cork Con), Jim Bowen (Cork Con), **Tony Ward** (St Marys), Donal Canniffe (Lansdowne), Pat Whelan (Garryowen), Les White (London Irish), Moss Keane (Lansdowne), Christy Cantillon (Cork Con) and Donal Spring (Dublin Uni).

*Munster 1978 – Legends all*
*Colm Tucker – Standing fifth from the right*
*Tony Ward – Sitting extreme left*
*Gerry McLoughlin – Standing third from the left*

Colm Tucker's Munster career spanned an incredible thirteen years. As well as beating the All-Blacks, he was on the side that beat the Wallabies at Musgrave Park in 1981. He also played in the defeats by Romania in 1980 and Australia in 1984.

His last game for the province was in the 1987 Interprovincial Championships. He played in the final game against Connacht at the Sportsgrounds. Munster won 12-17.

After retiring from playing, Colm Tucker became a selector for the Munster team in 1993 and by 1994 was the chairman of the selection committee. From that position Tucker oversaw Munster's success in the 1994 Interpro Championships and alongside coach Jerry Holland, managed Munster's transition into the professional era from 1995 onward.

It would be difficult to think of someone who had more impact on Munster Rugby than Colm Tucker during his career as a player and then as a manager.

*Munster team that defeated Australia in 1981*
*Colm Tucker - Standing on the extreme right*
*Gerry McLoughlin - Standing 2$^{nd}$ from left*
*Tony Ward - Sitting front left*

## International Rugby

Despite consistent performances for Shannon and Munster, Colm Tucker was overlooked repeatedly by the Irish Rugby team. In 1977 he was selected for the Ireland B team on a few occasions but not the full international team.

In August 1978, he was finally added to the Irish panel. He attended an all-day training session at Lansdowne Road after which he remarked *"I was pleased it went so well this early in the season"*.

Colm Tucker

To the joy of many, Colm Tucker got capped for Ireland for the first time on 20th January 1979 in a home game against France. That first game of the Five Nations saw four new caps. Colm was joined by clubmate Gerry McLoughlin, with Dick Spring and Mike Gibson (both of Lansdowne) also getting their first starts. Tucker scored a try that day but unfortunately it was disallowed for a knock on and Ireland drew 9-9.

Two weeks later, Tucker was again in the Irish team that went to Wales and narrowly lost 24-21 at the National Stadium in Cardiff. Match reports suggest he played excellently again but when the panel was selected for the third game of the season against England, Tucker had been dropped completely with his place going to Willie Duggan. Ireland beat England 12-7 at Lansdowne Road and finished the season with a draw in Edinburgh.

*Colm Tucker, on the left, during one of his Ireland appearances Gerry McLoughlin is on the right*

Colm Tucker

While part of the training squad for the 1980 Five Nations Season, Tucker was left out of the traveling party against England. Ireland lost 24-9 at Twickenham. He was, however, included as a substitute for the game at home to Scotland which Ireland won. Colm Tucker was again on the bench for the game against Wales, a home win.

In the third game of the 1980 season, he was again called up as a reserve against France in Paris. That game ended 19-18 to the home team. The match day programme that day said it all in terms of the IRFUs attitude towards Colm Tucker. Tucker's name was misspelt.

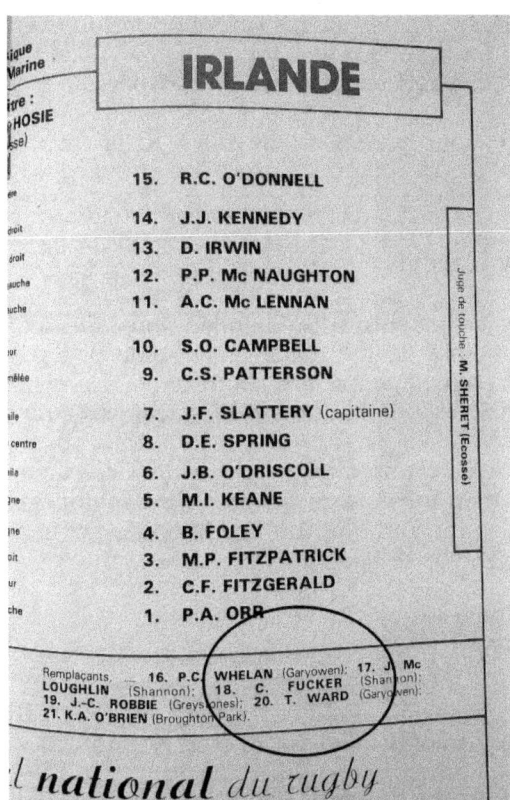

*The infamous mis-spelling of Tucker's name in the Ireland v France programme*

Later that year, Colm Tucker played on an Ireland XV against Romania at Lansdowne Road. The game ended in a 13-13 draw. At the time it wasn't classified as a test so no cap was issued, it has since been upgraded.

Colm Tucker played in the Ireland trial game at the start of 1981 but when the Five Nations games were played, Colm was playing for his beloved Shannon having been omitted again from the national team.

## The British and Irish Lions

Colm Tucker became the first Shannon player to represent the British and Irish Lions when, despite his lack of opportunity with Ireland, he was called up for the 1980 Lions tour of South Africa in 1980. On that tour he made nine appearances including two tests.

To read more about his 1980 Lions tour – Refer chapter South Africa (1980)

## Post Rugby Career

After he finished playing with Shannon and Munster, Colm Tucker worked relentlessly on the management side of the game to great success with both Shannon and Munster. He remained actively involved with Shannon right up until his death in 2012.

During his playing career, Colm worked with Coca Cola and Murphy's Brewery and then for most of his life in the motor trade with OHM Group. He also ran a pub next to the Milk Market named The Office which is now The Black Rabbit.

## Personal Life

Colm Tucker married Geraldine Hartery in 1978. They had three children, Colm Junior (Cullie), Rachel and Richard.

Colm Jnr has also had a rugby career. While his playing career was curtailed by injury, he has been very successful in coaching and is currently on the Connacht management team. Rachel Tucker also played rugby and like her father became an International, making her debut for Ireland in 2001.

Colm Tucker loved Kilkee and spent every summer down there with his family. He was also a keen golfer.

Colm Tucker died on 11th January 2012. He had been fighting lung disease for three years. He was just fifty-nine years old. He is buried at Castlemungret Cemetery in Limerick.

Colm Tucker

# Tony Ward
# Lion #573

**Tony Ward**
Born - 9 October 1954, Dublin

School – St Mary's College
Club – Garryowen
Ireland Caps - 19
Lions Tour(s) - 1980
Lions Appearances - 5
Lions Tests – 1
Position – Out-half

Perhaps a controversial inclusion as a 'Limerick' Lion but not for Tony Ward himself who proudly displays an 'Honorary Limerickman' certificate the wall of his home. Tony Ward is inextricably linked to the City of Limerick and, in particular, to sport in the city. He played League of Ireland and won the FAI Cup with Limerick Utd. He won the Munster Senior Cup twice with Garryowen. He was on the Munster 1978 team that defeated the All-Blacks. He was European Player of the Year. He won nineteen Ireland caps and was on the 1980 British and Irish Lions tour to South Africa. Limerick are proud to have this incredible sportsman as 'one of our own'.

## Early Life

Tony Ward has a fascinating back story which he outlines in his autobiography 'Twelve Feet Tall'.

Anthony Ward was born in Dublin on 9th October 1954. His father Danny Ward was from a Russian Jewish family who had fled anti-Jewish pogroms in Russia after the assassination of Tsar Alexander II. 'Danny' was born Saul Solomons in London and met and married Lily Gross in London in 1934. They had a child, Derek Solomons (Tony's step brother) before the marriage split up.

After the break-up, Saul Solomons moved to Dublin in the late 1940s. He changed his name to Danny Ward and converted to Catholicism. He met and married June Donnelly in 1952, married in 1953 and had a child Anthony (Tony) Ward who was born on 9th October 1954. The young family moved to Leeds but after the sudden death of his father on St Patricks Day 1960, June and her young son moved home to Dublin. Tony was brought up by June, living with his grandmother Lily in Harold's Cross.

## School

Tony Ward was educated at St Mary's College in Rathmines, Dublin. A sports all-rounder from an early age, Ward played football and rugby for St Mary's. In 1972, he captained the school's football team in the Leinster Schools Cup but they were knocked out by Beneavin in the first round. That didn't prevent Ward going on to play internationally with the Irish schools' team and also playing for Shamrock Rovers.

On the rugby field, Ward was on the Junior Cup team that got to the semi-final of the schools' cup in 1970. He scored a drop-goal in that game against Clongowes but his team were beaten and were knocked out of the competition. He played on the Senior Cup Team for three years and was captain in his final year (1972-73). He was also a reserve on the Leinster Schools' team that year.

After graduating from St Mary's, Ward moved to Limerick to study for a BA in Physical Education at Thomond College (now University of Limerick). While in Limerick, he began his tremendously successful club and representative rugby career.

## Club Rugby

### Garryowen

Tony Ward signed to play for Garryowen in 1975 when he moved to Limerick for university. Prior to that he was possibly better known as a Shamrock Rovers football player. He had played thirty-nine games as a winger for them and for a time continued to commute to games from Limerick.

*Ward (sitting third from left) with 1975 Garryowen Team*

In his first season with Garryowen, Ward won the Munster Senior Cup beating Cork Con in the final 6-4. Ward scored all of Garryowen's points that day. The Sunday Independent headline the following day roared *"Soccer star Tony wins it"*.

In both 1977 and 1978 Ward was on the Garryowen team that was beaten in the final of the Munster Senior Cup by a Shannon team featuring both Colm Tucker and Gerry McLoughlin. In 1977 Garryowen lost 6-3 and in 1978 it was 16-10.

Tony Ward got his hands on the Munster Senior Cup again in 1979 when Garryowen beat Young Munster 3-0 with Ward again scoring the Garryowen points.

In his final season with Garryowen in 1982, Ward won the Munster Senior League title.

*Ward (front 3rd from right) with 1979 Garryowen Team*

**St Mary's**

After the 1982 season, Tony Ward returned to live in Dublin and moved back to St Mary's for three seasons from 1982 to 1985. During this time, he continued to play for Munster.

**Greystones**

The emergence of Paul Dean at St Mary's led to Ward deciding in January 1985 to move to Greystones where he completed his playing career. After the move to Greystones, he also moved his provincial allegiance to Leinster. Ward played with Greystones until 1989.

Tony Ward

*Ward (sitting third from left) with St Marys Team*

## Munster Rugby

In August 1975, Tony Ward was called up for the Munster thirty-one-man panel to prepare for the upcoming season. He was a reserve in the initial games that took place from December that year and was named on the bench when Munster played the touring Australian team in January 1976 at Musgrave Park. However, a late injury to Munster captain and out-half Barry McGann saw Ward get his first provincial start against the Wallabies. Munster lost that game 13-15 in Musgrave Park but Ward played exceptionally well.

While with Munster, Tony Ward would famously be on the team that defeated the All-Blacks at Thomond Park in 1978. He scored eight of Munster's twelve points in that game; from a conversion and two drop-goals. In his autobiography, Ward called out this game as the highlight of his playing career.

> *"That was one of the greatest days of my life. It was also, and without any doubt, the highlight of my rugby career. I talked about this with a great many people over the years, but especially so with the great Moss Keane. Unlike me, Moss would later go on to be an integral part of the Ireland Triple Crown winning team in 1982. He was also capped by the British*

*and Irish Lions. But he, too, agreed with me: Munster's 12—0 win in 1978 was the undoubted high point of his career."*

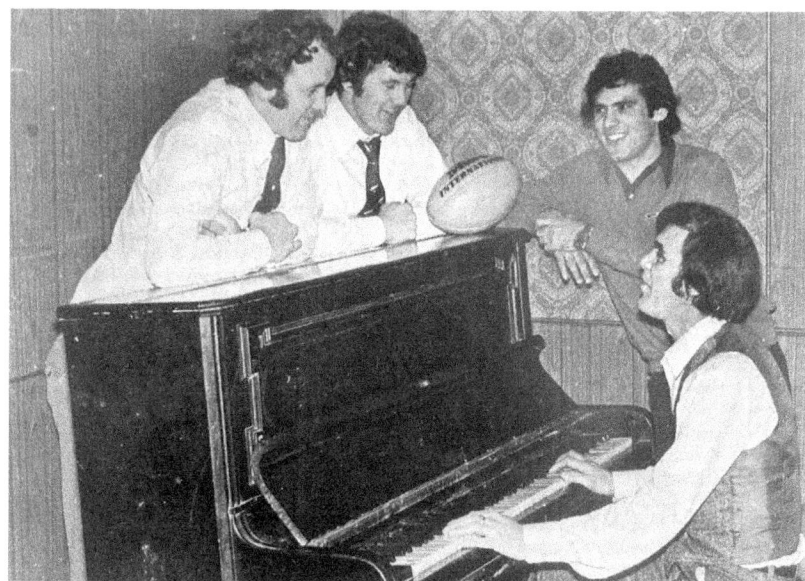

Ward enjoying a sing song with Ger Cusack (piano), Brendan Foley and Colm Tucker after Munster's 1978 victory over the All Blacks

With Munster, Ward won the Interpro Championship in 1975 and again in 1978 and while playing for Munster was voted the 1977/78 European Player of the Year.

He was also on the Munster team that lost to Romania 9-32 at Thomond Park in 1980, the team that beat Australia in 1981 (15-6 at Musgrave Park) and the team that lost to Australia 19-31 at Thomond Park.

Tony's last game for Munster was a defeat at Ravenhill against Ulster in December 1984.

*Tony Ward playing for Munster*

## Leinster Rugby

Ahead of the 1986 Interprovincial Championships, Leinster scheduled two games against Italian teams in Italy. The panel to tour was announced and Tony Ward was selected. However, a week before the tour was to take place, it was cancelled because of mismatched expectations as to the quality of the Italian teams they would face. Instead, Leinster played a home game against the Canadian team on 1$^{st}$ October and Tony Ward made his Leinster debut. Leinster won 13-3 at Lansdowne Road.

Tony Ward played for Leinster for three seasons from 1986 to 1988. Leinster came second in the Interprovincial Championships in 1986 and 1988 losing out to Ulster on each occasion.

## International Rugby

Despite being the first Irish rugby superstar and winning European Player of the Year, Tony had a love/hate relationship with the IRFU.

His time in the Irish jersey was steeped in controversy and curtailed as a result.

He made his debut at Lansdowne Road against Scotland in the 1978 Five Nations Championship. Ireland won that game 12-9. In a year in which Wales won a Grand Slam, Tony Ward played in all four games, including an agonising 10-9 loss in Paris, as well as losses at home to Wales and away at Twickenham.

In November 1978, a week after he had beaten them with Munster, Ward played the All-Blacks with the national team at Lansdowne Road. On this occasion he was on the losing side as Ireland lost 6-10.

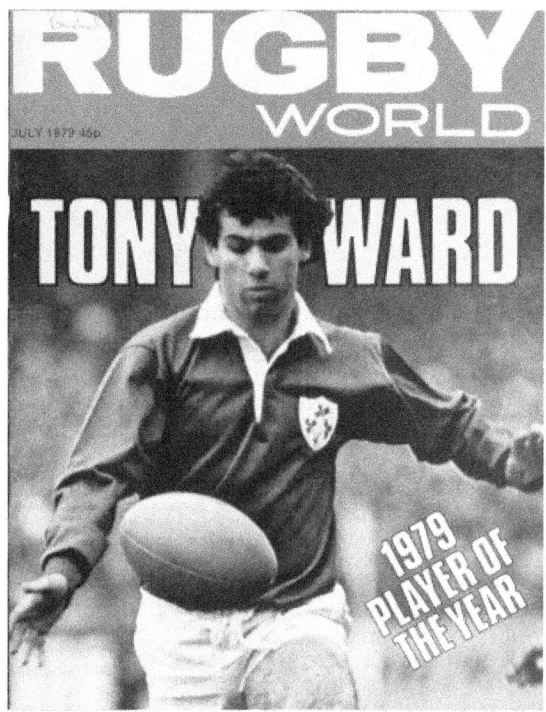

*Tony Ward on the cover of Rugby World having won 1979 Player of the Year*

Tony Ward again played in all four of the 1979 Five Nations Championship games. That year Ireland drew with France at home 9-

9, lost away in Cardiff, beat England at home 12-7 and drew 11-11 at Murrayfield. Just a few months later, in May 1979, Ward went on the Irish tour of Australia. Having played in all four of the Five Nations games, he was expected to be the first choice out-half. He wasn't selected for the first game against Western Australia. The Sunday Independent reported that *"Ireland's star out-half Tony Ward, is not exactly over the moon about missing the opening game. He would have preferred to play and get used to the conditions as quickly as possible"*. With Ollie Campbell in the number ten shirt, Ireland won comfortably 39-3.

In the second game of the tour, Tony Ward was back on the field and achieved a proud personal milestone by scoring his first try for Ireland. In all he scored nineteen points as Ireland beat Australian Capital Territory 35-7 in Manuka Oval in Canberra.

*Ward takes a kick for Ireland*

A few days later, Ward played again in the game against New South Wales at the Sydney Sports Ground and helped Ireland secure a 16-12 win. Tony was however again omitted for the game against Queensland at Ballymore. In that game Ireland secured a late 18-15 win ahead of the first test at the same ground a few days later.

For the first test match, the Irish selectors sensationally dropped Tony Ward from the test team. He was the incumbent for the Five Nations, he was two-time European player of the year and was a burgeoning superstar of world rugby but Ollie Campbell was selected ahead of him. Campbell at that point had only one cap under his belt. Strangely enough, that had earned against Australia when they had toured Ireland the previous year. There was consternation back in Ireland and for days the newspapers were awash with stories akin to the Roy Keane Saipan storm. The selectors were no doubt relieved when Ireland beat Australia 27-12.

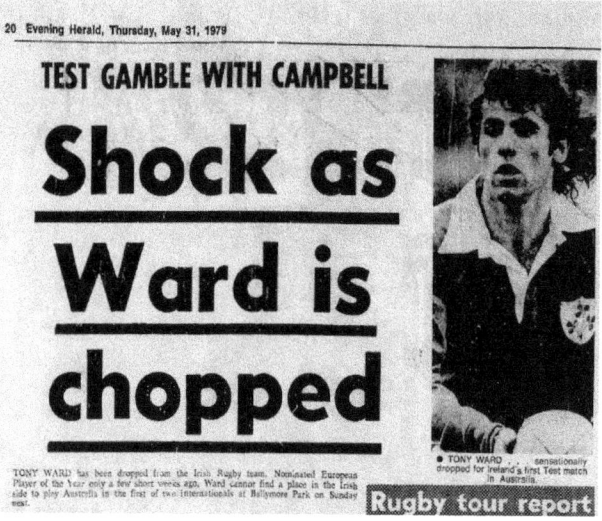

Tony Ward was restored to the team when Ireland played NSW Country in Orange. Ireland won 28-7 with Ward contributing twelve points. Ward was again in the team a few days later when Ireland suffered their only loss of the tour, against Sydney 12-16.

The tour's last game was a second test played at the Sydney Cricket Ground. Campbell was again played and Ireland secured a historic 3-9 win becoming the first country to win a test series in the southern hemisphere.

Tony is on record as saying that his treatment on that tour of Australia shattered his world. His relationship with Ollie Campbell remained positive but trust was completely broken with the Irish Manager, Noel Murphy, who would later be part of the 1980 Lions management team.

Tony Ward was left out of the Irish team for the 1980 Five Nations but was back in the team in 1981 when he played in three of the four games. Campbell played in the first game, a loss to France and Ward played in a 9-8 loss in Cardiff, a 6-10 loss to England and a 10-9 loss to Scotland.

Tony was again left out of the team for the 1982 championship but played one game in 1983 when he came on as a replacement for Campbell in the win against England at Lansdowne Road.

Tony Ward played two of the 1984 games. He scored all of Ireland's points in a 12-9 loss at Twickenham and he played in the away loss to Scotland. Ward's last Five Nations game was against Scotland in March 1986, a 9-10 defeat.

Tony was included in the Ireland squad for the inaugural Rugby World Cup in 1987. He played in the victories over Canada and Tonga but Paul Dean played in the all-important group game against Wales which Ireland lost.

## The British and Irish Lions

Tony Ward represented the British and Irish Lions on the 1980 Lions tour of South Africa. On that tour he made nine appearances including two tests.

To read more about his 1980 Lions tour – Refer chapter South Africa (1980)

## Soccer Career

In his youth, before he moved to Limerick, Tony Ward played soccer with top schoolboy team on Dublin's southside Rangers and then with Shamrock Rovers. He played over thirty times with Rovers including a pre-season game against Glasgow Celtic containing some of the Celtic European Cup winners from a few years previous. After moving to Limerick, Ward tried to continue playing in the League of Ireland but commuting to games was difficult and his studies and his rugby took priority.

In 1981, Limerick United qualified for the UEFA Cup and were drawn against Southampton in the first round. As preparation for this game, Tottenham Hotspur were invited to Limerick to play an exhibition game at Thomond Park on 10th August 1981.

Already a star in Limerick sport, Tony Ward was asked to make an appearance and played the second half of the game. Limerick Utd lost the game 2-6 against a team that featured two members of the 1978 World Cup winning team Argentina, Ossie Ardiles and Ricky Villa. Even with world cup winners on their team, Tottenham's star that day was Glenn Hoddle who scored four goals. Both of Limerick Utd's goals were scored by Des Kennedy.

*The Limerick team that played Tottenham Hotspur at Thomond Park
Tony Ward standing second from the left*

Tony Ward played so well in the game against Spurs that he was asked to sign for Limerick Utd for the season. He did so and played in both legs of the first round of the UEFA Cup against Southampton. The games were played in September and Limerick Utd lost three nil at home at the Markets Field but drew in the away leg at the Dell 1-1. That Southampton team featured Kevin Keegan.

Tony played the rest of the season with Limerick Utd and was on the team that won the FAI Cup in May 1982. Limerick beat Bohemians at Dalymount Park 1-0. It was Limerick's first title in ten years and only their second ever. Sadly, it remains that way today.

Tony Ward

*Tony Ward after Limerick played Southampton in the UEFA cup at Markets Field*

*Tony Ward with the Limerick Utd team that won the FAI Cup in 1982*

It is remarkable and of its time that Tony was able to play in two very high-level sports teams simultaneously. He played with Limerick Utd Soccer team on Saturday and with Garryowen on Sunday. Not only was he able to do it physically, but both teams were thriving.

## Life after Rugby

While living in Limerick, Ward had a sports store called Tony Ward Sports. He also had a gym on Thomas Street for a period. When he moved back to Dublin in 1982, he opened an equivalent there. Later he became a physical education teacher at St Andrews secondary school in Booterstown.

A true rugby star, he was in demand for media work after he finished playing and continues to be both a rugby pundit and a respected rugby journalist. He was also Director of Rugby at St Gerard's School in Bray near where he lives.

## Personal Life

Early in his playing career, Tony met and married Maura O'Regan. They had a daughter, Lynn, before going their separate ways. Later, during his playing days in Greystones, Tony met Louise Cole. They married and had two children together Nikki and Ali. Tony is also parent to Louise's son Richie. Tony Ward lives in Greystones, County Wicklow.

In 2015, he released an autobiography called 'Twelve Feet Tall'. It's a great read.

# South Africa (1980)

Since the British and Irish Lions had last toured South Africa in 1974, public concern about apartheid had gone up considerably. The Gleneagles Agreement, signed in 1977 by all Commonwealth countries, agreed to actively discourage their sports people and organisations from interacting with their South African counterparts. South Africa had been banned from the Olympic Games for twenty years and Australia had banned the Springboks from touring there. The 1980 tour was going to be a political minefield. There were arguments for and against the tour. Some felt that the tour could be used to enact change, while others felt that by excluding South Africa from sports competition pressure could mount for change from within.

On the South African side, in 1977 a new South African Rugby Board had been instituted. It took over from the previous all-white version and now included South African Rugby Football Federation, and the South African Rugby Association. They made an official statement that the SARB included all races and importantly, that national teams would be chosen on merit and not skin colour.

In 1979, a South African Barbarians team toured the United Kingdom. The team had eight white players, eight 'coloured' players and eight black players. The team played seven games and there were protests at all of them.

The Home Nations Rugby Unions were all of the view that, South Africa had started to make change by introducing some 'coloured' players to their teams and that a tour would encourage more of that. In January 1980, the decision was made by the Home Nations; regardless of the likely protests and public opinion, the tour was going ahead.

Irishman Syd Millar was appointed as the tour manager and Noel Murphy was his coach. Murphy had been the Irish manager who sensationally dropped Tony Ward during the 1979 tour of Australia. They had just four months to prepare. The 1980 Five Nations Championships was going to dictate who was selected for the tour.

Ahead of the 1980 Lions tour to South Africa, Ireland hadn't won the Five Nations in eight years. Wales had dominated the competition

1980 South Africa

winning two Grand Slams (in 1976 and 1978) and in 1980 England won a Grand Slam. Ireland were runners up to England that year. Bill Beaumont who captained the England team was subsequently named captain for the Lions tour.

Within the Irish camp, there was a real competition for the number ten shirt. Tony Ward had been the top point scorer in the Five Nations in 1978 but had been dropped in favour of Campbell during the 1979 tour of Australia. In 1980's Five Nations, Campbell was picked ahead of Ward and had been the championships top points scorer with forty-six. Tony Ward was not expecting to be picked for the tour and in the end wasn't.

When the thirty-man squad was announced on St Patricks Day, there were twelve Welshmen, eight English, five Scottish and just five Irish – Rodney O'Donnell, Ollie Campbell, Colin Patterson, John O'Driscoll and, in a surprise to many, Limerick's Colm Tucker. The Evening Mail reported, *"But it is the nomination of the 27-year-old Tucker which will have taken most by surprise. Tucker's only appearance in the Irish side this season was as a replacement in the match against France, in Paris, when John O'Driscoll was injured"*. It was true, at that point, Tucker had two Irish caps both won two years previous in 1978.

Around Limerick, there was joy at the selection of Colm Tucker and a real sense that his qualities had finally been recognised.

As with the Irish national team, Tony Ward had missed out on selection to Ollie Campbell. Moss Keane was also sounded out about being in the squad but because he was a civil servant, the Irish government's

1980 South Africa

ban on employees taking leave to travel to South Africa prevented him from taking part.

Twelve of those selected had been on the previous tour to New Zealand in 1977. Andy Irvine and Fran Cotton were going on their third tour having also been in the 1974 squad that toured South Africa and Derek Quinnell was going on his third tour having been in the 1977 squad and the 1971 squad which toured New Zealand. Quinnell's son, Scott, would also become a Lion when he toured in 1997 and 2001. His brother-in-law, Barry John, was also a Lion from 1968 and 1971.

Touring party

### Management
Manager Syd Millar (Ireland)
Coach Noel Murphy (Ireland)
Team Doctor Jack Matthews (Wales)

### Backs
Rodney O'Donnell (St. Mary's College and Ireland), Bruce Hay (Boroughmuir and Scotland), Andy Irvine (Heriots FP and Scotland), Mike Slemen (Liverpool and England), John Carleton (Orrell and England), Elgan Rees (Neath and Wales), Peter Morgan (Llanelli and Wales), Jim Renwick (Hawick and Scotland), Ray Gravell (Llanelli and Wales), David Richards (Swansea and Wales), Clive Woodward (Leicester and England), Paul Dodge (Leicester and England), Gareth Davies (Cardiff and Wales), Ollie Campbell (Old Belvedere and Ireland), **Tony Ward (Garryowen and Ireland)**, Terry Holmes (Cardiff and Wales), Colin Patterson (Instonians and Ireland), John Robbie

1980 South Africa

(Greystones RFC and Ireland) as replacement, Steve Smith (Sale and England)

**Forwards**
Peter Wheeler (Leicester and England), Alan Phillips (Cardiff and Wales), Fran Cotton (Sale and England), Clive Williams (Swansea and Wales), Ian Stephens (Bridgend and Wales), Phil Orr (Old Wesley and Ireland), Graham Price (Pontypool and Wales), Phil Blakeway (Gloucester and England), Bill Beaumont (captain; Fylde and England), Maurice Colclough (Angoulême and England), Alan Tomes (Hawick and Scotland), Allan Martin (Aberavon and Wales), John O'Driscoll (London Irish and Ireland), Colm Tucker (Shannon and Ireland), Jeff Squire (Pontypool and Wales), Stuart Lane (Cardiff and Wales), Derek Quinnell (Llanelli and Wales), John Beattie (Glasgow Academicals and Scotland), Gareth Williams (Bridgend and Wales)

*Colm Tucker (Middle 3rd from right) with the Lions*
*Tony Ward was a replacement and so is not in this photo*

## The Tour

Before the team had even left London, they had an injury problem to deal with. Andy Irvine had a hamstring problem that flared up the night before the team were due to depart. Elgan Rees was called in as cover. This was the start of a theme for the tour.

The Lions squad arrived in Johannesburg on May 4th. They were warmly greeted by a few hundred loud supporters, some travelling and

1980 South Africa

some ex-pats. There were six days before the first game against Eastern Province at Port Elizabeth.

The management had decided to do a few hard days of training at altitude to get the fitness levels up, so the team went to the town of Vanderbijlpark about forty miles from Johannesburg. In a sign of what was to come, the team had a fierce training session within hours of arriving at their hotel. For the first few days there were twice daily training sessions which, at altitude, were incredibly difficult. They also took a toll on the players. Ollie Campbell had to drop out of training on May 5th with a hamstring strain and Colm Tucker was amongst those who got severe blisters from the heat, their woollen socks and the new boots some were wearing.

*Tucker in his Lions gear*

1980 South Africa

After a few days the training eased a little and the Lions were able to recover enough energy to go and look around the host country. One of the first places they visited was Sharpville. It had just passed the twentieth anniversary of the Sharpville Massacre when sixty-nine people, mostly children, were shot dead by South African police as they protested outside the local police station. The Lions players found it confronting on two counts. Firstly, the scene was and is deeply troubling because of what had happened there but the players were also confronted by the poverty that still existed in the township. By the end of the tour, many of the players would be so disgusted by what they witnessed that they refused to visit South Africa on subsequent tours. For example, Tony Ward refused to travel when Ireland toured there in 1981 after what he witnessed on this tour.

## The Games

### Game One
### v Eastern Province
### Boet Erasmus Stadium, Port Elizabeth, South Africa 10/5/1980
### 28-16 - Win

Lions Team – Hay (Scotland), Rees (Wales), Gravell (Wales), Morgan (Wales), Slemen (England), Davies (Wales), Holmes (Wales), Beattie (Scotland), Lane (Wales), Martin (Wales), Beaumont (England), Squire (Wales), Price (Wales), Wheeler (England), Cotton (England)

Ollie Campbell had been named in the team to play the first game of the tour against Eastern Province but on the day before he felt a hamstring twinge and as a precaution pulled out of the game. Welsh out-half Gareth Davies played in his place.

This was supposed to be an easy first outing for the team and the score line suggests as much, however, it was anything but an easy game. Within the first minute of the game, Stuart Lane dislocated his knee, ending his tour. A penalty to Gareth Davies got the Lions off on the score board. Pretorius kicked an equaliser before Davies regained the lead for the Lions with a drop-goal. Another Eastern Province penalty levelled the scores again. A further Davies penalty, along with a try on twenty-five minutes, scored by Mike Slemen, gave the Lions a 15-6 lead. However, out-half Gareth Davies, who was only called in when Ollie Campbell cried off before the game, injured his shoulder badly in the lead up to the try. Despite a suspected dislocated shoulder, he successfully kicked the conversion before having to leave the field. Just on half time, Heunis scored for the Eastern Province but the Lions hit straight back when Holmes scored to give the Lions a 21-10 half time lead.

Elgan Rees scored for the Lions in the second half and Jim Renwick, taking over kicking duties from Davies, kicked a late penalty. The Eastern Province side scored when Campher capitalised on a Hay knock on inside the Lions' twenty-two but the Lions were too far ahead and won the game.

The tour was off to a winning start but already injuries were a concern, particularly at out-half. Ollie Campbell wasn't one hundred percent and it was later confirmed that Gareth Davies would be out for three weeks, leaving no cover at out-half for the first test.

The newspaper reports on the game come with headlines such as "Timid Lions Survive" and "Counting cost of ominous injuries".

*Game Two*
*v SARA Invitation XV*
*Border RU Ground, East London, South Africa 14/5/1980*
*28- 6 - Win*

**Lions Team** – O'Donnell (Ireland), Carleton (England), Renwick (Scotland), Woodward (England), Rees (Wales), Richards (Wales), Patterson (Ireland), Quinell (Wales), O'Driscoll (Ireland), Tomes (Scotland), Colclough (England), **Tucker (Ireland)**, Blakeway (England), Phillips (Wales), Williams (Wales)

Colm Tucker made his first appearance for the Lions in the second game of the tour against a SARA Invitational XV.

Welsh centre, David Richards, took on the number ten position because of the injuries to Campbell and Davies. Stand-in captain for the day was Derek Quinnell and he drove the Lions to a winning score that flattered his team. It was only in the last fifteen minutes that the score went from 16-6 to 26-6. Quinnell scored two of the Lions' three tries, the other scored by Elgan Rees. Clive Woodward took over kicking duties. His performance, with three penalties, two conversion and one drop-goal, was significant but there was concern about whether Richards could play at out-half at test level.

*Game Three*
*v Natal*
*Kings Park Stadium, Durban, South Africa 17/5/1980*
*21-15 - Win*

**Lions Team** – O'Donnell (Ireland), Carleton (England), Gravell (Wales), Richards (Wales), Slemen (England), Campbell (Ireland), Holmes (Wales), Beattie (Scotland), Squire (Wales), Martin (Wales), Beaumont (England), **Tucker (Ireland)**, Price (Wales), Wheeler (England), Cotton (England)

Three days after his first appearance, Colm Tucker was again in action in the game against Natal in Durban. Ollie Campbell was cautiously fit to play in the number ten shirt and he was instrumental in creating a last gasp try that won the game for the Lions.

This was a difficult game for the Lions. Played in sweltering heat and in front of 40,000 rabid Natal supporters, the home team put up huge resistance. With the score locked at 15-15 and the game slipping away, Campbell made a quick break and ran to within a few yards of the Natal line. From the ensuing ruck, the ball found its way to flanker Carleton who dove over the line. The Lions had won but the game was tighter than it should have been. After the game Syd Millar said, *"We are not playing anywhere near the way we can play, but we are not used to playing in this heat"*.

At a training session two days after this game, Ollie Campbell's hamstring flared up again. With ten days to go until the first test, cover

1980 South Africa

was needed and so Syd Millar called and asked for Tony Ward. It wasn't as simple as calling Tony and telling him to get on a plane. The Lions committee first needed to approve it. There had been media speculation for a few days but on May 19th Tony started to field calls. The first call came while he was at the vet with his dog. The press wanted to know whether he was being summonsed or not. At that stage he had no official call. It was only that evening that he was officially invited on the tour. He spent the next couple of days sorting out his personal business and then flew to London where he was measured up for his Lions suit. After a whistlestop London stop-off, Ward flew on to Johannesburg.

Two issues lay ahead for Ward as he prepared to join the squad. Firstly, he hadn't played any fifteen-man rugby for two months. He was instead playing sevens rugby and had travelled a lot in the previous four weeks. He had played in Bermuda, Amsterdam and Paris. All that travel wasn't ideal ahead of being thrust into the heat of likely test rugby. The second issue was, how would he deal with the fact that Noel Murphy, who had sensationally dropped him from the Irish team, was now the Lions coach? And vice-versa.

*Game Four*
*v South African Invitation XV*
*Olën Park, Potchefstroom, South Africa 21/5/1980*
*22-19 - Win*

**Lions Team** – Hay (Scotland), Rees (Wales), Woodward (England), Renwick (Scotland), Slemen (England), Richards (Wales), Patterson (Ireland), Quinnell (Wales), Williams (Wales), Tomes (Scotland), Colclough (England), O'Driscoll (Ireland), Price (Wales), Phillips (Wales), Williams (Wales)

Tucker sat out game four of the tour and David Richards was again stand-in stand-off. The South African Invitational XV were up 3-6 after twenty-five minutes. This was the first time the Lions had been behind in a game on the tour. The Lions recovered to win the game and the 23,000 spectators were given a show of what Lions Rugby was about when, with eight minutes remaining, Slemen scored a try for the Lions to win the game.

The extraordinary try started when David Richards made a break from a lineout. What followed was thirty-three consecutive passes over two minutes and forty-five seconds. On three occasions it looked like the move would break down but each time it was rescued before the ball finally got to Mike Slemen who scored. When he did, the spectators rose to their feet in unison to give a standing ovation that lasted for what felt like five minutes.

There was a big party to celebrate the try and the victory that night. There were sore heads on the bus the following day as the team moved from Potchefstroom to Bloemfontein.

While this game was going on, Tony Ward was on a flight south. He arrived in Johannesburg on 22$^{nd}$ May and met up with the squad at Potchefstroom. On arrival, a quick word with Noel Murphy solved the issue of any tension between the two. They were there to do a job. That was their agreed focus.

*Game Five*
*v Orange Free State*
*Free State Stadium, Bloemfontein, South Africa 24/5/1980*
*21-17 - Win*

**Lions Team** – Morgan (Wales), Carleton (England), Gravell (Wales), Renwick (Scotland), Slemen (England), Richards (Wales), Holmes (Wales), Squire (Wales), Williams (Wales), Colclough (England), Beaumont (England), O'Driscoll (Ireland), Price (Wales), Wheeler (England), Williams (Wales)

Heavy wind had a significant impact on this game with lots of Lions' kicking going astray. In the first half the Lions went behind when Gerber scored a try which was converted into the wind by Pienaar. There was no other score in the first half. The Lions woke up in the second half and scored fourteen points in fourteen minutes with tries to Slemen (2) and Holmes. Terry Holmes, however, dislocated his right shoulder mid-way through the second half and had to leave the field. Losing Holmes seemed to spur on the Lions. No sooner was he off the field than Jim Renwick scored a penalty and moments later hooker Peter Wheeler forced his way over the line for a try.

1980 South Africa

The team had only been in Bloemfontein for fifty-six hours. In a sign of what was going on outside of the rugby tour, in that time twenty protestors were arrested and one schoolgirl was shot dead in the local township. The day after the game, the team flew to Cape Town under cover of darkness to try and avoid the expected protests. A dozen police guarded the team hotel.

*Game Six*
*v South African Rugby Football Federation Invitation XV*
*Danie Craven Stadium, Stellenbosch, South Africa 27/5/1980*
*15-6*
*– Win*

**Lions Team** – O'Donnell (Ireland), Carleton (England), Richards (Wales), Woodward (England), Morgan (Wales), **Ward (Ireland)**, Patterson (Ireland), Quinnell (Wales), **Tucker (Ireland)**, Tomes (Scotland), Martin (Wales), Beattie (Scotland), Stephens (Wales), Phillips (Wales), Cotton (England)

Tony Ward had arrived in South Africa and, after just four days, he was officially a Lion. This was only his second game of rugby in two months. Colm Tucker, in a sign that he was unlikely to be in contention for the test team, was picked for his third appearance for the Lions.

The South African Rugby Football Federation (SARFF) was the union for coloured rugby players. Their team was known as the Proteas. They were not exclusively coloured and regularly augmented their ranks with a few white players up front in the pack.

This was a niggly game that is remembered more for what happened to English prop Fran Cotton than for anything else. The first few scrums of the game all ended with Cotton and his opposite number Hempies du Toit, wrestling and fighting.

As the game progressed things changed for Cotton. Just short of half time, he went down clutching his chest. There was immediate concern and he was taken from the field. He was rushed to hospital for tests amid fears that he had had a heart attack. That night Bill Beaumont, delegated his after dinner speaking role so that he could be with Cotton and so that he could call Cotton's wife to let her know what was happening.

1980 South Africa

The following day it was confirmed that Cotton had an infection in his pericardium (the lining of the heart). He was in hospital for four days before re-joining the squad having been ordered to rest for at least six weeks.

In the game itself, John Carleton scored a try for the Lions after seven minutes. Rodney O'Donnell dropped a goal and Tony Ward scored two penalties but missed six kicks. He was rusty. *"Kicking is in the mind. It all depends how well you kick that first one. If the first one goes over then you are so confident that you could kick all the rest. This was just one of those days"*, Ward said later.

The Lions looked strong and in control throughout. Early in the game, Ward got kicked on the leg during a tackle. It didn't impact his performance but there was damage done. Two days later he was named as the starting out-half for the first test and he needed strapping on his right thigh as a result of this injury.

On the day before the test match, Ward and Campbell went to Cape Town University for some kicking practice. Within minutes of arriving, students opposed to the tour, arrived and the two Irishmen had to abandon their plans.

*Game Seven*
*v South Africa (First Test)*
*Newlands Stadium, Cape Town, South Africa 31/5/1980*

1980 South Africa

## 22-26 – Loss

**Lions Team** - O'Donnell (Ireland), Carleton (England), Richards (Wales), Renwick (Scotland), Slemen (England), **Ward (Ireland)**, Patterson (Ireland), Quinnell (Wales), O'Driscoll (Ireland), Squire (Wales), Colclough (England), Beaumont (England), Price (Wales), Wheeler (England), Williams (Wales)

**South Africa** - Pienaar, Mordt, Smith, du Plessis, Germishuys, Botha, Serfontein, du Plessis, Stofberg, Louw, Moolman, van Heerden, le Roux, Kahts, Prentis

Ahead of the first test, there were demonstrations and protests around Cape Town all week. As a result, there was serious security around the game itself. Over a hundred policemen, all with Alsatian dogs, surrounded the pitch to ensure there was no invasion of the playing field. A real show of force.

Despite only being with the squad for a week and with just one game under his belt, Tony Ward was selected to play at out-half due to the continuing injury to Ollie Campbell. He very much justified his place with a remarkable performance in the first test.

Ward, who's leg was heavily strapped and who had painkilling injections to get him through the game, got his first shot at goal within the first minute. Kicking from the lefthand side of the field about thirty-five yards out, his penalty kick went just wide but that was his only miss of the day.

The Lions had the best of the game during the first twenty minutes. They put a lot of pressure on the Springbok try line but had no success. Then the Springboks came strongly into the game. Flanker Rob Louw picked up a kick ahead and, despite a tackle from O'Donnell, got over to score. The try was converted by Naas Botha.

Ward responded by kicking another penalty, before Willie du Plessis scored again for the Springboks after a chip ahead from Botha. Moaner

337

1980 South Africa

van Heerden then scored again from twenty yards just before half time. A third Tony Ward penalty made it 9-16 at half time.

Ward kicked a fourth penalty to make it 12-16 and then the Lions scored a try; Price winning a Springbok lineout five yards out and forcing his way over the line. The Lions then took the lead when Ward dropped a goal with his supposed weaker left foot. At 19-16, it looked as if the Lions had made an astonishing recovery but then Germishuys scored a try for the South Africans. Botha converted to give them a 19-22 lead.

Tony Ward kicked another penalty to level it. He had now kicked eighteen points which was a record for a Lion in a test game in South Africa but scrum-half Serfontein scored a try off the back of a maul to win it for the Springboks in the last minute.

In the aftermath of the game, the doctors confirmed that Ward would need a week to recover properly from his injury. They also confirmed that Campbell was almost ready to play again.

1980 South Africa

*Game Eight*
*v South African Country Districts XV*
*South West Stadium, Windhoek, Namibia 4/6/1980*
*27-7 - Win*

**Lions Team** – Hay (Scotland), Woodward (England), Gravell (Wales), Renwick (Scotland), Morgan (Wales), Davies (Wales), Robbie (Ireland), Beattie (Scotland), Williams (Wales), Martin (Wales), Tomes (Scotland), **Tucker (Ireland)**, Stephens (Wales), Wheeler (England), Orr (Ireland)

Colm Tucker got his fourth game for the Lions in the eighth game of the tour in Windhoek. Remarkably this game meant that he had appeared more often for the British and Irish Lions than for his own country. Such were the times in Irish rugby.

Gareth Davies had recovered from his injury and this was his first game back at out-half in four weeks. Campbell who had appeared to be almost ready to play, had suffered a mid-week training setback but was close. Tony Ward's future contribution to the tour was unknown.

The home team took an unexpected lead after three minutes when Errol Tobias kicked a penalty. Twelve months later, Tobias would become the first 'coloured' Springbok. He made his test debut against Ireland at Newlands on 30th May 1981.

Gareth Davies levelled the score after nine minutes and the Lions then took control of the game. John Beattie, Jim Renwick, Gareth Williams and Clive Woodward each scored tries for the Lions and Davies scored two more penalties to give the Lions the easy win they were expecting.

*Game Nine*
*v Transvaal*
*Wanderers Stadium, Johannesburg, South Africa 7/6/1980*
*32-12 – Win*

**Lions Team** – Irvine (Scotland), Woodward (England), Gravell (Wales), Richards (Wales), Hay (Scotland), Davies (Wales), Patterson (Ireland), Quinnell (Wales), O'Driscoll (Ireland), Beaumont (England), Colclough (England), Squire (Wales), Price (Wales), Wheeler (England), Orr (Ireland)

With the games coming thick and fast, Tucker and Ward both sat out the Transvaal game. In a game in which the newspapers said, the Lions could have scored fifty points, the injury jinx struck again. Centre David Richards dislocated his shoulder. His tour was over. It had already been interrupted when his father died and Richards made a dashing trip home for the funeral.

Tries from Richards, Price, Woodward and Davies gave the Lions a commanding lead. In the second half Woodward scored another try which he converted himself. The Transvaal side were a disappointment.

*Game Ten*
*v Eastern Transvaal*
*Pam Brink Stadium, Spring, South Africa 10/6/1980*
*21-15 – Win*

**Lions Team** – O'Donnell (Ireland), Carleton (England), Renwick (Scotland), Morgan (Wales), Hay (Scotland), Campbell (Ireland), Holmes (Wales), Beattie (Scotland), Williams (Wales), Martin (Wales), Tomes (Scotland), **Tucker (Ireland)**, Stephens (Wales), Phillips (Wales), Williams (Wales)

Colm Tucker was back in the mix for the tenth game of the tour against Eastern Transvaal. As it was just four days before the test, he was probably disappointed as it was an indication that he would again miss test selection.

Tony Ward had now recovered from his bruised thigh. Ollie Campbell was also fit and he got the nod for the out-half position and kicked seventeen of the Lions' twenty-one points; four penalties, one drop-goal and a conversion. John Carleton scored the Lions' only try.

*Game Eleven*
*v South Africa (Second Test)*
*Free State Stadium, Bloemfontein, South Africa 14/6/1980*
*19-26 - Loss*

**Lions Team** – Irvine (Scotland), Carleton (England), Gravell (Wales), Woodward (England), Hay (Scotland), Davies (Wales), Patterson

1980 South Africa

(Ireland), Quinnell (Wales), O'Driscoll (Ireland), Squire (Wales), Colclough (England), Beaumont (England), Price (Wales), Wheeler (England), Williams (Wales)

South Africa - Pienaar, Mordt, Smith, du Plessis, Germishuys, Botha, Serfontein, du Plessis, Stofberg, Louw, Moolman, de Klerk, le Roux, Kahts, Prentis

Neither of the Limerick boys were in the team for the all-important second test. Ward in particular had reason to be disappointed. He had played well in the first test and had kicked a record number of points in the game. Davies had been injured and only had two games under his belt since he returned. There must have been serious consideration about Ward playing. As it turned out, Davies would injure his knee in this game and miss the rest of the tour.

Springbokke
British Lions
TWEEDE TOETS          SECOND TEST
Stadion/Stadium, Bloemfontein    14/6/80

60,000 fans packed into the ground to watch the game and they were happy to see their beloved Springboks take a second victory in the series.

The Lions' forwards played well but the backs were nervous and it showed in some fumbles and poor kicking choices. After twelve minutes, Rob Louw scored a try for the Springboks after a poor defensive kick from fullback Irvine went straight to Germishuys who put Louw in for a try.

The Lions responded. Colin Patterson kicked ahead and the ball was picked up by John O'Driscoll who scored. The conversion by Davies gave the Lions an undeserved lead. However, Stofberg scored a second try for the Springboks after Hay had tackled Mordt but failed to hold him, allowing him to release to Stofberg. At half time the score was 9-16 to South Africa.

Two penalties for the Lions, scored by Davies and Irvine, brought the Lions back to within a point early in the second half. The score was 15-16 when Davies left the field to be replaced by Ollie Campbell. It is worth noting that the rules were changed to allow substitutions for injured players in 1968 and the first time the new rules were used was during a British and Irish Lions game in South Africa that year.

1980 South Africa

The Springboks responded when Pienaar released Germishuys who outpaced O'Driscoll and Carleton to score. The Lions suffered further when Pienaar launched a counter attack after Gravell was tackled and dispossessed. Pienaar went over to score a fourth try for South Africa. From being a point behind, the Lions were now down by eleven. Even a late try to Quinnell couldn't close the gap. The test series was gone. All the Lions could manage now was a draw and for that they would have to win the remaining two tests.

On the same day as the test match, another British Isles v South Africa competition was taking place. David Evans became the first Welshman to win the British Amateur Golf Championship when he beat South Africa's David Suddards. He got more headlines than the rugby team after their defeat.

On Monday 16th June, Colm Tucker damaged his ankle during training. He is quoted as saying *"I thought my tour was over"* that evening. Thankfully that wasn't the case. He hobbled around for a few days but recovered quickly.

*Game Twelve*
*v Junior Springboks*
*Wanderers Stadium, Johannesburg, South Africa 18/6/1980*
*17-6 - Win*

**Lions Team** – O'Donnell (Ireland), Rees (Wales), Renwick (Scotland), Dodge (England), Irvine (Scotland), **Ward (Ireland)**, Robbie (Ireland), Beattie (Scotland), O'Driscoll (Ireland), Martin (Wales), Colclough (England), Squire (Wales), Price (Wales), Phillips (Wales), Orr (Ireland)

With Davies' tour now over, Tony Ward was restored to the starting line-up for the game against the Junior Springboks. The home team were ahead at half time thanks to a converted try for Berger Geldenhuys. The Lions' only score was a drop goal, scored by Jim Renwick.

Three second half tries from Paul Dodge, Andy Irvine and Elgan Rees gave the Lions the win. However, even more casualties were added to the injured list.

1980 South Africa

Irish fullback Rodney O'Donnell was carried off after injuring his neck and Irish prop Phil Orr injured his thigh forcing him from the field. It was later confirmed that O'Donnell had dislocated his neck and needed surgery to wire the sixth and seventh vertebrae together. It proved to be a career ending injury. He was very lucky as it could have been a catastrophic and life changing injury. He later said, *"I'm lucky to be alive. You only get one life and I came bloody close to losing that. I thought I was paralysed after I had made the tackle. I owe a lot to referee Steve Strydom, who said he heard a click and told people not to move me. John O'Driscoll came off the field to attend to me and told me not to allow them to put me in any position that was uncomfortable. He also told me to keep squeezing my hands".*

O'Driscoll was to also play a potential lifesaving role for Tony Ward a few days later. In his book, Ward recounts a scary incident that happened not long after this game. The team moved to the Umhlanga Rocks Indian Ocean resort near Durban to recover and rest. While there, Ward went for a swim in the ocean along with Clive Woodward, Colm Tucker and John O'Driscoll. Ward was about twenty yards out and got caught in a current that swept him well out of his depth. He was struggling against a strong current and almost drowned. Luckily, John O'Driscoll noticed that he was in difficulty and alerted the lifeguard who came to his rescue.

*Game Thirteen*
*v Northern Transvaal*
*Loftus Versfeld Stadium, Pretoria, South Africa 21/6/1980*
*16-9 – Win*

**Lions Team** – Irvine (Scotland), Woodward (England), Gravell (Wales), Dodge (England), Hay (Scotland), Campbell (Ireland), Robbie (Ireland), Squire (Wales), **Tucker (Ireland)**, Colclough (England), Beaumont (England), O'Driscoll (Ireland), Price (Wales), Wheeler (England), Williams (Wales)

Tony Ward had been selected to be a replacement in this game however, he injured an Achilles tendon during a training session the day before the game. His place on the bench was taken by Welshman Peter Morgan.

Colm Tucker made his sixth appearance for the Lions against Northern Transvaal and the Lions maintained their unbeaten record against the provincial sides with a win. All of their points were scored in the first half and it was only in the second half that Northern Transvaal registered any score at all.

*Colm Tucker tracks a break by Clive Woodward*

Irvine kicked a penalty after sixteen minutes to give the Lions the lead. That was followed by a pushover try which shocked the 68,000 crowd who were not used to seeing the big Transvaal pack pushed backwards. Welsh number eight, Jeff Squire got the all-important touch over the

1980 South Africa

line. After thirty-three minutes, John O'Driscoll broke from a lineout near the half way line. He passed to Ollie Campbell who in turn passed to Maurice Colclough. With just ten yards to cover, the English second row made it to the line to score. While they didn't score in the second half, the Lions were comfortably in control and won easily.

*Game Fourteen*
*v South Africa (Third Test)*
*Boet Erasmus Stadium, Port Elizabeth, South Africa 28/6/1980*
*10-12 - Loss*

**Lions Team** – Irvine (Scotland), Woodward (England), Gravell (Wales), Dodge (England), Hay (Scotland), Campbell (Ireland), Patterson (Ireland), Squire (Wales), O'Driscoll (Ireland), **Tucker (Ireland)**, Colclough (England), Beaumont (England), Price (Wales), Wheeler (England), Williams (Wales)

**South Africa** - Pienaar, Mordt, Smith, du Plessis, Germishuys, Botha, Serfontein, du Plessis, Stofberg, Louw, Moolman, van Heerden, le Roux, Prentis

From the pre-tour newspaper reports that an *'unknown Irishman'* was surprisingly picked for the Lions' squad, to Colm Tucker starting in the critical third test match - that is an astonishing story.

Sean Diffley writing in the Sunday Independent opened his report with, *"The Lions of 1980 do not have any luck. They dominated this third test in wet and windy Port Elizabeth yesterday and led all the way until ten minutes from the end. Then a quick throw in from touch by South Africa, and a less than vigilant Lions side was caught napping as Gerrie Girmishuys, the Springboks left wing, scampered over for a dramatic try and a stunning revival of fortunes".*

Diffley continued, *"The Lions' pack, as it has been all through this tour, played magnificently. The back row of Irish flankers, John O'Driscoll and Colm Tucker, and the Welsh number eight Jeff Squire, did all that could*

345

1980 South Africa

*reasonably be expected of them. The front five drove forward with all the skill they have been exhibiting here, but unfortunately the backs just did not have the skill or speed to outwit the Springboks' back division."*

Ollie Campbell had opened the scoring with a penalty from thirty-five yards after just two minutes. The score stayed that way until mid-way through the half when Naas Botha scored a penalty to equalise. Towards the end of the half, the Lions scored a try when Scottish winger, Hay, capitalised on forwards pressure on the Springbok line to score a try. Campbell missed the conversion. The Lions were leading 7-3 at half time.

Botha scored a drop-goal early in the second half to reduce the Lions' lead to just a point. A successful penalty kick from Ollie Campbell put the Lions 10-6 ahead and it looked as if the Lions were on their way to victory. However, a quick lineout from Germishuys, thrown to flanker Stofberg who passed straight back, allowed Germishuys to go over and score. Late in the game, Ollie Campbell had a penalty chance from wide out on the left touchline but into a heavy wind, he missed. The test was lost, as was the series.

*Game Fifteen*
*v South African Barbarians*
*Kings Park Stadium, Durban, South Africa 2/7/1980*
*25-14 – Win*

**Lions Team** – Irvine (Scotland), Rees (Wales), Morgan (Wales), Renwick (Scotland), Carleton (England), **Ward (Ireland)**, Robbie (Ireland), Beattie (Scotland), Williams (Wales), Martin (Wales), Tomes (Scotland), Quinnell (Wales), Stephens (Wales), Phillips (Wales), Orr (Ireland)

The day after he had almost drowned, Tony Ward roared into this game scoring seventeen of the Lions' twenty-five points. He put on a man of the match performance in front of a crowd of 40,000, scoring a try, kicking three penalties and two conversions.

The Lions never looked in trouble during the game. Ward kicked three penalties and converted Alan Tomes try in the first half and he was the only scorer for the Lions in the second half when he scored a try and then converted it. This was a hugely important win for the squad's

1980 South Africa

morale and for Tony Ward's chances of making the team for the final test ten days later.

*Tony Ward launches one*

**Ward makes bid for Test recall**

BRITISH LIONS 25, SOUTH AFRICAN BARBARIANS 14

IRISH fly half Tony Ward scored a sparkling 17 points as the British Lions overcame the South African Barbarians in Durban yesterday.

Ward scored a try, three penalties and two conversions but the Lions did not

*Game Sixteen*
*v Western Province*
*Newlands Stadium, Cape Town, South Africa 5/7/1980*
*37-6 – Win*

**Lions Team** – Irvine (Scotland), Carleton (England), Gravell (Wales), Dodge (England), Hay (Scotland), Campbell (Ireland), Robbie (Ireland), Squire (Wales), **Tucker (Ireland)**, Colclough (England), Beaumont

(England), O'Driscoll (Ireland), Price (Wales), Wheeler (England), Williams (Wales)

After his strong performance in the test and a one game break, Colm Tucker was back on the field for the game against Western Province at Newlands.

Ollie Campbell was back in the out-half position and, almost as if to thumb his nose at Tony Ward, he scored twenty-two points as the Lions routed Western Province. Campbell kicked four penalties, two drop-goals and converted two tries. The Lions' tries were scored by Bruce Hay and Clive Woodward.

*Game Seventeen*
*v Griqualand West*
*De Beers Stadium, Kimberley, South Africa 8/7/1980*
*23-19 - Win*

**Lions Team** – Hay (Scotland), Rees (Wales), Woodward (England), Renwick (Scotland), Morgan (Wales), **Ward (Ireland)**, Patterson (Ireland), Beattie (Scotland), Quinnell (Wales), Tomes (Scotland), Martin (England), Williams (Wales), Stephens (Wales), Phillips (Wales), Orr (Ireland)

After Campbell's performance against Western Province, the ball was back in Tony Ward's court. He needed another big game to claim the test spot. Unfortunately, his scrum-half partner Colin Patterson was carried off with a knee injury after only six minutes. The change at scrum-half hampering his first half performance.

The Lions took an early lead when John Beattie scored a try after just two minutes. However, Patterson crashed to the ground while trying to stop Chris Oosthuisen from scoring a try. He failed, Oosthuisen scored and Patterson tore knee ligaments in the process. John Robbie came on as a replacement.

The Lions trailed 7-9 at the half time interval. Then after fifty minutes, Visagie, in difficult kicking conditions, kicked a penalty from thirty-five yards to make it 7-12. It was then that the Lions came alive and started their come-back. Welsh winger Peter Morgan scored a twenty-yard drop goal. He then scored a try which Tony Ward converted. The

1980 South Africa

Lions stretched their lead when John Robbie scored a try and then he too scored a drop-goal after Ward cleverly side-kicked the ball to him. Griqualand scored a late try to make the score look closer but by the end the Lions were in control after a slow start.

Victory in this game, gave the 1980 Lions the distinction of being only the second Lions team to go undefeated in the non-test games on the tour.

Near the end of the game, Tony Ward took a heavy knock and injured his right shoulder and knee. The following day he was sent along with two other players to see a physiotherapist. In an unusual experience, the players quickly found out that the physio was, in fact, blind.

*Game Eighteen*
*v South Africa (Fourth Test)*
*Loftus Versfeld Stadium, Pretoria, South Africa 12/7/1980*
*17-13 – Win*

**Lions Team** – Irvine (Scotland), Carleton (England), Gravell (Wales), Dodge (England), Hay (Scotland), Campbell (Ireland), Robbie (Ireland), Squire (Wales), O'Driscoll (Ireland), **Tucker (Ireland)**, Colclough (England), Beaumont (England), Price (Wales), Wheeler (England), Williams (Wales)

**South Africa** - Pienaar, Mordt, Smith, du Plessis, Germishuys, Botha, Serfontein, du Plessis, Stofberg, Louw, Moolman, van Heerden, le Roux, Malan, Prentis

When the test team was announced for the fourth test, Tony Ward had lost the battle with Ollie Campbell for the number ten spot. Colm Tucker had done enough to retain his place and earned his second Lions test cap.

The crowd of 68,000 were entertained by a curtain raiser featuring the Junior Springboks playing the South African Barbarians. With their Lions tours over, eight of the Lions players played for the South African Barbarian side; John Beattie, Jim Renwick, Peter Morgan, Elgan Rees, Alan Martin, Alan Tomes, Garreth Williams and Phil Orr. The Barbarians won the game 43-14.

1980 South Africa

In the main event, the Lions dominated the first half. The forward pack were astonishing good. Clem Thomas writing in The Observer had this to say, *"No praise can be too high for the performance of the forwards who, throughout, had the Springboks by the throat and they compare to any pack which has visited South Africa"*.

The first score of the game came from an Ollie Campbell penalty after thirty-two minutes. He was to have an off-day and this successful kick was one of just two out of his eight attempts. An equalising kick from Botha came shortly afterwards but right on the whistle of half time, Clive Williams crashed over for a try to the Lions and they went into the break with a 7-3 lead.

Willie du Plessis scored a try for the Springboks at the start of the second half and Pienaar also kicked two successful penalties to put the Springboks into the lead. It was beginning to look like the other test games until the Lions scored two magnificent tries. Irvine scored in the corner after passes from Gravell and Hay. The second try came from scrum near the Springbok line, scrum-half Robbie passed it long out to Ollie Campbell, who passed to Gravell and on to O'Driscoll who scored. It was a great victory and with three tries to the Lions against just one for the Springboks, the Lions deserved it. Captain Bill Beaumont was carried off the field on the shoulders of this forward pack at the end of the game.

SUNDAY INDEPENDENT, JULY 13, 1980

# THE LIONS ROAR IN!
### Irishmen the stars as 'Boks are broken at last

350

1980 South Africa

The team celebrated that night and were on the flight home the following day. It had been a long tour. The series had been lost but at least the Lions had not been whitewashed. Colm Tucker had made nine appearances and played in two tests. Tony Ward, omitted from the original squad, had played in five games including one test.

On their flight back to London, the Lions were joined by some high-profile soccer players. Ireland and Liverpool great Steve Heighway and the Manchester United manager, Dave Sexton had been following the team on the tour and were on the same flight home.

## Post Tour Game

In the aftermath of the tour, Bill Beaumont brought a Lions team to Ireland to play a game against a Cork Constitution Presidents XV. On the Cork Con team were some big names; Christy Cantillon and Moss Finn from the Munster 1978 team, as well as future Lions Ciaran Fitzgerald, Donal Lenihan and Limerick Lion **Gerry McLoughlin.**

*The Bill Beaumont's Lions XV team*

*Back row from left - D Healy (Referee), Dai Richards, Gareth Davies, Derek Quinnell, Maurice Colclough, Ollie Campbell, Clive Williams, Mike Rafter and Michael Keyes (Cork Constitution RFC President)*

1980 South Africa

*Front row from left - Rodney O'Donnell, Johnny Moloney, Colm Tucker, Bill Beaumont, Noel Murphy (Coach), John Carleton, Phil Blakeway, Allan Phillips and Fran Cotton*
*Seated Tony Ward, left, and John Robbie.*

The game was played on September 28$^{th}$ 1980. Cork Con threatened the shock of the rugby year and were leading for the first forty-five minutes. In an exhibition game, where flair is what is expected, the Lions resorted to an Ollie Campbell penalty kick to level the scores at 17-17 before captain Bill Beaumont scored a decisive try to win the game 23-17 for the Lions.

# 1983
# New Zealand

Gerry McLoughlin

# Gerry McLoughlin
# Lion #599

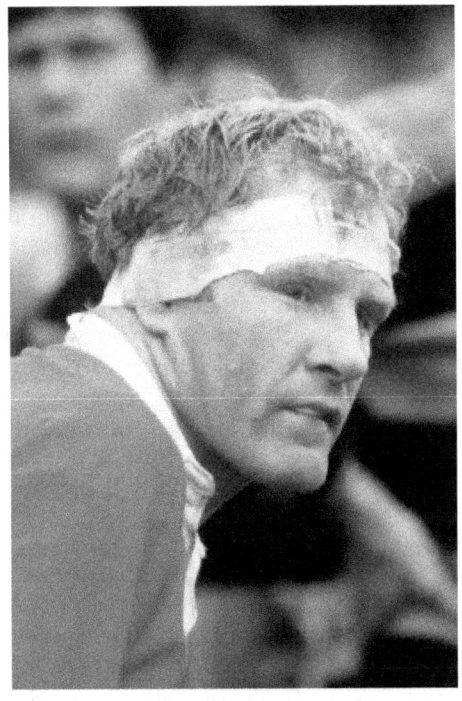

**Gerry McLoughlin**
Born - 11 June 1951, Limerick

School – Christian Brothers
Club – Shannon
Ireland Caps - 18
Lions Tour(s) - 1983
Lions Appearances - 2
Lions Tests – n/a
Position – Prop

Gerry McLoughlin was a people's champion of Limerick rugby and is much loved. Munster Senior Cup wins with Shannon, playing for both Connacht and Munster, beating the All-Blacks would be enough for most. Add to that single-handedly taking on the English pack in 1982 and scoring the try that probably won Ireland a first Grand Slam in decades and you have a legend. He was also held at gun point while in Argentina. Never beaten in an Irish jersey at Lansdowne Road, later he even became the Mayor of Limerick.

## Early Life

Gerry McLoughlin was the eldest child of Mick McLoughlin, a CIE bus driver and his wife Bridget (nee Cross). Mick and Bridget had four children in all, three boys and a girl. Gerry's brothers Pat and Mick also played for Shannon. His sister's name is Jackie. At first the McLoughlin family lived at 60 Clare Street, ironically next door to the family of another Limerick Lion, Tom Reid. The family later moved to the Roxboro Road.

## School

Gerry McLoughlin was educated by the Christian Brothers. While there, he dabbled in sports. He later said in an interview, *"As a young man, I dabbled with hurling and Gaelic football as a full-back or full-forward with St. Patrick's CBS. I had no great skill at either code; I simply mullocked and laid into guys. My destiny was certainly never to be a skillful, All-Ireland winning hurler with Limerick. Rugby was always going to be my game"*.

While he was at school, he considered becoming a priest - *"As soon as I entered Sexton Street CBS, my admiration for the role that the Christian Brothers played in Irish society saw me develop a vocation to become a Christian Brother. I spent a three-year novitiate between Carriglea Park in Dun Laoghaire and St. Helens in Booterstown and was within three weeks of taking my vows of poverty, chastity and obedience before deciding that I wanted to opt out. Had I taken the vows, I would have entered a world where there was no television, no newspapers and would not be able to take holidays or see my family for the best part of five years. That's the way it was in those days. I was at a young impressionable age and, in the end, I got stage fright and returned to Sexton Street as a pupil."*

# Club Rugby

Gerry McLoughlin started his rugby career with St Mary's. With them he won the 1966/67 Juvenile League.

In 1968/69 McLoughlin captained the St Mary's team to the Juvenile League.

*Gerry McLoughlin (standing 4$^{th}$ from left) with St Marys 1966/67*

## Shannon

Gerry's father Mick had played for Shannon and indeed had won a Transfield Cup with them. It was only natural therefore that Gerry should join Shannon. He started with them when he was sixteen years old.

Within two years Gerry had progressed and was part of the Limerick team that played in the Intercity games against Cork.

Gerry McLoughlin left Shannon for a brief spell (1971-1973) while he was being educated in U.C.G. and U.C.C getting a teaching qualification. He returned for the 1973 season.

*"In my early days with Shannon, we hardly rated on the rugby map. Teams like Trinity and Wanderers didn't want games against us.*

Gerry McLoughlin

*Garryowen were the standard bearers in Limerick and our aim was to become as good as them. After I returned from U.C.G. in 1973, Shannon, with Brian O'Brien pulling the strings, had begun to assemble a powerful team. Brendan Foley was a fine second-row and an inspirational captain. Colm Tucker was the best ball-carrying wing-forward I ever played with.*

*For twenty years we trained, two hundred scrums a night with another pack of forwards. I'd go and get fellas out of bed to come over and go on the machine against us. Those scrums sessions were tougher than you'd find at Lansdowne Road.*

*We were never going to have a backline that would be able to take on Garryowen. It wasn't that we didn't have confidence in the backs, it was that they were better tacklers than passers.*

*We devised a way of playing with seven forwards. Our full back was Terry Fitzgerald, he was a great goal kicker but he wasn't the fastest full back in the world. So, we took Eddie Price out of all the forward exchanges and played Eddie as a second full back so there was no option for anyone to kick the ball behind us. We played with seven forwards for about five years and it worked."*

Gerry McLoughlin

Gerry McLoughlin was on the Shannon team when they had remarkable success through the late 70s and 80s. He won the Munster Senior Cup five times, 1977, 78, 82, 86 and 87. He was also a beaten finalist on three other occasions. He also captained the club in the 1978/79 season.

*Gerry McLoughlin (standing 4$^{th}$ from left) with the 1986 Shannon Team*

Gerry McLoughlin

*Mick McLoughlin (seated 2<sup>nd</sup> right) and Pat McLoughlin (front row on the left)*
"Tony Ward played for Garryowen against Shannon on twelve occasions and lost every one of them. That is a statistic for you. We played thirty-five matches in 1986. We won thirty-four and drew one. Then 1987 came and the cup final was in Cork. That was huge, to go to Cork and take the cup out of Cork. We beat Highfield in the final. I won five medals but it wasn't about the medals. It was about the challenge that was there all the time.".

Gerry McLoughlin

"Playing the Lions and winning cup medals, it didn't affect me one bit. To be honest with you, beating Garryowen was probably my greatest achievement of all time because that was with my friends and with my club.

359

*I'd have been nothing without the Brian O'Briens and the Michael Noel Ryans of this world. They put everything in to us."*
Gerry McLoughlin

U.C.G.

After school, Gerry went to U.C.G. to further his education. He played on the U.C.G. team with Ciaran Fitzgerald beside him in the front row.

*"At 18, I was in the Shannon senior-cup team and I knew that I had some ability. After Sexton Street, I went to U.C.G. to do my BA and that gave me the opportunity of further developing my rugby skills as I joined Ciaran Fitzgerald in the Colleges senior front-row".*
Gerry McLoughlin

## Connacht Rugby

Within a year of leaving Shannon to further his education in Galway, Gerry McLoughlin was playing on the U.C.G. team with Ciaran Fitzgerald beside him in the front row.

Very quickly he was also called into the Connacht squad and he made his debut against Ulster at Ravenhill in November 1972. He got a handful more Connacht caps before he played his final game for them in March 1973. He was on the Connacht team that beat Spain 11-10 at The Sportsground in Galway. That win, ended a near ten year losing run for Connacht.

## Munster Rugby

Gerry McLoughlin made his Munster debut in a fierce game against Argentina at Thomond Park. The game was played on 31$^{st}$ October 1973 and ended in a 12-12- draw. Munster were leading 6-0 at the break but Argentina played tough rugby in the second half to level the score. The game was described as a *"Controversial Irish debut for the touring Argentinians".*

Gerry McLoughlin

Gerry would go on to play for Munster for over a decade. With Munster he won the Interprovincial Championship in 1975 and again in 1978.

Four touring sides would come to Munster during Gerry's career:

**Australia**

In January 1976, he was on the Munster team that played the touring Wallabies at Musgrave Park. Playing alongside Seamus Dennison, Tony Ward, Donal Canniffe, Moss Keane and Brendan Foley, Munster put up a tremendous fight. The Australians were lucky to get away with a win. The game ended 13-15.

*Newspaper Headlines after the Australia game in January 1976*

**New Zealand**

Gerry McLoughlin was one of the legendary Munster team that toppled the All-Blacks at Thomond Park in October 1978.

*"It wasn't a fluke by any means as that was a superb Munster team. For starters, the usual Cork/Limerick selectorial carve-up didn't apply as twelve of the Munster team picked themselves. We had leaders and quality players all over the field. Wardie (Tony Ward) was under pressure all day, but still managed to kick brilliantly for position; Canniffe gave him a great service; Dennison and Barrett never stopped tackling; Larry Moloney was himself at full-back; Andy Haden might have won the line-out battle, but we matched the All-Blacks forwards everywhere else; in the end, we fully deserved our 12-0 victory."*

Gerry McLoughlin

Gerry McLoughlin

*Gerry McLoughlin in a lineout during the All-Black game 1978*

## Romania

In October 1980, Gerry was on the Munster team that played Romania at Thomond Park. On that day there were none of the 1978 heroics and Munster were well beaten 9-32.

*Munster v Romania in Oct 1980*

The only defence for the poor performance against Romania was that a week earlier, Bill Beaumont had brought the 1980 Lions team to Cork to play Cork Con and a few of the team had played in that game and no doubt enjoyed the after-game party.

*Gerry McLoughlin playing for Munster*

**Australia**

Australia again came to Munster in 1981. This game was played in Musgrave Park in November and Munster again took down one of the big names by beating the Wallabies 15-6. The Australia team featured distinguished names such as Mark Ella and Simon Poidevin.

*Newspaper Headlines after the Australia game in 1981*

Almost thirteen years to the day after his first appearance for Munster, Gerry McLoughlin played for the province for the last time against Ulster in Cork on 25$^{th}$ October 1986. Munster were defeated 6-17.

## International Rugby

Gerry McLoughlin was a late bloomer in international rugby terms. He was called up for the Irish trials in 1978.

> *"In the final trial, they went according to dimensions in those days. I was only thirteen stone ten. I had to get to fourteen stone so I put lead in my jock strap. Then I was getting old at that stage, I was nearly twenty-seven so I went back to twenty-five. I became a six foot, fourteen stone, twenty-five-year-old. That was my first excursion up to Dublin. We weren't heard about in Limerick you know."*
>
> Gerry McLoughlin

You can still find Gerry McLoughlin's birth date recorded as 1952 because of this fudge to make the Irish team. Just three months after beating New Zealand and a successful Irish trial with the 'probables', McLoughlin made his international debut in the Five Nations clash against France at Lansdowne Road on 20$^{th}$ January 1979. Ireland drew 9-9. He went on to play in all four games of that campaign. Ireland lost in Cardiff, beat England at home and drew in Scotland.

In June 1979 Gerry went on the **Irish tour to Australia**. In a very successful tour, Ireland won eight of their nine matches including both tests and became the first northern hemisphere team to win a test series down under. Their loss came against a Sydney team.

In the first game against Western Australia in Perth, Gerry McLoughlin wasn't originally selected to play but Ned Byrne was the victim of a hit and run accident, breaking his leg and was unable to play.

> *"I scored the first try on that tour. I didn't know until nine o'clock that morning that I was playing. I wouldn't be able to tell you what time I went to bed the night before. I was rooming with Ned Byrne. I was waiting for him to come in. No sign of him. He had gone for a walk with Slattery and Duggan. The Blackrock boys."*
>
> Gerry McLoughlin

Gerry played in the 39-3 win but went off injured towards the end with a groin strain.

*Gerry McLoughlin and Moss Keane*

Three days and three thousand kilometres further east in Canberra, Ireland played Australian Capital Territory. Gerry was scheduled to play despite being injured but Mick Fitzpatrick, who had been called out as injury cover, arrived in time and played in Ireland's 35-7 win.

A few days after that, Gerry McLoughlin was recovered to play the game against New South Wales at the Sydney Sports Ground and Ireland secured a 16-12 win.

Gerry sat out the game against Queensland at Ballymore. Ireland secured a late 18-15 win in that game ahead of the first test at the same ground a few days later.

There was serious contention when Tony Ward was dropped for the first test. He was two-time European player of the year and was a burgeoning superstar. Ollie Campbell was selected ahead of him and McLoughlin played when Ireland beat Australia 27-12 in the first test.

Gerry McLoughlin was again in the team that made it six wins out of six on the tour when they played NSW Country in Orange. Ireland won 28-7.

Perhaps the fall out over Tony Ward played a small part in Ireland's only loss of the tour when they lost to Sydney 12-16. Ward was back in the team and Gerry McLoughlin played his sixth game of the tour.

The tour's last game was a second test played at the Sydney Cricket Ground. Again, Gerry was in the side as Ireland secured a historic 3-9 win.

The following season, McLoughlin played in the first game of the Five Nations, a loss away to England who would go on to win a Grand Slam that year. He was on the bench for the rest of the games that season.

*Gerry McLoughlin (standing 2nd Left) with the Irish team*

Ireland's 1980/81 Five Nations tournament was shrouded in controversy. Ahead of the games, it was announced that Ireland would undertake a tour to South Africa in April and May of that year.

In 1977, the Gleneagles Agreement was signed by all members of the Commonwealth. That agreement pledged that each country would discourage contact and competition between their sporting organisations and those of South Africa in protest against the apartheid system. While Ireland was not a commonwealth country, all of the other major rugby nations were and so Ireland by extension was expected to comply. The IRFU's decision to undertake the tour sparked massive protests. No government officials attended the Ireland games that year and the pitch at Lansdowne Road had to have a wire fence installed to keep protestors off the field. Ireland had an awful campaign and lost all of their games. Gerry McLoughlin wasn't in the squad for those games.

While it is easy from today to look back and condemn it, the game was an amateur sport and the players wanted to represent their country.

*"Nelson Mandela was encouraging Errol Tobias to play for the Springboks. If he was supporting them, why wouldn't we go?"*
Gerry McLoughlin

Before the Five Nations campaign, the IRFU sent out letters to forty players enquiring about their availability for the tour. Some opted not to go citing various reasons. Gerry wanted to play rugby and made himself available. He even quit his job so that he could go on the tour.

*"I was teaching in Sexton Street at the time and initially got approval from the school to travel. However, just a week before we were due to depart, a change of management took place within the school and my permission to travel was withdrawn. It left me with a very difficult decision to make. I was married with a young family, but I dearly wanted to represent my country. Also, I felt that South Africa were making advances on apartheid. Errol Tobias, in fact, became the first non-white player to wear the Springboks jersey in a full-international against Ireland. In the end, I resigned my teaching position and travelled with Ireland."*
Gerry McLoughlin

The tour went ahead. Ireland played seven games including two test matches against the Springboks. Ahead of the tour, the IRFU stipulated that in four of the seven games, the South Africans should field multi-racial teams.

Gerry McLoughlin played in the first three games of the tour. The tour opened with a game against South African Gazelles at Loftus Versfeld. Ireland lost 15-18. Ireland got their tour back on track by beating a South African Mining Invitation XV at Potchefstroom 7-46.

Ireland again won the third game against a President's Trophy XV at Kings Stadium Durban 3-54.

Gerry McLoughlin was rested ahead of the first test and watched on as Ireland were beaten 16-17 by South African Country Districts at Boland Stadium in Wellington.

The first test at Newlands on 30th May 1981 was historic due to the fact that Erroll Tobias became the first coloured Springbok player. Gerry McLoughlin was on the field that day as Ireland lost 15-23.

Gerry was again rested for the second last game of the tour against a Gold Cup XV in Oudtshoorn. Ireland easily won 51-10. He was back on the pitch for the final game, the second test played at Kings Park in Durban on 6th June. Ireland narrowly lost 10-12.

The decision to tour South Africa in 1981 had a dramatic effect on McLoughlin's life. When he returned, he was out of work and blacklisted because of his decision to play rugby.

> *"On my return from South Africa, I was advised that I had a solid legal case against my former employers in Sexton Street but I decided against taking any action as I had a great love of the Christian Brothers and had witnessed the benefits which their dedication gave to generations of children. They were put under severe pressure at the time as apartheid was a political and social time-bomb.*
>
> *I wrote to every school in the country and couldn't get an interview, never mind get a job. The IRFU had plenty of people in positions of power, but the support from that quarter was nil. Ray McLoughlin and Mick Molloy did offer considerable help at the time. Other than that, I was largely left to fend for myself. It was my decision to travel to South Africa – I had to accept the consequences."*
>
> Gerry McLoughlin

It took time before Gerry McLoughlin found a part time job. Jerry Burke, principal of the Tech on O'Connell Ave, gave him the opportunity he needed.

While Gerry felt the impact of the tour, the Irish public were quick to forget when Ireland had a historic 1981/82 Five Nations championship, winning the Triple Crown for the first time in thirty years. Gerry McLoughlin was to play a huge role in that success.

Ireland got their campaign off the ground with a home win over Wales (20-12). McLoughlin was on the bench for that game. Ireland then went to Twickenham and one of the highlights of Gerry McLoughlin's career.

Ireland were ahead 10-3 at half time thanks to a try from scrum-half Robbie McGrath. England closed the gap at the start of the second half with a penalty. Then, after Ollie Campbell had a drop goal attempt charged down, Ireland gathered the ball and McLoughlin led a charge to the line and scored his one and only try for Ireland. In a thriller, England pulled the score back close to the end and the game ended 15-16 to Ireland.

WE'RE ON FOR THE TRIPLE CROWN! . . . Ireland's thrilling 16-15 rugby win over England at Twickenham yesterday leaves only Scotland to beat in a fortnight's time for the Triple Crown, which has eluded Ireland for over 30 years. Gerry McLoughlin is pictured here about to touch down for Ireland's second try yesterday. Full report, page 28.

*Gerry McLoughlin's famous try against England in 1982*

Newspaper headlines after Irelands win at Twickenham

"At the time, I was misquoted as saying I dragged the Irish pack over the line with me. In fact, I dragged the entire Irish and English forwards across the line that day! Also, I never got the credit for creating the free which led to my try. As Steve Smith was about to put-in at an English scrum, I whispered to Ciaran Fitzgerald that I intended to pull the scrum, which I did successfully with the result that Smith was penalised for crooked-in. After the free was taken, I took over."

"In the dressing room after, Moss said to me that they were after giving that try to Willie Duggan. I said, fuck off Moss, I pulled them all over. The best thing about that try was, I knew I wouldn't get dropped for the next match. I played eighteen times for Ireland and I was a substitute twenty-two times, so I knew how it felt to be dropped."

Gerry McLoughlin

Two weeks after his heroics at Twickenham, Gerry played in the home victory of Scotland. Ireland's defeat away in Paris in the final game of the campaign is overlooked as Ireland had won their first Triple Crown since 1949 and had won the Five Nations.

Gerry McLoughlin was also central to Ireland's Five Nations campaign in 1983. He played in all four games as Ireland shared the championship with France. Ireland opened the campaign with a win away in Scotland (13-15). They then beat France in Dublin by 22-16. A disappointing loss in Cardiff (23-9) was followed in the final game with a 25-15 win over England at Lansdowne Road.

*John O'Driscoll, Moss Keane and Gerry McLoughlin 1983*

*Gerry McLoughlin with the Ireland forward pack*

Ahead of the 1984 Five Nations, McLoughlin was suspended for two months by the Munster Branch.

## Two months suspension for prop McLoughlin

BRITISH LIONS prop forward Gerry McLoughlin has been suspended for two months by the Munster branch of the Irish Rugby ~~F~~ ~~~~ of the inter-provincial series as well as the final Irish trial on December 17.

McLoughlin was a late replacement for the Lions' tour

McLoughlin can appeal, however, and will take part in the Irish squad training session on Sunday.

● The All Blacks will com-

*"I was playing against Old Crescent in the Munster Senior League. Someone was holding on to my boot so I couldn't get away and the ball had gone. So eventually I got away and I tapped your man (Ken Lyons) on the arse. I never kicked anyone in my life. I tapped him in the arse.*

*Two days later the Limerick Leader had an article saying that I kicked a guy in the ruck and the referee had missed it. So, I was called up by the Munster Branch. Ken Lyons even went to the meeting with me and vouched for me but they suspended me. That cost me a few caps in the end."*

Gerry McLoughlin

The two-month ban meant that McLoughlin missed the interprovincial series and the Irish trial ahead of the five nations. He was selected to play in the opening round of the Five Nations in Paris on 21st January 1984. Ireland were beaten 25-12 on that occasion. That was the last time Gerry McLoughlin would play for Ireland.

*"Playing for your country is all you ever go out to achieve. All I ever wanted was to play for Ireland. After that, nothing ever mattered. To pull on the green jersey, just for five minutes, is all you want. You don't hold on to it but it's all you ever want. Knowing, this is it. Nothing ever matters after that".*

Gerry McLoughlin reflecting on his Irish career

### Penguin International Rugby Football Club

The Penguin International Rugby Football Club was formed in 1959. Similar to, but much less well known than the British and Irish Lions, the Penguins are an international invitational touring team. Their objective is to foster the development, goodwill and camaraderie of

Rugby Union worldwide. Since their inception, the team have travelled to over eighty countries and have drawn on players from over thirty-five.

Gerry McLoughlin was invited to tour Argentina with the Penguins in August 1980. A touring party of twenty-nine players and management set off from Gatwick airport on 31$^{st}$ August. Ahead of them were seven scheduled games.

Two days after arriving, on Sunday 3$^{rd}$ August, they played their first game against La Plata in the outskirts of Buenos Aires. They won the game easily with a score of 21-0.

On Thursday 7$^{th}$ August they played and beat Cordoba Province in Cordoba a few hundred miles inland from Buenos Aires.

## PROGRAMA
### DOMINGO 10 DE AGOSTO DE 1980
15,30 HORAS

| PENGUIN R.F.C. | C.A. BANCO NACION ARG |
|---|---|
| 1. MC LOUGHLIN, Gerry A. | 1. CORDEIRO, Carlos |
| 2. FISHER, Colin D. | 2. ORTEGA, Jorge |
| 3. MACKENZIE, Gregor | 3. N ARRON, Alfredo |
| 4. MARTIN, Nick (CAPITAN) | 4. CARDONATO, Daniel |
| 5. HAKIN, Ronaldd F. | 5. FAHEY, Alberto |
| 6. HANRAHAN, Desmond | 6. CATO, Juan C. |
| 7. ROBERTS, Garetti | 7. LEDO, Horacio |
| 8. PAXTON, San M. | 8. N ASTROCOLA, Oscar |
| 9. MC. GRATH, Robert F. | 9. CONTARDI, Alberto |
| 10. HORTON, John | 10. PORTA, Hugo (CAPITAN) |
| 11. MC. LENNAN, Alfred | 11. DI SALVATORE, Omar |
| 12. IRWIN, David G. | 12. LORENZO, César |
| 13. WILSON, Frack | 13. DE VARGAS, José M. |
| 14. SWIFT, Anthony | 14. CAPPELLETTI, Adolfo |
| 15. HUTCHINS, Neil | 15. IGLESIAS, Mario |
| 16. MORAN, John P. | 16. GIORDANO, Mario |
| 17. CANTRELL, John L. | 17. ALONSO, José A. |
| 18. NIMES, Barry | 18. FIORIOLI, Marcelo |
| 19. DOUGLAS, Mark | 19. EHRN AN, Ramiro |
| 20. SPARKS, Conor G. | 20. FERRARIS, Claudio |
| 21. COAKLEY, Gary | 21. AZTIBIA, Eduardo |

*Gerry McLoughlin listed on the Penguin team-sheet for the third game of their tour*

Their third game was against C.A. Banco Nacion back in Buenos Aires on Sunday 10$^{th}$ August. This was a tougher game with the Argentina out-half Hugo Porta playing as their captain and a number of other Pumas also on the team. The Penguins again won the game. After the game there was a reception where the teams socialised and ate. After the reception, the team split off into groups and headed out to enjoy Buenos Aires. Willie Anderson brought his bagpipes and spent the evening moving between bars with a few other players.

On his way back to the team hotel, Anderson passed a government building that, as was usual, an Argentine flag flying. Anderson had souvenired a Canadian flag the previous year while he was there and decided that that Argentina flag would look good on his wall at home too. With the help of Frank Wilson and one other unnamed accomplice, Anderson freed the flag from its flagpole and joyously walked back to the hotel. As other players also arrived back, a party broke out in the room of David Irwin. There were about then players there including Gerry McLoughlin, and Willie Anderson was showing off his new possession.

Not long later, the players heard sirens outside and joked that Anderson was going to be arrested for theft. Little did they realise that it was true. After another few minutes, armed police entered the room and the players all had a gun pointed at their heads.

> *"A few of the lads went out together but eventually split up. When I got back to the hotel at 2am, a dozen policemen stormed in and said someone had stolen a flag. The flag was under a bed. I don't think it was realised that the flag was taken just as a souvenir. Later the British Embassy told me that taking a national flag is the equivalent of stealing the Crown Jewels."*
>
> John Palmer

> *"Guns to our heads. Where's the flag? Next thing was, they were looking for English passports. There was one brave man, John Palmer from Bath. One of the players being called up Irishman Conor Sparks. Sparks was a solicitor. He said 'if I get arrested, I'll lose my job'. So, John Palmer volunteered and went instead of him. The four of them (Willie Anderson, David Irwin, Frank Wilson and John Palmer) were taken away."*
>
> Gerry McLoughlin

The four players were whisked away in four police cars and locked up. Gerry followed them to the station to give them morale support.

> *"The next day we were feeding them in a cage"*
>
> Gerry McLoughlin

On Tuesday 12th August, the news broke back home that the players had been arrested. The Argentine RFU suspended the tour and the four prisoners were brought before a magistrate. Willie Anderson took full responsibility for the theft of the flag but all four were remanded.

This incident took place not long before the Falklands war and while there was a military junta in control of Argentina. The case became a major international incident between Britain and Argentina.

On Wednesday 13th August, James Palmer was released as it was evident that he wasn't with Anderson when the flag was taken. He was freed in time to board a flight home with the rest of the party. They flew out leaving the three Northern Irishmen in prison.

After a refuelling stop in Rio, the team arrived back in London on Thursday 14th. Meanwhile, in Buenos Aires, hundreds turned out to watch as the recovered flag was raised again outside the government building.

After two weeks in prison, the judge ordered that Wilson and Irwin be released without charge. He ordered Willie Anderson face trial on a charge of "Stealing a flag and demeaning a national symbol". The punishment for that charge could have been as much as ten years prison. Anderson was released on £13,000 bail on condition that he didn't leave the country.

For three months Anderson stayed in a hotel in Buenos Aires waiting for a court case. He was eventually convicted on 18th November but was given a two-year suspended sentence allowing him to travel home.

## The British and Irish Lions

Gerry McLoughlin was called up for the 1983 British and Irish Lions tour of New Zealand. On that tour he played in just twice.

To read more about his 1983 Lions tour – Refer chapter New Zealand (1983)

In 1980, in the aftermath of the Lions tour to South Africa, an unofficial Lions team came to play a game in Cork against a Cork Con Presidents' XV. Gerry was selected to play in the historic game. Technically he has played for and against the British and Irish Lions.

> *"I don't really consider that game to be against the Lions. It was more a game against Bill Beaumont's team. It was for charity. I'll never forget Maurice Colclough looking for expenses. I didn't like him on the Lions tour then a few years later. He gave Fitzy an awful time. If he couldn't win the ball, he would blame Fitzy. Fitzy is a quiet individual and he was captain."*
> Gerry McLoughlin

*Gerry McLoughlin with the Cork Con Presidents XV v The Lions in Cork 1980*

## Life after Rugby

Gerry McLoughlin was an Economics teacher at Christian Brothers Sexton Street when he resigned to go on the Ireland tour of South Africa in 1981. He struggled to find work when he returned. He had a part time teaching job with the Municipal Institute of Technology and for a time he had a pub called The Triple Crown on Athlunkard St.

An economic downturn led to financial difficulties so he made the difficult decision to close the pub and move to Wales.

*"In all, I spent 13 years in Wales, teaching in Gilfach Goch near Pontypridd during the day and running a pub in the evenings before deciding to return to Ireland."*

*"I coached a team to win the Welsh schools cup when I was in Wales. Cardinal Newman School. The smallest school in Wales. My sons and my nephew were on the team. They'd never won it before. We went all the way to the Arms Park and beat Neath in the final. There were only twenty-five kids in sixth year. All the boys were from fifth year and third year. We trained and trained and trained. Everything was about speed on the ball."*
Gerry McLoughlin

*Gerry McLoughlin behind the bar of his wine bar in Wales*

When he returned to Ireland, McLoughlin started a political career. He felt that Ireland had changed a lot with the Celtic Tiger. Some people were being left behind and needed help. He stood as a candidate in the 2004 Local Elections and was elected. He later joined the Labour Party and represented them on the council for a number of years. In 2012 he had the honour to be elected Mayor of Limerick.

*Gerry McLoughlin – Mayor of Limerick*

*"I was on all the committees in St Marys. When I came back from Britain I was like a lost soul. I had nowhere to go, no community to go to so I went back down to St Marys. I knew everyone up there, all the families. I went in as independent. I remember going to do the novena in June. I wouldn't be that religious but I came out of the novena and I got a phone call asking if I wanted to be Mayor. I hadn't even considered it. I consider that to be my greatest, not achievement, but honour. Bigger than any Lions. Bigger than beating Garryowen. I love Limerick."*

Gerry McLoughlin

## Personal Life

Gerry McLoughlin lives in Garryowen. He has four children with Colette O'Donovan, Orla, Cian, Fionn and Emmet.

His daughter, Orla, was the South Wales Rose of Tralee entrant in 2000. After returning to Ireland, she was for a while a Labour Party Councillor in Limerick.

His son, Fionn, also had a rugby career playing for Shannon, and Munster. His talent was evident early when he was on the Pontypridd

Welsh Schools under-11 rugby sevens competition at the National Stadium in Cardiff in 1994.

Another son, Emmet, also played for Shannon and Munster. Both Fionn and Emmet were on the Pontypridd Schools U-11 KO Cup winning team in 1993 and both were also on the Cardinal Newman team that won the Welsh schools cup at the Cardiff Arms Park in May 2000.

Mcloughlin was inducted into the Rugby Writers' Hall of Fame in 2018.

*McLoughlin's induction into the Rugby Writers' Hall of Fame*

Gerry McLoughlin

# New Zealand (1983)

France won a Grand Slam in the 1981 Five Nations championships with Ireland finish with a wooden spoon under the cloud of the proposed tour to South Africa that year. Ireland bounced back the following year winning the championship and the Triple Crown thanks to Gerry McLoughlin's try at Twickenham and in 1983, coming into the Lions tour to New Zealand Ireland had again won the championship (shared with France). It had been a good year and Ireland expected strong representation in the tour squad.

On the home front, Shannon were in the middle of their decade of success in the Munster Senior Cup winning it in 1981 and being runner up in 1982. Young Munster won it in 1983.

Irish rugby great Willie John McBride was appointed as the team manager for the tour and Gerry McLoughlin's Ireland front row colleague Ciaran Fitzgerald was appointed captain. With his heroics at Twickenham still fresh in people's minds McLoughlin was strongly tipped to be selected.

*The 1983 British and Irish Lions*

## Touring party

When the squad was announced there were ten English, nine Welsh, eight Irish and eight from Scotland. McLoughlin was omitted. One of

1983 New Zealand

the Irish was Gerry McLoughlin's Muster teammate, Donal Lenihan who was diagnosed with a hernia and missed the start of the tour.

Gerry McLoughlin was not in the original squad selected ahead of the tour. He was told he was to be on standby.

*"I knew I was in contention but I didn't think too much about it. I was getting on a bit. It didn't bother me too much. To me it didn't feel as important as playing for Ireland. You were told you might get called but you never expected to get called. We couldn't even follow the tour. It wasn't even on the television back then".*

Gerry McLoughlin

**Management**
Manager Willie John McBride (Ireland)
Coach Jim Telfer (Scotland)
Doctor Donald McLeod
Physio Kevin Murphy

**Backs**
Robert Ackerman (London Welsh and Wales), Roger Baird (Kelso and Scotland), Ollie Campbell (Old Belvedere and Ireland), John Carleton (Orrell and England), Gwyn Evans (Maesteg and Wales), Dusty Hare (Leicester and England), Terry Holmes (Cardiff and Wales), David Irwin (Instonians and Ireland), Mike Kiernan (Dolphin and Ireland), Roy Laidlaw (Jedforest and Scotland), Hugo MacNeill (Oxford University and Ireland), Nigel Melville (Wasps), Trevor Ringland (Ballymena and Ireland), John Rutherford (Selkirk and Scotland), Steve Smith (Sale and England), Clive Woodward (Leicester and England)

**Forwards**
Steve Bainbridge (Gosforth and England), John Beattie (Glasgow Academicals and Scotland), Steve Boyle (Gloucester and England), Eddie Butler (Pontypool and Wales), Jim Calder (Stewart's Melville FP and Scotland), Maurice Colclough (Angoulême and England), Colin Deans (Hawick and Scotland), Ciaran Fitzgerald (capt) (St Mary's College and Ireland), Nick Jeavons (Moseley and England), ST 'Staff' Jones (Pontypool and Wales), Donal Lenihan (Cork Constitution and Ireland), **Gerry McLoughlin (Shannon and Ireland),** Iain Milne (Heriot's FP and Scotland), Bob Norster (Cardiff and Wales), John O'Driscoll (London Irish and Ireland), Iain Paxton (Selkirk and Scotland), Graham Price (Pontypool and Wales), Jeff Squire (Pontypool

1983 New Zealand

and Wales), Ian Stephens (Bridgend and Wales), Peter Winterbottom (Headingley and England)

## The Games

Gerry McLoughlin joined the tour late having been called in to replace Ian Stephens. He missed the majority of the games as a result. He joined the group at game thirteen of eighteen in Christchurch.

The following is a list of games played ahead of Gerry joining the tour.

*Game One*
*v Wanganui*
*Spriggens Park, Wanganui 15/5/1983*
*47-15 - Win*


*Game Two*
*v Auckland*
*Eden Park, Auckland 18/5/1983*
*12-13 - Loss*

*Four future world cup winners played on the Auckland team – Gary and AJ Whetton, John Kirwan and Grant Fox.*

*Game Three*
*v Bay of Plenty*
*Rotorua Stadium, Rotorua 21/5/1983*
*34-16 - Win*


*Game Four*
*v Wellington*
*Athletic Park, Wellington 25/5/1983*
*27-19 - Win*

*Stu Wilson who was on the losing side at Thomond Park in 1978 played this game for Wellington.*

1983 New Zealand

*Game Five*
*v Manawatu*
*Showgrounds, Palmerston North 28/5/1983*
*25-18 - Win*


*Game Six*
*v Mid Canterbury*
*The Showgrounds, Ashburton 31/5/1983*
*26-6 - Win*


*Game Seven*
*v New Zealand (First Test)*
*Lancaster Park, Christchurch 4/6/1983*
*12-16 - Loss*

**Lions Team** - MacNeill (Ireland), Ringland (Ireland), Irwin (Ireland), Ackerman (Wales), Baird (Scotland), Campbell (Ireland), Holmes (Wales), Stephens (Wales), Fitzgerald (Ireland), Price (Wales), Paxton (Scotland), Winterbottom (England), Norster (Wales), Colclough (England), Squire (Wales)

**New Zealand:** - Hewson, Wilson, Pokere, Fraser, Taylor, Dunn, Loveridge, Mexted, Hobbs, Haden, Whetton, Shaw, Ashworth, Dalton, Knight

Coming into the first test the All-Blacks were slight favourites. There was very strong Irish representation in the test team when it was announced.

Pundits felt that the All-Black pack would dominate the Lions and use that as a platform for victory. In the game itself this didn't prove to be the case with Ciaran Fitzgerald and the Lions pack giving as good as they got. The Lions were in the game right up until the end.

All of the Lions' points were scored by Ollie Campbell. Nine came from penalties and the rest from a drop-goal. The All-Blacks got the only try of the game in the second half, scored by Mark Shaw in the second half. It was all to play for with the All-Blacks leading 12-13 into the closing stages. The Lions had chances but didn't take them and with two

1983 New Zealand

minutes left on the clock, the All-Blacks closed the game with a Hewson drop-goal.

Gary Whetton and Warwick Taylor on the New Zealand side would go on to win the first Rugby World Cup in 1987.

*Game Eight*
*v West Coast*
*Rugby Park, Greymouth 8/6/1983*
*52-16 - Win*

> *This was the only game on tour without Irish representation on the Lions team.*

*Game Nine*
*v Southland*
*Rugby Park, Invercargill 11/6/1983*
*41-3 - Win*

*Game Ten*
*v Wairarapa Bush*
*Memorial Park, Masterton 14/6/1983*
*57-10 - Win*

*Game Eleven*
*v New Zealand (Second Test)*
*Athletic Park, Wellington 14/6/1983*
*0-9 - Loss*

**Lions Team** – MacNeill (Ireland), Carleton (England), Irwin (Ireland), Kiernan (Ireland), Baird (Scotland), Campbell (Ireland), Laidlaw (Scotland), Jones (Wales), Fitzgerald (Ireland), Price (Wales), Paxton (Scotland), Winterbottom (England), Norster (Wales), Colclough (England), O'Driscoll (Ireland).

**New Zealand** - Hewson, Wilson, Pokere, Fraser, Taylor, Smith, Loveridge, Mexted, Hobbs, Haden, Whetton, Shaw, Ashworth, Dalton, Knight

1983 New Zealand

There were six Irish men on the test team showing the strength of Irish rugby at the time. Andy Dalton won the toss for the All-Blacks and decided to play with the breeze at their backs in the first half. With the wind advantage, the All-Blacks ran out to a 0-9 half time lead. The Lions were continually under pressure. The New Zealand points coming from a Loveridge try and a Hewson penalty.

There was no change in the second half and the game ended the same way as the first half with the Lions down by nine points.

The Lions were under pressure at this stage. While they had won all but one of the provincial games to this point, they had lost the two opening test matches and the best they could now do was draw the series. Injuries were also beginning to mount up.

On the Thursday before the game against North Auckland, the team were training at a school ground in Whangarei when Ian Stephen's knee gave way. He was strapped up and taken from the training field. He had x-rays done and it was confirmed that his tour was over. Later that evening it was announced that **Gerry McLoughlin** would be joining the tour. Donal Lenihan who was in the original squad but who had been recovering from a hernia, was also on the way, as was Steve Smith.

> *"I started wheeling wheelbarrows of muck, of clay, from down by Woodview Park, up the hill into my own back garden. I had to get myself wound up. You wouldn't lose that much fitness but at the same time you wouldn't be fit after being off for a couple of months. I wouldn't have been drinking and I had four kids so I was kept busy".*
> Gerry McLoughlin

With re-enforcements on the way, the Lions continued their tour with a game in North Auckland, before traveling on to Christchurch for a game against a Canterbury side featuring Robbie Deans who would later be Crusaders and Wallabies coach and who scored eighteen of his team's twenty-two points that day.

In his book 'My Life in Rugby', Donal Lenihan recounts a story of the long journey from Shannon, via London, Los Angeles and Auckland to Christchurch. On their stop-off in Los Angeles airport Gerry McLoughlin went missing. With a flight to catch, Lenihan and Smith went in search of him. They found him in the middle of a crowd of

386

1983 New Zealand

Lions supporters who had gathered around him as he was doing pull ups on a construction scaffolding in the terminal. *"That used to happen to me a lot"*, Gerry said with a smile when asked about it.

**Game Twelve**
**v North Auckland**
**Okara Park, Whangārei 25/6/1983**
**21-12 - Win**

**Game Thirteen**
**v Canterbury**
**Lancaster Park, Christchurch 28/6/1983**
**20-22 - Loss**

Gerry McLoughlin, Steve Smith and Donal Lenihan arrived in Christchurch on the morning of the Canterbury game. Two hours later Smith was thrown in at the deep end and sat on the bench for the game. McLoughlin and Lenihan were given a more lenient start.

The Lions moved on to Dunedin for the third test. They were in town for five days and had appalling weather the entire time. The test was played in hail, sleet and wind, not what the Lions needed to play open running rugby.

McLoughlin hadn't trained for two months after being omitted from the touring side originally. Donal Lenihan was also unfit as he was recovering from his hernia. The duo quickly got down to work and the Irish Independent reported –

> *"The two Irish replacements, Gerry McLoughlin and Donal Lenihan train on their own, doing lap after lap around the perimeter of the training area. They are supervised and encouraged by the team doctor, Donald McLeod, a rather stern Scottish gentleman, with a stop watch in hand. Ginger McLoughlin's expression at being exhorted by the team doctor makes it patently clear that it was adding a new dimension to his experience of training. As the Irish pair bend their strides into the wind and rain, I could not help thinking of Captain Scott and gallant Captain Oates. The suffering was comparable".*

Gerry McLoughlin

1983 New Zealand

Scott and Oates both froze to death on the Terra Nova Antarctic Expedition in 1912.

*Game Fourteen*
*v New Zealand (Third Test)*
*Carisbrook, Dunedin 2/7/1983*
*8-15 - Loss*

**Lions Team** – Evans (Wales), Carleton (England), Kiernan (Ireland), Rutherford (Scotland), Baird (Scotland), Campbell (Ireland), Laidlaw (Scotland), Jones (Wales), Fitzgerald (Ireland), Price (Wales), Paxton (Scotland), Winterbottom (England), Bainbridge (England), Colclough (England), Calder (Scotland)

**New Zealand** - Hewson, Wilson, Pokere, Fraser, Taylor, Smith, Loveridge, Mexted, Hobbs, Haden, Whetton, Shaw, Ashworth, Dalton, Knight

None of the three recently arrived players were picked to play in the test and they watched on from the relative comfort of the stand.

The Lions scored two tries to one in the floodlight game at Carisbrook but lost to a powerful All Black pack. The Lions led by 8-6 mid-way through the second half but a converted All Black try gave them a lead they didn't relinquish. The Lions tries were scored by Roger Baird and John Rutherford. Neither converted. The All-Blacks' Stu Wilson scored a try which Allan Hewson converted and he also kicked three penalties. The test series was lost.

*Game Fifteen*
*v Hawke's Bay*
*McLean Park, Napier 6/7/1983*
*25-19 - Win*

**Lions Team** – Hare (England), Ringland (Ireland), Irwin (Ireland), Woodward (England), Ackerman (Wales), Rutherford (Scotland), Smith (England), Milne (Scotland), Deans (Scotland), **McLoughlin (Ireland),** Lenihan (Ireland), Boyle (England), Winterbottom (England), Beattie (Scotland), Jeavons (England)

388

1983 New Zealand

A week to the day after they landed in New Zealand, Gerry McLoughlin and Donal Lenihan became Lions when they were picked to play against Hawke's Bay in Napier. Up against them on the local side was Frank Shelford, four time All Black and uncle of Sir Wayne (Buck) Shelford.

The message from Jim Telfer to the team was clear *"The tour is far from over. The lads haven't packed up or given up after the test on Saturday. They're naturally disappointed that they've lost the series, but they done believe that signals the end of anything. We still have a point to make on this tour, and we hope to do so by playing good rugby".*

McLoughlin looked a little rusty in the first half but in the second half his performance dramatically improved, as did that of the Lions team as a whole.

The strength of McLoughlin's scrummaging was evident when Paxton scored from a pushover try and the Lions also scored a try when Deans blocked down a clearance kick. However, Hawkes Bay's scored three tries in the first half. Holmes scored one of the tries of the tour and both Allen and Porter went over to give them a 13-19 lead at the break.

In the second half, the Lions lifted their game and Irwin scored a try. On top of that Rutherford scored a drop-goal and Clive Woodward kicked a penalty. McLoughlin had won his first Lions game.

*Game Sixteen*
*v Counties*
*Pukekohe Stadium, Pukekohe 9/7/1983*
*25-16 - Win*

**Lions Team** – Evans (Wales), Carleton (England), Kiernan (Ireland), Rutherford (Scotland), Baird (Scotland), Campbell (Ireland), Smith (England), Price (Wales), Fitzgerald (Ireland), Jones (Wales), Bainbridge (England), Lenihan (Ireland), Winterbottom (England), Jeavons (England), O'Driscoll (Ireland)

1983 New Zealand

The Lions selected a strong team for the next game in Pukekohe. Twelve of the Lions had played in the third test. McLoughlin was excluded. The game itself was an easy win for the Lions. Ollie Campbell kicked five penalties and two drop-goals and Carleton scored a try.

As he hadn't played in the game, McLoughlin along with Colin Deans and Eddie Butler did a little bit of training on the pitch after the game. As they jogged along, an intoxicated spectator ran up behind McLoughlin and tripped him from behind. McLoughlin got up and chased after the guy who escaped into the stadium and out the gate. As the three got on with their jog, another man ran at them and punched Deans knocking him down. A scuffle broke out in which McLoughlin and Butler both threw punches in defence of their teammate. It died down quickly with the intervention of security and local officials but the tabloids got wind of it and it was in the papers the following day. The Lions players were innocent victims but the press made it sound otherwise. It also made front page news back home in Ireland.

*"These wouldn't be typical New Zealand supporters. They were just fellas who had too much alcohol. What can you do? I don't know what got into them. One of them tripped me and there was a few digs thrown. When you are caught from behind like that, you don't know what you are facing. What can you do? There were no repercussions. I wasn't going anywhere on that tour with the coach anyway so it made no difference".*

Gerry McLoughlin

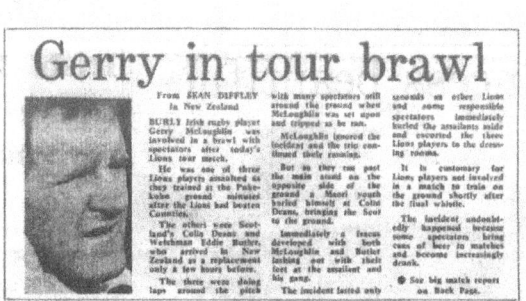

Front page of the Evening Herald

1983 New Zealand

*Game Seventeen*
*v Waikato*
*Rugby Park, Hamilton 12/7/1983*
*40-13 - Win*

**Lions Team** – MacNeill (Ireland), Ringland (Ireland), Irwin (Ireland), Woodward (England), Baird (Scotland), Campbell (Ireland), Laidlaw (Scotland), Milne (Scotland), Deans (Scotland), **McLoughlin (Ireland)**, Bainbridge (England), Colclough (England), Winterbottom (England), Butler (Wales), Driscoll (Ireland)

Ahead of McLoughlin's second game for the Lions, against Waikato in Hamilton, there was speculation that he might be in line for a test spot. Despite only being in the country for a little over a week, his performance in the second half of his first game, coupled with the poor performances of Staff Jones, might see him get selected.

A disappointing performance from Waikato in front of 30,000 of their fans but a huge game for Ollie Campbell who scored twenty-four of the Lions' points. He had seven kicks at goal and only missed one. It could have been even more had he not left the field with a hamstring twinge.

McLoughlin performed really well and the Lions won five scrums against the head. The newspapers reporting favourably on his performance – *"Gerry Mcloughlin did well too, in the loosehead prop position and I have no doubt that the selectors will give much thought to giving him the place in the Test where Staff Jones has not been setting the world on fire".*

When the test team was announced for the final game of the tour, the speculation that Gerry McLoughlin might have done enough in his two outings to earn a test spot, failed to materialise on the team sheet. He was named as a replacement so was on the bench.

1983 New Zealand

### LIONS '83 – Sean Diffley reports on the rugby tour
## McLoughlin to win Test spot

*Test spot speculation back home*

**Game Eighteen**
*v New Zealand (Fourth Test)*
*Eden Park, Auckland 16/7/1983*
*6-38 – Loss*

**Lions Team** – Evans (Wales), Carleton (England), Irwin (Ireland), Kiernan (Ireland), Baird (Scotland), Campbell (Ireland), Laidlaw (Scotland), Jones (Wales), Fitzgerald (Ireland), Price (Wales), Paxton (Scotland), Winterbottom (England), Bainbridge (England), Colclough (England), O'Driscoll (Ireland)

**New Zealand** - Hewson, Wilson, Pokere, Fraser, Taylor, Dunn, Loveridge, Mexted, Hobbs, Haden, Whetton, Shaw, Ashworth, Dalton, Knight

With Gerry McLoughlin watching from the sidelines, the Lions were hammered by the All-Blacks in the fourth test. The New Zealand side scored six tries setting a record for the most points conceded by a Lions test team. All the Lions could muster in response was two penalty goals.

*"I was on the bench for the last test but I knew I wouldn't get a game. I swapped jerseys at half time. They were destroying us. Fraser was all over the place. So, I went over to the All-Blacks side and I never came back over to the Lions bench. I swapped my jersey over there. Someone's leg would have had to come off for us to have a chance to play in those days. I should have had a cap in 1978 against Scotland and Willie Duggan's shoulder*

1983 New Zealand

*went. The doctor, the physio, the referee, the coach, the captain all said, Willie you have to go off. Willie wouldn't go off for anybody. He told me he'd break my neck if I came on. Willie was a giant of a man. Willie was brave. Unbelievably brave."*

Gerry McLoughlin

After the game, during the end of tour celebrations in the dressing room, McLoughlin dislocated his toe in the jacuzzi.

*"I must have hit something, some bit of timber or something. I was probably never in one in my life. It was probably my first time in a jacuzzi. I supposed we were availing of the after-game hospitality. I wasn't carried out. It was small. I managed to get out ok."*

Gerry McLoughlin

## Tour Reflections

*"It was a very disjointed tour. The Scots never gave Fitzy a fair crack of the whip out there. He had been captain of Ireland for four years. Won the triple crown. He did a great job as captain.*

*The Irish were very good mixers because we don't have any airs and graces. The Scots wanted their hooker, Colin Deans, to play instead of Fitzy. When myself and Lenihan arrived on the scene, I could see Fitzy was down. He had been my captain at U.C.G, when I was with Connacht and in the Irish team. We went back, to the 70s. Fitzy was unbelievable. Fitzy would put his head where most people wouldn't put their boots. He was another Peter O'Mahony. When we arrived, he was delighted to see us and we were going to enjoy ourselves out there as well.*

*Jim Telfer. The coach. Never said a word to me for six weeks. Never said a word to me. The coach. Sure, we knew we were dirt trackers.*

*The camaraderie was very important because you are talking about bringing a pile of guys together from different clubs, provinces, countries and even different positions on the field. The front row forwards would sit together. Front five would sit together. They had nothing in common with the backs. They had nothing in common with the back row because you'd be sick of telling them to stay down in the scrum."*

Gerry McLoughlin

1983 New Zealand

# A team of Limerick Lions

Everyone loves to debate who should make the Lions team. An all-Limerick team is an impressive unit. The below team of Limerick Lions would have one hundred and sixty-nine appearances including forty-four test caps. There are another thirty-six appearances and six caps on the bench.

*An all-Limerick British and Irish Lions Team*

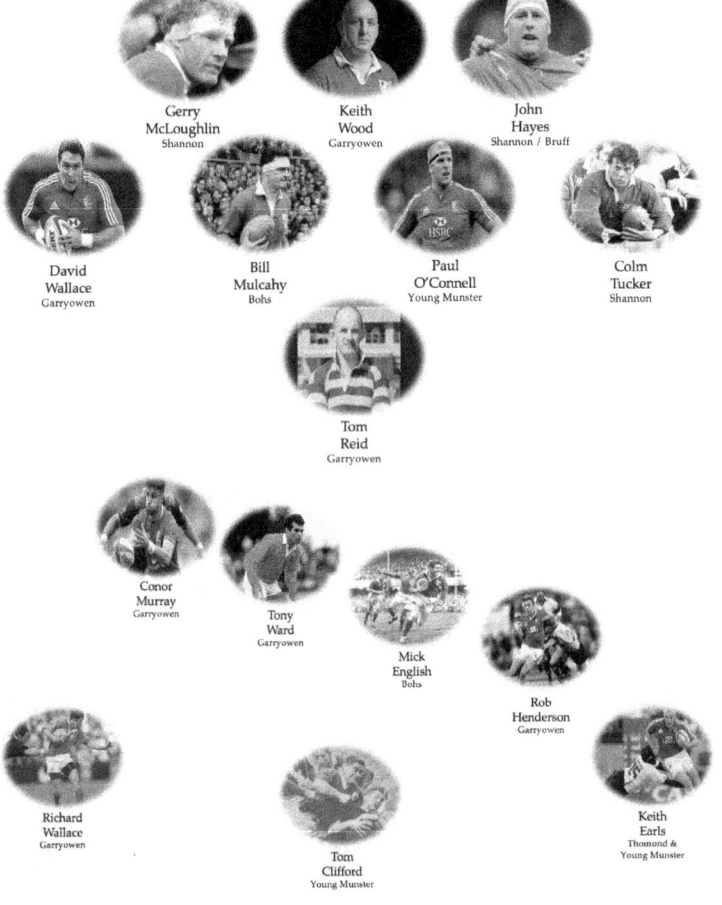

Gerry McLoughlin
Shannon

Keith Wood
Garryowen

John Hayes
Shannon / Bruff

David Wallace
Garryowen

Bill Mulcahy
Bohs

Paul O'Connell
Young Munster

Colm Tucker
Shannon

Tom Reid
Garryowen

Conor Murray
Garryowen

Tony Ward
Garryowen

Mick English
Bohs

Rob Henderson
Garryowen

Richard Wallace
Garryowen

Tom Clifford
Young Munster

Keith Earls
Thomond & Young Munster

A team of Limerick Lions

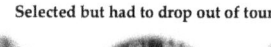

Substitutes

| William Roche | Gordon Wood | Mick Galwey | Paul Wallace | CJ Stander |
|---|---|---|---|---|
| UCC and Newport | Garryowen | Shannon | Garryowen | Munster |

Selected but had to drop out of tour

| Peter Clohessy | Alan Quinlan | Jerry Flannery |
|---|---|---|
| Young Munster (Injured) | Shannon (Suspended) | Shannon (Injured) |

*Note - Includes 'honorary Limerick men' Tony Ward, Mick Galwey, CJ Stander, Rob Henderson, Paul Wallace and Richard Wallace. All of these are Lions and all played a significant portion of their careers in Limerick.*

*Note - Tom Clifford is selected in the position he first played in for Young Munster. He could play anywhere.*

*Note – Paul O'Connell would be our captain.*

So, now that you have the insight into the first one hundred years of Limerick and the British and Irish Lions, who would be your pick for the team?

A team of Limerick Lions

www.ingramcontent.com/pod-product-compliance
Lightning Source LLC
Chambersburg PA
CBHW050336010526
44119CB00049B/575